PCV
I

D0501425

ALEXANDER THE GREAT

AND HIS TIME

AGNES SAVILL

BARNES
& NOBLE
BOOKS

NEW YORK

This edition published by Barnes & Noble, Inc.

All rights reserved. No parts of this book may be used or reproduced in any manner whatsoever without the written permission of the Publisher.

1993 Barnes & Noble Books

ISBN 0-88029-591-0

Printed and bound in the United States of America

05 M 19 18 17 16 15

QF

PREFACE TO THE SECOND EDITION

IN this edition I have amended several of the errors discovered by kind reviewers. The pages dealing with the *Phaedrus* and the *Symposium* have been completely rewritten after further study of these remarkable Dialogues.

Alexander was one of the few men who deserve the title "The Great". Most of his defeated enemies, astonished by his clement and magnanimous treatment, became his devoted followers. It is believed that Alexander's ideas of culture and of religion surpassed those of any other supreme conqueror. His private life was of a quality so noble that Sir William Tarn, the most profound of the Alexander historians, said of him that "he gave the strange impression of one whose body was his servant."

When several schoolmasters wrote that my book should be in every school library for the benefit of upper form pupils, I realized that my work had been rewarded. In this disturbed modern world, with idealism and religion being regarded as out-of-date, the young should be encouraged by learning the record of a man who was successful in battle, who loved the Arts, who respected every form of religion, and who was the first to advocate the brotherhood of all mankind.

AGNES SAVILL

PREFACE TO THE FIRST EDITION

THE introductory pages of Chapter 1 explain the reasons which induced me to begin to write for the general reader a short study on perhaps the most remarkable figure in history. But no brief summary could do justice to the subject —the meteoric career and the development of the aims and the character of Alexander the Great.

The book is divided into two parts: Part I describes the military achievements of Alexander, the break-up of his Empire and the changed condition of the world. Quotations from both appreciative and hostile authors are given in Chapter XII; if the latter were omitted, some readers might question why the fame of the victor of Asia remained so long under a cloud. Both points of view are presented; in any case, every estimate will be accepted or rejected according to the temperament of the reader.

Part II is necessary because the character and the lifework of Alexander cannot be understood without some knowledge of his background—his education, the surroundings in which his youth was passed, the religion and the culture of his time. Greek and Latin used to form the basis of education in our schools and universities, but to-day the growing demand for training in science is displacing the classics; many students are ignorant of their value to life. However, in recent years excellent English translations, broadcast talks and representations of Greek dramas have aroused so much interest that the general public is beginning to turn to the treasures of ancient Greece. It is hoped that the final chapters of this book—mere headlines of a vast subject—may induce many to continue further study of Hellenic culture; its noble teaching, which Alexander the Great endeavoured to spread throughout his Empire, remains to this day an inspiring ideal for our unhappy modern world.

Apart from the exhaustive research of Sir William Tarn, the books which have given most aid for Part I were Arrian's *Anabasis*, the French translation of Droysen's *Alexandre* and the volume of Lieutenant-Colonel Dodge. Arrian, with military and administrative experience in Roman days, and access to ancient works now lost, was able to pronounce reliable judgment on the victories and character of Alexander. Droysen had insight into the psychology of the King, the Hellenes and the Oriental races. Dodge, a professional soldier, a profound admirer of Alexander as a captain, stated that no man could have been so successful without nobility of nature and supreme intellectual gifts. C. G. Jung's studies on the unconscious and the driving force which in individual men brings about the great movements of history, shed a new light on Alexander's work and character. Dr. Gilbert Murray's *Five Stages of Greek Religion, The Rise of the Greek Epic* and translations of Greek plays, C. Seltman's *Twelve Olympians*, Werner Jaeger's *Paideia* and many of the Dialogues of Plato, all contributed to provide the material for Part II.

I am grateful to Messrs. Houghton, Mifflin and Company, publishers of Lieutenant-Colonel Dodge's book, for permission to reproduce the sketch of the opponents in the battle of Gaugamela, and to copy the tabular list of the long march through Asia, the Punjab and back to Babylon. A map of the route was drawn by Mr. Tresadern, who grudged no time nor trouble to ensure its accuracy. The dates inserted on the arrowed lines help readers to follow the steps of the eleven years' campaign.

I have profited by the encouragement, advice and criticism of many friends. I mention gratefully these names: Mr. John Hunt, who read every chapter; Dr. Redvers Ironside, who gave special attention to the chapter on the city-state. Mr. and Mrs. Donald Phillips aided in many ways; without the assistance of Mrs. Phillips, a student of the C.G. Jung Institute of Zurich, the pages dealing with the myths and Jung's philosophy would not have been clearly expressed for the general reader. Valuable help was given by my nephew, R. L. S. Blackadder; others whose useful suggestions were adopted should be mentioned—Mrs. Van Somern Godfery, Dr. Elizabeth Senior, Dr. Patricia Jevons, Mr. Peter Hunt, Miss Elise McMichael, Dr. Ethel Browning and Mrs. Gina Franklin ; their interest and appreciation encouraged me to continue an apparently interminable task.

I am indebted to Mr. Cuthbert Wilkinson for help with the reading of proofs and the compilation of the index, and to the following publishers who have kindly permitted me to use quotations from their books:

> The Cambridge University Press
> Jonathan Cape Ltd.
> Chatto & Windus
> The Clarendon Press
> Constable & Co. Ltd.
> J. M. Dent & Sons Ltd.
> The Encyclopædia Britannica Ltd.
> The English Universities Press Ltd.

Hodder & Stoughton Ltd.
Henry A. Laughlin
Routledge & Kegan Paul, Ltd.
Longmans, Green & Co. Ltd.
Methuen & Co. Ltd.
The Oxford University Press
Paul R. Reynolds & Son, New York
C. A. Watts & Co. Ltd.
The Thinkers' Library
I should also like to thank most warmly the staff of the London Library for their assistance in tracing quotations from ancient authors, and my publishers for helpful co-operation throughout the passage of this book from the typed MS to the completed volume.

AGNES SAVILL

CONTENTS

A. Burn—Sir William Tarn—Legend and
romance.

PART II

LIST OF BOOKS CONSULTED

ARISTOTLE	*Politics*, translated by Sir Ernest Barker, Clarendon Press, 1948
	Ethics, translated by J. A. K. Thomson, Allen & Unwin, 1953
	The Art of Poetry (many translations available)
ARRIAN	Three translations: Rooke (2 vols.), 1859; Chinnock, Hodder & Stoughton, 1884; Iliff Robson, Jonathan Cape, 1933
Atlas of Classical Geography, Everyman Library, 1950	
BERNARD BERENSON	*Aesthetics and History*, Constable, 1950
HENRI BERGSON	*Les Deux Sources de la Morale et de la Réligion* and other works, Felix Alcan, 1933 (English translation, Macmillan, 1935)
EDWIN BEVAN	*The House of Seleucus* (2 vols.), E. Arnold, 1902
SIR E. WALLIS BUDGE	*Introduction to Pseudo-Callisthenes*, C. G. Clay & Sons, 1896
	Translation of Pseudo-Callisthenes, Oxford University Press, 1933
W. G. DE BURGH	*The Legacy of the Ancient World*, Pelican, 1947
A. R. BURN	*Alexander the Great and the Hellenistic Empire*, Hodder & Stoughton, 1947
C. DELISLE BURNS	*Greek Ideals*, Bell & Sons, 1917
G. BURY	*The Hellenistic Age*, Cambridge University Press, 1923
Cambridge Ancient History: Articles by Sir William Tarn and Sir Ernest Barker	
GORDON CHILDE	*What Happened in History*, Pelican, 1948 (last edition 1950)
QUINTUS CURTIUS	Loeb edition, Heinemann (2 vols.), translated by T. C. Rolfe, 1946
LOWES DICKINSON	*The Greek View of Life*, Methuen & Co. (many editions since 1924)
	Plato and his Dialogues, Pelican, 1947
DIODORUS	Extracts from his *History*
LT.-COL. THEODORE DODGE	*Alexander*, Houghton Mifflin & Co., 1890
J. D. DROYSEN	(French translation by Benoist

Méchin of the Alexander section of *Hellenismus*) *Alexandre le Grand*, Bernard Grasset, Paris, 1934

VICTOR EHRENBERG — *Alexander and the Greeks*, Basil Blackwell, 1938
Sophocles and Pericles, Basil Blackwell, 1954

Encyclopaedias, Chambers' and *Britannica* (latest editions)

ANDRÉ-JEAN FESTUGIÈRE, O.P. — *Personal Religion among the Greeks*, University of California Press, 1954

W. WARDE FOWLER — *The City-States of Greeks and Romans*, Macmillan, 1893

E. A. FREEMAN — *Historical Essays*, Macmillan, 1873

KATHERINE FREEMAN — *Greek City-States*, Macdonald, 1950

FRONTINUS — *Strategamatigon*, Loeb edition, Heinemann, translation by C. E. Bennett, 1925

A. FOUCHER — *L'Art Gréco-Bouddique du Gandhara* (vol. I, 1905, vol. II, 1918)

A. W. GOMME — *Essays in Greek History and Literature*, Cambridge University Press, 1937

GEORGE GROTE — *History of Greece* (vol. XII), 1948 edition, Everyman Library

W. K. GUTHRIE — *The Greek Philosophers*, Methuen & Co., 1950

History of Greece, Published by the Society for the Diffusion of Useful Knowledge, 1829

WERNER JAEGER — *Paideia; Ideals of Greek Culture*, Basil Blackwell (vol. II, 1944, vol. III, 1947)

WILLIAM JAMES — *Varieties of Religious Experience*, Gifford Lectures, 1901-2 (last reprint 1944), Longmans, Green & Co.

Journal of Hellenic Studies, 1939, LIX, 124, 229

C. G. JUNG — *Modern Man in Search of a Soul*, Kegan Paul, 1941
Essays on Contemporary Events, Kegan Paul, 1947
The Secret of the Golden Flower, Kegan Paul, 1931

H. D. F. KITTO — *The Greeks*, Pelican, 1951

HAROLD LAMB — *Alexander of Macedon*, Robert Hale, 1946

L. LÉVY-BRUHL — *La Mentalité Primitive*, Felix Alcan, Paris, 1922, and further editions

xvi

	(English translation, Allen & Unwin, 1923)
SIR RICHARD LIVINGSTONE	*The Pageant of Greece*, Oxford University Press, 1923
	Greek Ideals and Modern Life, Oxford University Press, 1935
	The Peloponnesian War, World Classics, 1943
J. McCRINDLE	*Invasion of India by Alexander the Great*, Constable, 1893
J. P. MAHAFFY	*Progress of Hellenism in Alexander's Empire*, Unwin, 1905
SIR JOHN MARSHALL	*Taxila* (vol. I), Cambridge University Press, 1951
DR. GILBERT MURRAY	*Five Stages of the Greek Religion*, Thinker's Library, 1946
	The Rise of the Greek Epic, Clarendon Press (4 editions) 1907
	Euripides and his Age, Home University Library, (1918 and further editions)
	Translations of Greek Plays
F. H. MYERS	*Human Personality*, Longmans, Green & Co., 1903
PLATO	Translations of many of the Dialogues by Jowett, Carey, Burges, and others
	The Republic, Golden Treasury Series, Macmillan, 1852, and many editions.
	Trial and Death of Socrates, Golden Treasury Series, 1880, and many editions.
PLUTARCH	The *Lives*
PLUTARCH	*Moralia*: (several translations, revised by W. W. Goodwin, 5 vols., 1870) (vol. II), *Orations on The Fortune of Alexander the Great*, Little, Brown & Co., Boston and a translation in 14 vols. (vol. IV), *On the Fortune of Alexander*, Loeb Library, Heinemann, 1936
POLYBIUS	Extracts from his *History*, translations: Loeb Library, Heinemann; and Shuckburgh, Macmillan, 1889, (Books V, 10 and VIII, 12).
GEORGES RADET	*Alexandre le Grand*, Paris, 1931
C. A. ROBINSON, JR.	*History of Alexander the Great*, Brown

	University, Providence, Rhode Island, 1953
ILIFF ROBSON	*Alexander the Great*, Jonathan Cape, 1929
JOHN RUSKIN	*The Crown of Wild Olive*, 1866 (and further editions)
C. SELTMAN	*The Twelve Olympians*, Pan, 1952
	Woman in Antiquity, Pan, 1956
SIR AUREL STEIN	*On Alexander's Track to the Indus*, Macmillan, 1929
J. C. STOBART	*The Glory that was Greece*, Sidgwick and Jackson, 1911 (and further editions)
STRABO	Extracts from his *Geography*
SIR WILLIAM TARN	*Alexander the Great* (vol. I, 1947, vol. II, 1950), Cambridge University Press
	Hellenistic Civilisation, E. Arnold, (last edition 1952)
	The Greeks in Bactria and India, Cambridge University Press, (last edition 1951)
BISHOP THIRLWALL	*History of Greece* (vol. VII, pp. 119-20), Longmans, Green & Co., 1852
ARNOLD TOYNBEE	*Study of History* (abridged by D. C. Somervell), Oxford University Press, 1946
K. J. UJFALVY	*Le Type Physique d'Alexandre le Grand d'après les auteurs anciens et les documents iconographiques*, 1902
ARTHUR WEIGALL	*Alexander the Great*, Butterworth, 1933
H. G. WELLS	*Short History of the World*, Thinker's Library, 1929
B. IDE WHEELER	*Alexander the Great*, Putnam, 1900
ULRICH WILCKEN	*Alexander the Great*, Chatto & Windus (English translation 1932)
PROFESSOR WRIGHT	*Alexander the Great*, Kegan Paul, 1934
PROFESSOR A. ZIMMERN	*The Greek Commonwealth*, Oxford University Press, 1911 (and other editions)
XENOPHON	*Memorabilia*, Heinemann, 1923
	The Symposium, Heinemann, 1922

IMPORTANT DATES[1]*

Some of the distances in miles are given by Lieutenant-Colonel Dodge. The back and forward hasty travelling, necessitated by the revolts and attacks from several directions in Bactria, Sogdiana and adjacent territories, add up to 3,900 miles.
The mileage in the region of the Five Rivers mounts up to 1,070.
The miles traversed from the starting point of Pella to Alexander's death at Babylon amount to 21,900.
In Asia minor, from the Hellespont to the Granicus was fifty miles.

558–529		Conquests of Cyrus
336		Alexander became King
335	Autumn	Thebes
334	Spring	Alexander starts for Asia
334	May	Battle of the Granicus
333	March	Left Gordium
333	Summer	Cicilian Gates
333	November	Battle of Issus
333–332	Mid-winter	Tyre siege begun
332	August	Tyre taken
332–331	Winter	Egypt
331	Early summer	Euphrates
331	October 1st	Battle of Gaugamela
331	October	Babylon
331	November	Susa
331	Early December	Uxian campaign
331	December	Persian Gates taken
331	December	Persepolis
330	March	Left Persepolis
330	May	Ecbatana
330	July 1st	Death of Darius
330	August	Tapurian Campaign
330	September	Caspian Gates Campaign
330	October	Drangiana and Arachotia
329	January to March	Alexandria-ad-Caucasum built
329	April	Passage of the Parapamisus
329	May	Oxus crossed
329	Summer	Scythian Campaign

[1] Taken from the Table of Lieutenant-Colonel Dodge, published in his *Alexander*, by kind permission of Messrs. Houghton, Mifflin & Co.

* Important Dates continued after map

xix

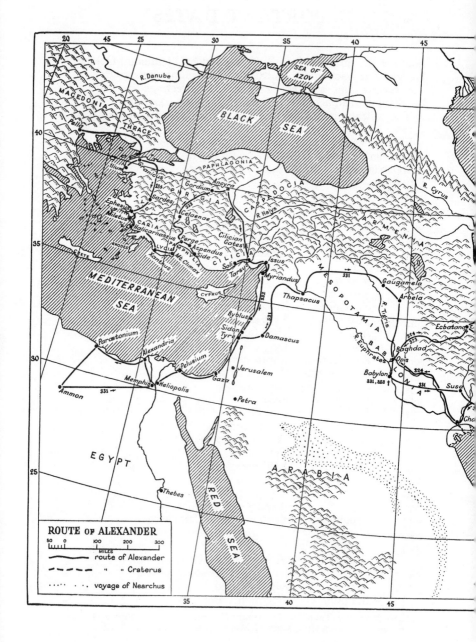

ROUTE OF ALEXANDER

50 0   100   200   300
|⎍⎍⎍⎍⎍⎍| | | |
MILES

———— route of Alexander
— ― — — "   " Craterus
· · · · · · · voyage of Nearchus

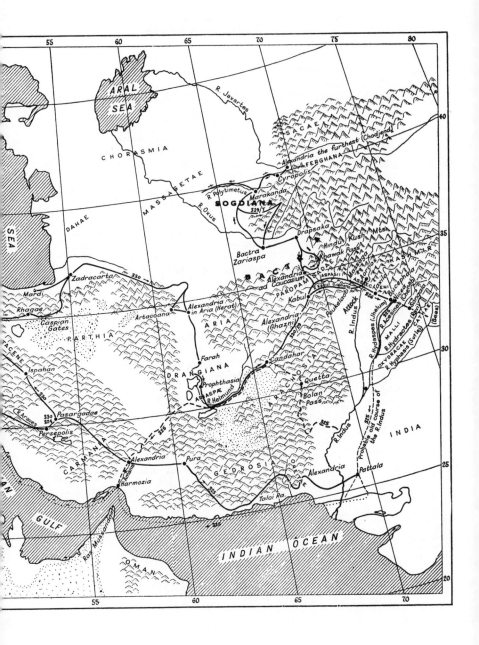

329	Autumn	Back to Maracanda
329	Autumn	Success of Spitamenes
329–328	Winter	In Zariaspa
328	Spring to Summer	Five Column Campaign
328	Autumn	Final Sogdian Campaign
327	Early	Sogdian Rock and Rock of Chorienes
327	Spring	Back to Zariaspa
327	May	To Alexandria-ad-Caucasum
327	July	Left Alexandria and Nicea
326	Late Winter	Campaigns of Cophen and Aornos
326	Early Spring	Crossing of Indus
326	April	In Taxila
326	May	Crossing of Hydaspes river and battle
326	June and July	Five Rivers Campaign
326	End of July	At Hyphasis
326	August	Back to Hydaspes
326	October	Start down river
326	November and December	Mallian Campaign
325	January to June	Campaign lower Indus
325	July	Pattala
325	August	Indus delta
325	September	Oreitian Campaign
325	October and November	Desert of Gedrosia
324	January	In Persepolis
324	Spring	In Susa
324	July	Mutiny at Opis
324	Autumn	Ecbatana
324–323	December to January	Cossean Campaign
323	Spring	Babylon
323	May	Funeral rites of Hephaestion
323	June	Death of Alexander

PART I

CHAPTER I

INTRODUCTION : ACCESSION TO CROSSING OF THE HELLESPONT

Contradictory estimates of Alexander—His world-wide influence—Greece before the rise of Philip of Macedon Marriage with Olympias—Alexander enters the school of Aristotle—Isocrates' influence on Philip— Philip becomes Head of the League of Corinth— Assassination of Philip—Claimants to his throne— Alexander takes prompt action—Oracle of Delphi tells him he is invincible—Northern tribes subdued— Destruction of Thebes—His army—Departure for Asia.

ALEXANDER THE GREAT has had a magnetic attraction for many writers who have approached the subject from angles varying with their emotional reaction. All history is coloured by the temperament of the individual who selects the facts which to him appear relevant or important. No doubt, I am no exception. Puzzled by the contradictory accounts of the character and the aims of Alexander of Macedon, I delved into many volumes, both hostile and friendly, but found no convincing evidence that a man with such enchanting promise in youth had degenerated into the drunken tyrant and megalomaniac depicted by his detractors. Such attributes were inconsistent with the fact that whether present or distant he could always rely on the implicit obedience of his officers, strong and remarkable men,

Of few, if of any, great captains has that been recorded. For over 21,000 miles his army, joined by volunteers from many nations, followed him through Persia and the Punjab. Several able Romans essayed to repeat his march, but none reached further than 1,800 miles behind his turning-point.

The books of Sir William Tarn and Ide Wheeler gave reliable clues for an understanding of the complex personality of the great Macedonian—conqueror, explorer, dreamer of visions. Thus it happened that during a period of convalescence I had time to ruminate over the extraordinary story, and was impelled to compose a summary which might interest the general reader, who in these days knows too little of the history of Greece. Nor am I the first to have found consolation from the fascinating subject. Ujfalvy's tome on the statues of Alexander tells of the sickness of King Alphonse of Naples; despairingly, he called for something to distract his mind from his sufferings. His physician sent him a book on Alexander which was read aloud to him. "Fi des médecins!" he exclaimed, as the narrative was continued.

Alexander passed his boyhood in an atmosphere of unrest, rumours and fear of war with neighbours, frontier tribes and Persia. It is in such times of recurring crises that people demand a strong leader, an ideal hero whom they can trust without reserve. We have seen in modern Europe how the people have been led astray by false idols who brought about disillusionment and destruction. In ancient Greece wise philosophers declared that when one man excelled all others in intellect and character he should be regarded as a god among men, and the people should gladly obey him. The Youth of the future, seeking for such a guide, should measure him by comparison with Alexander of Macedon. Of him it has been said that not only do his achievements captivate the imagination of both old and young, but his perseverance, his assiduous devotion to duty, his indifference to the pleasures of the body, his insatiable pursuit of the pleasures of the mind, his longing to unite the nations and his religious attitude to life, set an example which should inspire us all in this troubled century. In the thirteen years of his reign he so altered the whole outlook of the world that historians

divide the civilisation of that epoch into that which pre-
ceeded and that which was created during his brilliant and
meteoric career.

Modern politicians can learn much by a study of the
history of Greece during the centuries before Christ when
that virile nation developed democratic government. In a
later chapter is described the high standard of the civilisation
enjoyed in the fifth century B.C. by that remarkable people,
so few in number, so eminent in every intellectual and
artistic sphere.

Alexander of Macedon lived in the century which followed
the great days of Greece when Athens, under the guidance of
Pericles, her leading statesman, had gained a deservedly
high reputation as the chief city in Greece. Contest with
Sparta had led to a prolonged war which left her exhausted
both by land and sea, subject to a ruthless and oligarchic
Spartan domination. This was so resented that after a few
years democratic rule was restored, but it had not the high
traditions of public life which had characterised the time of
Pericles. However, during the fourth century B.C. international trade prospered; games and festivities were
organised to please the populace; paid members of the
Tribunal incited class antagonism; a proletariat developed,
impoverished and workless. As Greeks were known to be
splendid warriors, many were hired as "mercenaries",
soldiers who fought bravely, even against their own countrymen. For that matter, some of the larger city-states were
bribed or otherwise induced to take up arms on the side of
the Persian enemy. Thus it had not been difficult for Persia
to force upon Greece in 386 B.C. a humiliating peace; Persia
acquired control over the Greek cities on the Asiatic coast
and gained the right to interfere in the affairs of the Greek
communities.

Just before the advent of Alexander many eminent
thinkers tried to bring about a healthier condition in Greece.
In *The Republic*, Plato advocated an ideal form of government,
but later in life, in *The Laws*, he advised monarchy, the King
to be a man of noble character, bound to work for the good

of his subjects. The pressing problem of the age absorbed another philosopher, Isocrates, who urged that, as Greece represented the highest civilisation in the world, its numerous city-states should cease to fight each other; if united in a common aim, they could meet the recurring menace of Persian invasion. Looking round, in vain, for a strong Greek leader, he believed that the suitable man was Philip, King of Macedonia, who combined the high qualities of both warrior and statesman.

Who was Philip? And how had he risen to eminence? The Macedonians were a hardy folk, who lived the simple life of agriculturists; their monarchy was hereditary, but the people had the right to elect their King. The King was assisted in his duties by men of noble family, aristocrats, who ruled over their own territories. These were the "Companions" of the King; they spent their lives in hunting, fighting and caring for the welfare of their subjects, chiefly shepherds, peasants and labourers. From youth they were accustomed to give orders; they had the dignity, poise and assurance of men born in a ruling caste; without effort they commanded the willing obedience of their subjects. The title "Companion" was also used in connection with the hypaspists, the chief foot-soldiers; the bodyguard of the King was composed of a number of both groups of Companions. In Sparta the aristocracy treated the peasants with severity, as if slaves, but in Macedonia no such humiliating relationship existed; the peasants received kindly consideration from their overlords.

When Thebes was a great power in Greece several Macedonian nobles were taken there as hostages; one of these was Philip, heir to the throne of Macedonia. When he became King in 359 B.C. Philip found his country beset by danger on every side, but by 356 B.C. he had quelled the majority of his frontier foes. Improving on the lessons of war learned in Thebes, Philip built up the strongest army in the world. Having observed that one could never rely upon mercenaries as one could on soldiers recruited on a voluntary system, he constructed a force of 40,000 men who were severely disciplined, trained to march long distances in full equipment, carrying their baggage and food sufficient for three days. The officers, young aristocrats, were rewarded for special merit; tested for endurance, they competed and eagerly sought the appreciation of their King.

Isocrates wrote several letters to Philip, explaining the urgent need for the unification of all Greek cities. As a lover of Athens, he begged Philip to be friendly with that great city; if they worked together they could extend Greek culture over the world. But Demosthenes, the famous Athenian orator, disdaining Macedonia as barbaric, repudiated the suggestion. Persia placed bribes and spread propaganda in suitable quarters so that a tense situation arose between Macedonia and Greece whilst Philip defeated adjacent tribes and encroached on Greek coastal towns. War ensued, and in 338 B.C. the battle of Chaeronea made Philip master of Greece; with Philip as Head, the Greek cities became united under a treaty known as the League of Corinth. Only Sparta stood out for independence; this led to trouble in future years.

Meanwhile Philip had introduced Greek culture into his country. Guests from Greece and other countries found the royal Court at Pella, his capital, conducted with so much dignity, style and luxury that the social life and manners of the Macedonian aristocracy compared favourably with those of Athens. Isocrates praised Philip because, by treating his foes with generosity, he gained their co-operation; a more fruitful method than the destruction of their cities. Isocrates also told Philip that if he could force the King of Asia to obey him he would be "as a god"—an expression destined to have consequences when his son, Alexander, became King of Persia.

Philip married Olympias, the sister of the King of Epirus, and from their union was born, in 356 B.C., Alexander, and in the following year a daughter, Cleopatra. Philip could trace his descent from Hercules; Olympias was in the direct line from Achilles. That Olympias was not a Macedonian princess, but came from Epirus, a "foreign" land, was a fact which in the future caused bitter trouble with those of the Macedonians who regarded such a marriage as illegal.

The research of Francis Galton on heredity proved that high intellectual power runs in families, apart from environmental influences; certainly Alexander had a distinguished inheritance from both his parents. He combined the best qualities of Philip and Olympias; from his father came his sober judgment, clear intellect, reliable, systematic and practical methods of work; from his mother was derived his passionate, warm-hearted, romantic, emotional nature.

Olympias is said to have followed the cult of Dionysus which prevailed in her country; it was rumoured that she roamed the woods at night, joining in the wild songs and dances indulged in by the Dionysian worshippers when his rites were due. The story of Dionysian orgies may be true or false, but it is undoubted that Olympias was impulsive, independent and very outspoken; throughout his life Alexander remained devoted to her, but never permitted her to take any part in political affairs. That she had much to suffer from the frequent marital infidelities of her husband and his habits of overdrinking may in part excuse some of her unrestrained actions. She is reported to have dreamed, just before her marriage to Philip, that Zeus impregnated her in the shape of a serpent; it may be true that she believed in the symbolical conception of Alexander that night, and that she taught him in childhood to regard himself as the son of the god. He had too much common sense to credit this in manhood, but the tale was spread about in order to discredit him as a megalomaniac in later life.

Alexander received his first education, with other youths of noble birth, from Leonidas, a relative of his mother. The boy was readily persuaded, impossible to drive, but always approachable when given a reason which he could understand. That this characteristic remained with him to the end of his life is mentioned by Aristobulus, the Greek architect who accompanied him throughout the Asiatic campaign. When Alexander reached puberty Philip was so impressed by his ability that he decided that his son must have the best tuition, and for this purpose he selected Aristotle, who at that time was attracting attention by his wise methods of instruction. At about thirteen Alexander was sent to Meiza, where Aristotle had his school, and there he remained until seventeen, when military duties claimed most of his time. No wiser choice of tutor could have been made, for Aristotle gave the young man much advice concerning the duties of kings and encouraged him to follow his father's projects in Asia. Until the early death of Alexander master and pupil maintained a friendly intercourse, corresponding regularly during the eleven years in the East.

When Alexander was fourteen Isocrates wrote to tell him how delighted he was to hear excellent reports of his love of good literature and his choice of associates with high character and intellect, and added that if he continued on such lines he would become as outstanding as his father. Just before he died in 346 B.C., when over ninety years old Isocrates wrote to Philip saying that he was happy to have lived to see that his hopes at last were to be fulfilled—Philip would avenge the wrongs which had been inflicted upon Greece by the Persians. But, just as he was beginning his preparations for the invasion of Asia, Philip met a sudden death by assassination in 336 B.C.

The accumulation of events which led to this murder of a distinguished king had a small beginning to which no one at the time had attributed much importance. Philip had divorced Olympias when he became enamoured of Cleopatra, the beautiful young niece of Attalus, one of his generals. Pausanias, a youth of good birth, had been insulted in public by Attalus, and had asked Philip to obtain satisfaction for this rude conduct. Philip tried to soothe the youth, gave him a gift and retained him in his personal service. Seeing that he would obtain no retribution, Attalus being the uncle of Philip's second wife, Pausanias nursed his grievance, and while brooding over it he sought the advice of a Sophist, who glibly informed him that he would gain glory if he attacked some prominent man. While festivities were being held at the wedding of his daughter to the King of Epirus, Philip was walking alone at the head of a procession, when Pausanias rushed from the crowd of spectators and killed the King with his poignard. Pausanias fled, but was pursued and slain by Perdiccas, Leonnatus and other nobles.

The accession of Alexander was not undisputed. Philip's second wife had borne a child and many Macedonians considered that this infant was the legal future sovereign. Rumours spread that Olympias was so unresigned to the second marriage that she was involved in the plot which led to the murder of Philip. She had tried to induce Epirus to revolt against him, but that move had been countered when Philip gave his daughter as wife to the King of Epirus. Attalus claimed that his niece had the prior right to the throne because she was a Macedonian; he urged that he should act as Regent until her infant became of mature age. But at that time Attalus and Parmenion were in Asia Minor, where Philip had sent them to attempt to gain over the Greek coastal towns. Attalus was accused of treason and executed; too late it was discovered that he had not been disloyal.

Other applicants for the throne came forward. The Lyncestian brothers pled that they had the right to the crown because their family had formerly possessed Macedonia; they promised to restore the old customs of the country and protect the people from becoming involved in a fruitless war with Persia. But it was proved that they had accepted money from the King of Persia.

Now the sympathies of the people, after the murder of Philip, lay with Alexander, who had so admirably carried out his duties as Regent during the temporary absence of his father. Although many of his friends advised him to come to terms with the various claimants to the crown, the young man refused to listen to such counsel and acted with promptitude. All who were incriminated in the assassination of Philip were severely dealt with. The Lyncestian Alexander was pardoned because, finding he was in danger, he hastened to swear that he was loyal. Alexander never harboured a grudge; he accepted the apology and gave the man a post in his army; this led to trouble in Asia in a later year.

The news of Philip's death caused consternation throughout the country. Greece claimed independence of the League of Corinth. Letters from Attalus, then in Asia Minor, arriving too late to save his life, provided proof that Demosthenes was inciting Athens and other Greek cities to break their agreement with the League of Corinth. He claimed that the treaty bound no city to any leader except Philip; who could believe in the ability of the new King of Macedonia, untried, unknown, only a boy of twenty? Alexander realised that he was in peril on every side: from the northern tribes who had not been completely subdued by his father, from Asia, and from Greece. An immediate decision must be made as to which task should be undertaken first. Considering that it was essential to consolidate his position as Head of the League of Corinth, Alexander took the reins with characteristic rapidity and confidence. He had good reason to feel sure of himself, for at sixteen he had been entrusted with the government of Thrace and Macedonia during the absence of his father, and at eighteen had been so successful with the management of the left arm of the army at the battle of Chaeronea that after the contest Philip had embraced him, declaring that he would not be able to leave to his son a kingdom extensive enough for his exceptional gifts.

Alexander lost no time in starting out for Thessaly. Aware that the dissentient troops would gather to prevent his passage through the formidable Pass of Tempe, he cut steps up the high mountain of Ossa, and with this "ladder of Alexander" he turned the dangerous defile and descended to the plain beyond the enemy without having to strike one blow. The fine Thessalian cavalry became his possession; a gain of high importance, for this competent body was destined to play a prominent part in the campaign in Asia for many years. To an Assembly of the Thessalian nobility Alexander explained that he desired to be recognised as Head of the League of Corinth in the place of his father; he would protect their country and carry out all the plans contemplated by Philip. Booty which might come from the war against Persia which they would be fighting together would be shared. With a characteristic romantic touch Alexander reminded the Thessalian aristocrats that they were, like himself, descendants of Achilles. Favourably impressed by the sincerity of the speaker, his audience assured him that he could rely upon their loyalty and assistance in furthering the unification of Greece. This meeting had the happy outcome that all the adjoining states agreed to acknowledge the position of Alexander as Hegemon (Head) of the League, and at Thermopylae he was unopposed. He convoked the Amphictyonic Council (combination of States) and was appointed Hegemon of Greece in the place of Philip; but no representatives came from Thebes or Athens, and Sparta refused to join. Demosthenes continued to inveigh against Alexander, but no fortifications were prepared against possible attack on Athens. The spirit of the populace was with Alexander; in him, they felt, lay their sole chance of safety in the event of Persian invasion of Greece.

At Corinth, Alexander was met not only by politicians, but also by artists and thinkers who desired to converse with a King who had been a pupil of Aristotle. Here too he visited Diogenes the Cynic, and received the famous reply to his offer of help: "Only stand out of the sunlight." To the courtiers who objected to this discourtesy Alexander responded that if he were not Alexander he would like to be Diogenes. This popular story may have a basis in fact.

On his homeward journey, Alexander consulted the Oracle at Delphi, and rejoiced to learn from the priestess that he was "invincible". On his return to Macedonia he was shocked to learn that during his absence Olympias had taken a cruel measure in order to prevent any further claim to the throne; she had brought about the death of Cleopatra, the widow of Philip, and her infant. Alexander remonstrated with his mother, but later he was to realise that her impetuous action had removed future trouble.

Until the submission of the tribes on the frontiers Macedonia was so insecure that there could be no question of an invasion of Asia. Preparations therefore were at once begun for an expedition to the northern border. Leaving Antipater at Pella to keep the Illyrians in check, Alexander marched to the Danube to meet the dangerous Triballians. In ten days he reached the Balkan range of mountains, where the enemy awaited him, ready to repulse his approach through the passes. When the Macedonian infantry advanced, the enemy tribe rolled heavy waggons and chariots upon the close formation of the phalanx. Alexander at once issued orders that the solid front of soldiers should disperse to right and left, leaving a passage along which the waggons would roll; those who could not separate should lie flat, holding above their bodies their interlocked shields. This surprising device succeeded; the vehicles rolled down the open pathways on the top of the firm shields; not a man was killed. Meanwhile the archers on one flank attacked the waggons and chariots, and followed them up with vigour while Alexander completed their defeat by striking from the other side.

Thence the King marched to the Danube; on the opposite bank the Getae tribe awaited him with a strong force. His inventiveness was called into action. His fleet being too small, he gathered hollowed logs such as were used by fishermen, hides and coverings for the protection of hay and agricultural produce, and with these constructed rafts; other skins, blown out, provided floats for the rafts and for individual soldiers during their passage by night. In the early morning the Getae, horrified to find beside them the enemy whose river crossing had not been expected for several days, fled hurriedly in disarray. Thus rapidly was the Danubian menace removed. This success brought many messengers and ambassadors from adjacent tribes seeking alliance with the new King.

Without loss of time Alexander turned south and encountered the fierce resistance of the Illyrians. Pelium, their chief city, being situated in the gap of a mountain range on the western border, was a constant threat to Macedonia. At one stage of this struggle Alexander was placed in a dangerous position, being so cut off that his army rations were unobtainable and his communications severed. He instituted an ingenious plan to confuse the enemy; it is said that never before or since has such a method been employed. In full sight of the foe, the army carried out drilling manoeuvres, marching to right, to left, up and down, wheeling slowly and rapidly, as if practising for battle. Thus the enemy were kept wondering from which direction an attack might come and when the drill might develop into a battle. Suddenly the phalanx charged and Pelium was captured. The enemy realised that even a greater king than Philip had arrived.

During the delay caused by the northern campaign rumours had spread that Alexander had been killed. Certainly he had received a severe wound from a club and a stone and Demosthenes produced a witness who was certain that the King could not recover. Thebes claimed independence, and other Greek cities promised to aid her against Macedonian supremacy. In Cadmea, the citadel of Thebes, two officers of the Macedonian garrison were murdered. Alexander realised the serious import of such news; if he were obliged to dispute his right as Hegemon of the League of Corinth, the departure to the East might be long postponed. The Theban rebels must be dealt with before their example spread throughout Greece. With his usual precipitation he marched south, choosing the route over the higher hills, where the rivers were readily forded. Within a fortnight, before anyone had heard of his approach, he encamped some six miles' distance from Thebes. In fact, the Thebans declared that Alexander could not have come so far in so brief a time; they believed that they saw the troops of Antipater.

The rapidity of the march struck Athens with dismay; recalling the troops sent to aid Thebes, the Athenians decided to await results. Thebes found that all her promised allies vanished, and feared that the Boeotians, Phocians and Plateans whom they had ruled with severity would probably assist Alexander if war broke out.

Ptolemy tells us that Alexander was extremely loath to fight with Thebes, the great town which Epaminondas had raised to such power that she had twice defeated Sparta. He postponed attack and awaited an apology for the murder of the two officers. Thebes refused admission; no one for a moment believed that so young a general could win a contest with Thebes. Every conciliatory approach being rejected Alexander reluctantly prepared to attack the city.

Perdiccas found a weakly guarded position in the wall, and made a breach through which his men and those of Amyntas entered; fearing that the two brigades would be in danger if unsupported, Alexander sent archers and light troops to their assistance. Although gravely wounded, Perdiccas drove the Thebans to the Temple of Hercules; the Cadmean garrison swept down to aid them and terrible slaughter ensued. The Theban cavalry fled early in the combat as they were powerless in the city.

At nightfall a halt to the struggle was called; next day those members of the League of Corinth who had joined Alexander's forces were summoned to a conference and told that as sufferers under the cruelty of Thebes they had the right to declare her punishment. To their demand that the city should be razed to the ground Alexander unwillingly consented, on condition that the house of Pindar, the poet, and the temples should be spared. Records state that the ruin of Thebes was carried out not by the Macedonians, but by the Boeotians and others who had long groaned under its dominion; they seized the opportunity to avenge their wrongs with equal ruthlessness, and showed no mercy to men, women and children. The devastation of this great city made a profound impression upon the victor; the memory of the toll of deaths and slavery troubled his conscience for many years; in Asia, when Theban mercenaries were taken prisoner, special terms were always shown toward them.

Terrible as had been the price paid by Thebes, the result of her fate was that all other cities hastened to submit. The greatest clemency was shown to all. Athens, who had temporised, was afraid of what might happen to her. But as Alexander loved that beautiful city and the culture it represented, he made no demand except that nine men who had inveighed against him should be delivered up as hostages; one of these was Demosthenes. After some discussion Alexander was persuaded to modify his terms, and exacted that only one man, Charidemes, should be exiled; he escaped to Persia and joined Darius.

Thus, at the age of twenty, the young King had within

one year made himself master of Greece. Now, at last, the
road seemed clear to prepare for the expedition to Asia.

Nothing certain being known of the topography of Asia
beyond the Euphrates, Alexander made thorough investigation before setting out from Europe. For years he had
been making enquiries from every source—mercenaries who
had fought for Persia, travellers, tradesmen, sailors and
prisoners. When still a boy he had even interrogated
Persian ambassadors who had visited the Court of his father.
He knew the weak and the strong points of the Persian
army, something of their roads and communications, the
lack of cohesion of the nation under a King without any
warlike instinct, and corruptible satraps who reigned as
kings in their own territories, widely scattered over the
immense expanse of Persia. Having inherited from his
father the best equipped and trained army in the world
Alexander was confident of victory, and had the enthusiastic
support of the troops whom he had led to the Danube and
to Thebes.

Some of Philip's preparations for the invasion of Persia
should be briefly mentioned. He had built up his incom-
parable army on a basis of the phalanx formation which he
had studied when in Thebes. The phalanx was composed of
closely packed rows of heavily armed infantrymen; the
number of ranks varied with differing circumstances; some
tell of sixteen rows of eight men arranged so that the points
of the lances held by the fifth rank reached as far as the
front row. These heavily armed infantry soldiers were
known as the hoplites; they wore a helmet, a cuirass of
leather studded with metal scales, and carried a shield large
enough to cover the whole body; their weapon was a pointed
spear, the sarissa, about thirteen to fourteen feet long,
exaggerated by some writers to sixteen or eighteen feet, and
a short sword. The hypaspists, an integral part of the phalanx,
were not so heavily armed. In his great battles, Alexander
placed them on the right of the heavy infantry, next to the
cavalry.

In Macedonia the phalanx was the mainstay of the army;
its tightly packed rows struck terror into all who opposed it;

none could face its long pointed spears. It could march in a square, could turn or wheel into an oblique position; it could also disperse, allowing lanes of passage to open out, then fall on those who had hurried through its ranks. Such movements required special training to be effective when ordered to be carried out with swift precision during battle. On even ground the phalanx was formidable, but on rough, irregular slopes and in hilly country it was at a disadvantage; where mobility and rapidity were required it was so unmanageable that Alexander divided it into smaller units. Indeed, the famous phalanx of Philip was rarely used in Asia; Alexander's phalanx was composed of battalions of heavy infantry, 1,500 men under separate commanders. Six of such crossed the Hellespont and six remained with Antipater in Macedonia. The army formations were often modified to suit the different conditions of warfare in Persia, Iran and the Punjab.

Alexander relied chiefly upon the cavalry for attack; he placed his horsemen on both wings whilst the infantry were in the centre as a strong reserve force of defence. His usual method was to entice the enemy to try to force back the infantry while he harried their left wing with his horsemen. The cavalry originally consisted of nobles, friends of the King, expert in the use of their lances; there being then no saddles or stirrups great skill and experience were required in close combat. The special guards of the King, both cavalry and foot soldiers, were known as the Agema, who acted as his bodyguard both in war and peace. The picked Agema of the hypaspists were trained to support the heavy cavalry, the Companions of the King. At one time the Companion cavalry consisted of eight squadrons; each unit of 1,000 men constituted a hipparchy. Later, one was known as the Royal Squadron, and from this body Alexander drew his generals and governors; hence, as the years passed, he became short of good officers of Macedonian birth.

Arrian tells how the Companion cavalry "rode at the double", a vivid description which conveys to the reader their swift charge, with Alexander always at the head, apparently reckless in daring, but taking in at a glance where and when to push the attack, irresistible by any infantry or horsemen. Elephants and chariots in comparison seemed to him cumbersome, often even useless. He introduced new weapons; battering rams and siege engines were not always so effective as catapults which threw large stones and darts as far as 300 yards. A huge bow could be mounted on an improvised platform constructed of wood obtained from neighbouring forests; pikes and arrows could travel a distance of almost half a mile and red hot balls could be cast with terrifying result over a long range; these missiles often dispersed an enemy force. Enormous mounds could be built up with remarkable speed; in about twenty-four days they could rise to eighty feet high and 300 feet wide; during the siege of a city they were used to fill up ravines or ditches and reach to the summit of ramparts. Cranes containing fully armed men could be lifted and swung over high walls.

The expedition into Asia did not consist of only military equipment. With Alexander went architects, engineers, surveyors, sinkers of wells, experts in all branches of natural science: zoology, botany, forestry, soil composition; rudimentary medicine; specialists to estimate the position and the course of rivers, bays, gulfs, coast outlines and possible harbour sites. Poets, musicians and artists joined the army later, when in Asia. All that was finest in the period of the supreme blossoming of Athens was an absorbing passion with Alexander; Greek culture appealed to him throughout life. In his youth Achilles was his military hero; he followed the example of that Homeric warrior in many of his most daring adventures. Subsequent pages describe how his devotion to Greek civilisation and his advocacy of its culture completely altered the world of ideas for many succeeding centuries and still influence modern Europe.

Knowledge of geography was at that time very imperfect. It was believed that the Habitable Earth was encircled by a great Ocean; drawn toward it as by a magnet, long did Alexander attempt to find its margin, and ever did it recede just as he hoped that he had reached it. The history of his uniform success in battle has unfortunately given rise to the opinion that he was only a military genius; his high qualities of intellect, as evidenced by his achievements in administration, exploration, and his foresight for the development of commerce and the founding of cities, were equally remarkable. One historian of antiquity, Polybius, declared that he was in advance of most of the thinkers of his generation.

Before setting out for Asia it was essential to leave as Regent in Macedonia a man loyal to the throne and competent as a general. Such a man was Antipater, an elderly and tried commander of austere life, who carried out his duties with scrupulous care and later became the faithful guardian of the widow and the posthumous son of his King. Antipater and Parmenion were troubled about the royal succession and at a Council Meeting decided to advise Alexander to marry before he left Europe; for if he fell in battle and left no heir, there would be trouble in the country. But the young King dismissed the suggestion; how could he contemplate marriage whilst preoccupied with preparations for Asia? The immense Persian army was growing larger every day; in such circumstances marriage could not be considered.

The day of departure at length arrived; Alexander quitted Pella, his capital, which he was never to see again, early in 334 B.C. Passing along the coast on his way to the Dardanelles, he arrived in twenty days at Sestus, 200 miles away. Across this narrow part, just over 4,000 feet in width, Xerxes had built a bridge of boats when he invaded Greece. On the opposite side Parmenion had gained possession of a strip of land under Philip's order; hence the disembarkation was undisputed when the Macedonian army crossed the Straits. Alexander took the opportunity to land at Ilium with his friend Hephaestion; there he placed a garland of flowers on the tomb of Achilles, the swift-footed hero of Homer's epic poem. From the temple Alexander took the famous shield of Ilium which in a future year was to be the means of saving his life when wounded, prostrate and unconscious, he lay surrounded by enemies.

In ancient Greece war was so usual that men went to battle, returned home to take up their ploughs and in a few months or years were ready to engage in fresh combat.

There was none of the total warfare of modern times; men were not slain from afar by unseen artillery or missiles thrown from above the clouds. From Homer's *Iliad* we can understand the glory and excitement of combat between individual warriors. Modern mass destruction has robbed the soldier of this exhilaration, but we catch an echo of it when we listen to vivid broadcast narrations of the exploits of our air force.

Alexander was a hero to his army, revered and beloved because he had proved himself to be a captain of men who discounted danger, who overcame every obstacle and had always been victorious. All accounts agree that he possessed rare personal charm and magnetism. As regards his physical appearance, Ujfalvy's volume analyses every statue, bust and coin which has been traced as representing Alexander the Great. He was just above medium height; the complexion white and rosy; the hair, ruddy gold, thick and curling, stood up like the mane of a lion; across the forehead ran a deep transverse furrow above prominent eyebrows. The eyes were deep-set; some say that one was coloured a piercing blue, the other somewhat darker; they had a penetrating gaze when he considered a place or an individual, but when at rest they were soft, with a "melting, liquid" expression. The chin was strongly moulded; the mouth not large, the lips full, yet finely curved; his body very muscular, strongly built, but of perfect proportion. To a stranger he presented a striking appearance of immense power and brilliance; this impression is confirmed by several of the best statues. He was accustomed to carry his head slightly turned to the left shoulder, looking upward; many of his officers copied this attitude and it is said that even the Emperor Augustus, who deeply admired him, began to adopt that position of his head. It is believed that Alexander had received a wound in the neck during the war in Illyria, and that the inclination of the head dated from that time. Add to the beauty of his personal appearance his frank, open manner of speech, his generosity, his high standard of morality, his absolute confidence in victory, his infinite capacity for work and endurance; it is obvious that all these endowments of body, mind and spirit were bound to gain for him the adoration of his troops. One can enter into their spirit of exaltation when one hears a great actor chanting the lines of the *Iliad*. The version which Aristotle revised for his pupil was his military guide; by night he kept it under his pillow, beside his sword.

Ptolemy, Hephaestion, Seleucus, Antigonus, Leonnatus, Craterus, Perdiccas, Nearchus, Coenus, Eumenes (his secretary) and many others of that brave team obeyed him loyally through eleven long years of terrible trial, far from home and kindred. After his early death they could never accomplish what he had achieved with such apparent simplicity. Not one of them showed a tithe of his swiftness in decision, his imaginative foresight, his ability to inspire and to maintain the co-operation of his subordinates; yet they all became intelligent, able and conscientious rulers and kings in their own dominions.

To some readers the above may appear too glowing an estimate; but even higher praise has been given by many historians. Here I shall quote only the enthusiastic words of Lieutenant-Colonel Dodge:

At the head of these Generals, and in a sense which no captain has ever since reached, stood Alexander, in every respect the leader of his army; its pattern, its hardest worked, most untiring, most energetic, bravest, most splendid member. What he did and the way he did it, roused the emulation of his lieutenants to an unexampled pitch. With Alexander it was never "GO!" but "COME!" . . . None could vie with him in courage, bodily strength, expert use of arms or endurance. And in every detail of the service, from hurling the Agrianian javelin to manoeuvring the phalanx, from the sarissa drill to the supreme command of the army, he stood without a peer. In his every word and deed he was easily master from his qualities of body, mind and heart.

CHAPTER II

ASIA MINOR, EGYPT, GAUGAMELA

*Cyrus the Great—Cambyses—Darius I takes Thrace
and Macedonia—Darius defeated at Marathon—The
religion of Zoroaster—Xerxes invades Greece but is
defeated at Salamis and Plataea—Darius II has
advocates in Greece, especially in Sparta—Darius III
—Alexander enters Asia Minor and Persia—His army
formations—Battle of the Granicus—Miletus, Halicarnassus—Caria—the Taurus Mountains—Mount
Climax—Battle of Issus—Siege of Tyre—Egypt;
Oracle at Siwah—Sparta defeated by Antipater—
Battle of Gaugamela—Alexander becomes Great King
of Asia*

PHILIP and his son were determined to remove the recurring threat of Persian invasion of Greece. Cyrus the Great,
founder of the Persian Empire, reigned from about 558 to
529 B.C. It is believed that he was a Persian, but his early life
is wrapped in legendary obscurity. Seeing the indolence of
the Medes, he put before his people a serious choice: would
they be luxury-loving idlers, or would they prefer to become
a strong nation? The agriculturists of the Bactrian and the
Parthian heights, hardy races, responded to this appeal;
Cyrus conquered the Median Empire, Babylonia and Lydia,
and became "master of the world". He was a great warrior,
a wise statesman, and a magnanimous ruler.

His son, Cambyses (reigned 529-522 B.C.) added to the
already large empire Egypt, Ethiopia and part of North
Africa. Then, as so often happens in history, people wearied
of austerity and toil, and disorders occurred in many regions
until a strong leader arose—Darius I—who after much

trouble was accepted as King of Persia. During his reign (521-485 B.C.) he quelled revolts in Media, Babylonia, Armenia and Egypt, then turned east and reached the Indus. In 512 B.C. he seized Thrace and Macedonia, but in Greece was twice defeated, finally and decisively at Marathon in 490 B.C. When arranging a third attempt to conquer Greece, he died, and the task was undertaken by his son, Xerxes. Throughout the empire Darius constructed military roads and fortresses commanding strategic positions; so efficient was his system that a messenger could travel 300 leagues, from Susa to Sardis, in ten days. He carried on the policy of Cyrus; his rule was strict, but he permitted every land to preserve its own language, customs and religion. Persia was governed with twenty satraps who were treated as independent rulers of their own territory on condition that they ensured the fertility of their soil and did not oppress their subjects.

Under Darius I the religion of Zoroaster became firmly established; it dated from some fifteen centuries before Christ. It taught that a divine law exacted high purpose both in word and deed, and respect for truth and duty. It was based upon the eternal struggle between Ormuzd, the god of goodness, with his seven Archangels of light, and Ahriman, the spirit of evil, with his demons of darkness. Every good thought and action impaired the power of the god of evil. Both gods desired to capture mankind, but every man was free to choose on which side he would fight during his brief sojourn on earth. A holy fire burned continuously on the altar of the temple where the sacrifices and the ceremonies were celebrated.

Xerxes (reigned 485-465 B.C.) invaded Greece and wrought much destruction on Athens; he ruined many of its fine buildings and temples but was defeated at the naval battle of Salamis in 480 and at Plataea in 479 B.C. Though Darius I and his son had failed, the threat of a future Persian invasion hovered over Greece like a dark thunder cloud which at any time might burst. History tells us that in subsequent years Persia degenerated, lost her adventurous spirit and tried to stave off a Greek war of revenge. For a time Darius II found a ready ally in Sparta, who was jealous of the growing reputation of Athens, and in other city-states Persian bribes influenced men even of high standing who believed that the Greek standard of life could be maintained only by alliance with the Great King of Asia. Even in Macedonia Persia found accomplices. After the apparent success of this diplomacy, Persia had a breathing space. Some Persian officers became anxious about the future when they learned that Alexander had passed unscathed over the high mountain range at Ossa, but no one dreamed that Philip would have a successor still greater than himself in the person of his son. However, their efforts to stir up rebellion among the tribes on the frontiers of Macedonia had roused these hardy fighters, and Persia relied on them to keep Alexander occupied in Europe for a considerable time. But when the news came that the rumour of Alexander's death was false, and that the young King had unexpectedly appeared before Thebes and destroyed that proud town, the Persians realised that here was a new enemy who might be a danger if he intended to follow the designs of his father.

Before describing Alexander's entry into Asia, some of the facts upon which he based his confidence should be explained. With little money and few troops he yet felt certain that he had good grounds to expect victory over an army much larger than he could muster. After the Greek naval victory at Salamis in 480 B.C. the people of Persia had steadily deteriorated under a succession of weak kings. The satraps, left without the control of a strong monarch, became insolent and corrupt, and no longer carried out their duties to the provinces which they governed. Suffering under wrongs which could not be remedied, the people grew hopeless; they had no means of approach to a central authority; the King, far away, lived in luxury with his royal court, ignorant of the unhappy condition of his subjects.

When Darius III came to the throne Persia required the guidance of a strong king who could pull his people together and infuse into them some of their ancient energy. But Darius III was not a man to stir the spirit of a nation which had lost faith in itself. He was universally liked for his amiable and benevolent qualities, but little could be expected from him as a ruler. He was unaware that any danger could come from Macedonia, and his opinion was shared by his nobles and the majority of his military staff. What could a nation with so small an army hope to accomplish when faced with the enormous forces of the great Persian Empire? They decided that the quickest way to deal with the threatened invasion was to concentrate on killing Alexander.

But Alexander knew the weaknesses of that empire. The races who dwelt in the mountainous regions would be strong opponents, but those of the warm plains were lazy and indolent, spoilt by luxurious living. In the cities of Asia Minor there was passive resignation to the yoke of oligarchic and tyrannical governors; only a few had been left independent, because they were of use for Persian trade. Thus many of the Phoenician cities remained virile, not because of loyalty to the Persian King, but because they were kept alert by rivalry and jealousy of adjoining neighbours. Egypt resented the domination of Persia, but was powerless to dispute her supremacy.

Alexander could compare his army with satisfaction; small as it might be numerically, its training and discipline were superior to that of any army in the world. Moreover, it was united under one commander, himself; that of the enemy was under the control of many leaders. That the Persian soldiers were so numerous was a disadvantage on a field of battle; with divided leadership it was impossible to meet emergencies with a swift change of tactics. Even in the past, Persian generals and soldiers had proved inferior in their encounters with the more alert and resourceful men of Greece.

Alexander acted as if he had some premonition that it would be long before he again set foot in his native land. To his friends he gave away so many of his personal possessions that Perdiccas asked what he had left for himself. "Only my hopes", was the reply; to which Perdiccas responded that they all would share his hopes. Alexander must have had many a conversation with his father concerning his plans for the invasion of Asia Minor and Persia. As the Treasury was reduced to some sixty talents, several writers have denounced the young King as a foolhardy adventurer who set out with no definitely formed plans for conquest. But there is evidence that his preparations had been so complete that he had even considered a scheme for the improvement of the monetary system. Silver was used in Greek currency; gold in Persia. Philip had introduced bi-metallism; but this subject is too complicated for consideration here.

Antipater was left as deputy in Macedonia while Alexander was absent in Asia. He took with him, it is said, 30,000 foot soldiers and 5,000 horsemen. For the heavy cavalry, a horse was required for an equerry and the baggage; thus much forage had to be obtained from the country through which they travelled. With the advance into Asia reinforcements of good horses were sent from time to time.

The composition of the foot soldiers was considered in the first chapter. Soon after the entrance into Asia, Alexander found that the altered terrain, with its hills and mountains, demanded modification of the infantry equipment and battalions. In the chief battles, the hypaspists were placed near the cavalry; on the march they were employed to occupy passes, to force river crossings and to withstand the charges of enemy horses and elephants. The Agema, forces selected by the King for important expeditions and serious battle manoeuvres, were drawn from both the hypaspists and the cavalry. The infantry Agema included the famous "shield-bearing guards" who provided the special body-guard of the King and could be relied upon in every emergency. The Agema of the cavalry were the flower of the Companions, the nobles who, even in Macedonia, were proud to be called upon to aid their King in his public as well as his military duties. The Agrianians, frequently employed for arduous work in war, were light troops of high quality, "barbarian" because not of Macedonian origin, but chosen for their loyalty and courage during frontier fighting when Alexander succeeded to the throne.

In Asia the cavalry had a prominent rôle. The finest cavalry came from Thessaly and Macedonia; the riders were specially trained members of the nobility whose bravery rivalled that of their King. The Persian cavalry, renowned in the days of Cyrus the Great, had become less disciplined and were unaccustomed to hard endurance on the field. Alexander's cavalry were not only superior as fighters, but they were united in devotion to their King. Thus Alexander calculated that although his army was numerically inferior to that of Darius, it was more highly organised for war when initiative was demanded in unexpected situations.

Memnon, a Rhodian, was in command of the Greek mercenaries who served under Darius. He knew that Alexander had a high military reputation, but was hampered by the fact that he had entered Asia with little money and food for his army. As a favourite with Darius, Memnon could speak freely to the King; he counselled that Persia should avoid any encounter with Alexander, for even if successful, the struggle could not be decisive. The wise strategy was to utilise the fleet, send a force into Macedonia and retreat in Persia, laying waste the countryside so that Alexander would find no food for his troops nor fodder for his horses. But this sensible suggestion was disregarded. Both the nobles and the military authorities deemed it unworthy of their great empire; it would be construed as evidence that they were afraid of a young King who so far had never met his match. The fact that they were jealous of the influence of Memnon, a Rhodian in a subordinate position, strengthened their opposition. Yet Memnon had dealt successfully with Parmenion and Attalus when Philip had sent them to Asia Minor. Realising that Memnon was checking the progress of these able generals, Alexander had recalled them soon after his father's death; Asia Minor, he had decided, must wait until he could give its invasion his undivided attention. For, with all his impetuosity of temperament, Alexander never hurried until all preparations were complete; then, and then only, did he strike with that swiftness which his critics so often had mistaken for foolhardiness or reckless daring and love of danger.

BATTLE OF THE GRANICUS, MAY, 333 B.C.

The Persians made a stand on the right bank of the river Granicus and the plain beyond. In some parts the river was fordable; in other regions its current was too swift and deep to permit the passage of infantry or cavalry. The banks were so steep and slippery that men and horses would find it hard to keep a foothold as they tried to scramble up, faced with a shower of enemy darts, arrows and sharp javelin knives.

There are no reliable figures concerning the size of the Persian army. Ptolemy, whose Journal is consulted for military information, sometimes exaggerated the number of enemy forces and minimised the Macedonian losses; this encouraged the troops. Only the seriously wounded were counted; cuts, abrasions and injuries which scarcely incapacitated the soldier were not mentioned. At the Granicus it is probable that the Persian cavalry was four times as numerous as that of the Macedonians; among them were many horsemen from the mountainous districts of Iran, fierce fighting men with extensive experience in war.

Hearing from his couriers that the Persian forces were drawn up on the right bank of the Granicus, Alexander pushed ahead to meet them. On his right he placed the bowmen and the Agrianians; next these, the Companion cavalry with himself as leader; then came the hypaspists and the heavy-armed infantry, usually referred to as the phalanx; on his left were the Thessalian, Thracian and Greek cavalry. As he approached, Alexander saw at a glance that the Persians had committed the error of stationing their infantry, the Greek mercenaries, strong fighters, on rising ground behind the cavalry. This was a faulty arrangement; the infantry ought to have been placed along the river bank in front of the cavalry, where they would have contended the Macedonian passage over the river. But, being on the rear of the cavalry, the mercenaries were reduced to become mere spectators of a struggle in which they could offer little assistance.

Alexander decided that immediate attack was the correct strategy. Parmenion argued that the day was far advanced, that if checked, the effect upon the morale of the army would be disastrous; he pressed his opinion that they should wait until the morning. Alexander answered that he had

taken all these points into serious consideration, but preferred his own plan. Despatching Parmenion to command the
left wing, he moved forward to the right. Recognising
Alexander, the Persians realised that the chief and decisive
attack would come from his side; reinforcing their cavalry
to meet him, they stood firm on the bank. Alexander
scrutinised their ranks closely, searching for the region most
favourable for his charge. Raising the battle cry, and to the
sound of trumpets, the Macedonians advanced, Ptolemy
and Amyntas toward the Persian right, where Memnon
resisted their heroic endeavour to cross the river.

Intent on concentrating on Alexander, the Persians
watched him; his glittering armour and white plumes made
him a conspicuous target for their missiles. Alexander sent
in advance a contingent of cavalry and infantry, then slanted
his Companion cavalry to the right, opening the horses out
so that they presented a broad front to the enemy. A shower
of javelins and arrows met them as they forced their way
over the river; scrambling up the bank the horses slipped
in the mud while the opposing Persian riders fell over them.
A desperate struggle followed as Persian and Macedonian
cavalry met in a close tussle, horse pressing against horse.
The infantry fared severely until Alexander came to their
aid, driving off the Persians who were covering them with a
hail of darts. Slowly but steadily the Macedonian infantry
made progress, having the advantage, at close quarters, that
their spears were longer than the short Persian weapons.
Always in the thick of the *mêlée* were seen the white plumes
of Alexander. His lance was splintered; he called to his
equerry to bring him another; his, too, had been shattered.
With his truncheon Alexander inflicted fatal injuries on all
who came near him. Mithridates, the son-in-law of Darius,
wounding Alexander in the shoulder, at once was slain. A
relative of Mithridates, who cleft the King's helmet with his
sword, was also killed. A third man raised his arm to deal a
fatal blow, but Alexander's foster-brother, Black Cleitus as he
was called, diverted his stroke by severing the arm from the
body. And still, with increasing intensity, the bitter warfare
continued.

That the Persians fought with courage was evidenced by their heavy casualties; at last they wavered, and when their centre broke, flight followed. Memnon escaped. Among the dead were a son-in-law and a brother-in-law of Darius, the Governor of Cappadocia and the Viceroy of Lydia. In comparison, the Macedonian losses were few, about 115 slain, and twenty-five of the Companion cavalry.

Lieutenant-Colonel Dodge analysed the numbers and compared them with the killed and wounded in the wars of the Middle Ages and of the American Civil War. When an army ceases to resist, the ensuing scramble during the time of demoralisation and flight leads to many injuries and deaths; men push forward, maddened by fear, unaware of what they do as they trample upon those in front. So also, when an outbreak of fire occurs in a crowded hall, the frightened mob, rushing for safety, treads on the fallen bodies of weaker individuals in its path.

Captured Greek mercenaries were sent to Macedonia to till the soil; no mercy could be shown to men who had broken their oath to the League of Corinth by serving under Persians and fighting against their own countrymen. But the Theban prisoners were given freedom. On the day after the battle Alexander ordered statues to be made to the memory of the twenty-five Companions. All who had fallen in battle, including the Persian dead, were buried with high military honours; the families of the Macedonian victims were exempted from taxation. Alexander visited his men in hospital and examined their wounds; his gracious sympathy endeared him to his troops.

As a thank-offering to the gods, and in especial to Pallas Athene, 300 suits of armour were sent to Athens, with this inscription: "Alexander, son of Philip, sends to the Greeks, except the Lacedaemonians [Spartans], this tribute from the barbarians dwelling in Asia." Many times, in later years, he made similar friendly overtures to Athens, but there is no record that his gifts were ever welcomed.

After the Granicus Alexander could have travelled further east, but rejected that plan because it would have jeopardised his communications; his supplies could have been cut off by the Persian fleet. To gain possession of the coast of Asia Minor was the most important strategic consideration. Alexander announced that to every city he would restore a democratic form of government and abolish Persian tribute money and oligarchic rule. When Sardis, the capital of Lydia, surrendered voluntarily, it was rewarded with a freedom which it had not enjoyed for centuries. Ephesus, a prosperous centre of commerce with Phrygia, Lydia and Caria, revolted against its Persian authorities when it heard of Alexander's approach. He took severe measures to control the excesses of the mob, and delighted the citizens by ordering that the Temple of Diana, destroyed by fire on the day of his birth, should be rebuilt. Persian money was employed to construct new harbours, moles and necessary buildings in many cities.

Miletus refused to submit. Without Miletus, Persia could not retain mastery of the sea; owing to its importance for trade Persia had left it free, with its own government. Parmenion advised the King to try conclusions with the Persian navy, but Alexander refused to risk failure. As ships were obliged to enter a harbour almost daily for provisions or protection from the weather, he maintained that it was more important to deprive the enemy of shelter bases. Parmenion argued that as an eagle had settled on a rock near the ships, the omen was favourable for a trial of strength; but Alexander said that this indicated victory on land, not on sea. Before the surrender of Miletus the mightiest engines, battering rams and other destructive weapons were required.

Memnon, whose advice to Darius had been ignored, had escaped to Ephesus, thence to Halicarnassus; under his command that great town sustained a long siege. Eventually he reached the fleet and stirred up disaffection in cities still hesitating whether to resist or to support Alexander. Especially in Sparta had he gained adherents. Then, suddenly, Memnon died. This news told Alexander that the menace of the Persian fleet need no longer be feared.

Ada, widow of the King of Caria, deprived of her right to the throne by her brother, welcomed Alexander, treating him as a son. Espousing her cause, Alexander appointed her Viceroy of Caria. At last the march east had no danger to flank or rear. Parmenion was sent to Phrygia with the baggage and heavy transport whilst Alexander turned to the Taurus mountain range, earning the gratitude of many coast towns by ridding them of robbers in the adjacent hills. During the winter spent at Phaselis games and other festivities afforded relaxation and much needed rest to both the King and his men.

About this date Parmenion intercepted a letter from Darius to the Lyncestian Alexander suggesting that if he could bring about the death of his King he would be rewarded with the throne of Macedonia. This was the man who had disputed Alexander's accession, but had been pardoned when he swore fealty. After the Granicus he had been given a high post in the Thessalian cavalry; but the Companions had never trusted him, and regretted that he had not been branded as a traitor. Reluctant to punish the Lyncestian, Alexander only degraded his rank and kept him under guard; some three years later he again came under suspicion.

Now came the episode of the Mount Climax march which has been embellished by romantic writers. Mount Climax was a precipitous cliff rising about 7,000 feet above a narrow beach some miles long. This path was often covered by tidal sea waves which rendered it impassable except when a strong northerly wind blew the water from the shore; then for some hours the coast could be traversed in safety. On one such occasion the Macedonians marched without accident along the beach. This was regarded by the soldiers as a special mark of favour shown by the gods. Callisthenes, the flattering historian, described how the very waves bowed down before the mighty King with the Oriental ceremonial *proskynesis*. But Alexander wrote home quite simply that he had crossed along the sea path below the Pamphylian ladder.

As yet neither Greece nor Persia had realised Alexander's strength and perseverance. Athens believed that Memnon had allowed him to proceed so that he would have a long way to retreat when, sooner or later, the Persians cut his home communications. But Destiny had removed Memnon just as he was rousing revolt in hesitating and disapproving city-states.

Plans were made to meet Darius. The various columns of the army met at the village of Gordium: Parmenion with transport and baggage, siege engines and other formidable machines; officers from many directions; newly married soldiers who had been on home leave during the winter— all happy to renew their comradeship, confident, joyously anticipating fresh adventures and victory.

Now at Gordium there was a local legend that the whole of Asia would belong to the man who succeeded in untying a complicated knot attached to a waggon. It had baffled so many examiners that Alexander was curious to investigate the puzzle. An often repeated story tells us that Alexander solved the problem by cutting the rope with his sword, but after minute scrutiny of the scources of every statement derogatory to the reputation of Alexander, Tarn could not find any evidence to support this discreditable account. Ptolemy and Aristobulus are acknowledged as trustworthy writers on the campaign; Ptolemy was an able general, Aristobulus, an architect and engineer; both accompanied the King throughout the campaign in Asia. Neither of these men, who knew Alexander intimately and kept careful note of his exploits, made any mention of the knot having been cut with a sword. On the contrary, Aristobulus tells how Alexander pulled out the pole connected with the waggon yoke, carefully examined the hidden ends of the cord and then untied the knot. Throughout the centuries run several versions of this tale, the sword-cutting being too attractive to discard. Tarn asks whether a man so scrupulous in the observance of religious customs would have thanked the gods, as Alexander did, for success achieved by trickery.

After the unravelling of this famous knot, Alexander proceeded east to the Cilician Gates, a defile in the Taurus mountain range, where severe opposition was expected in a gorge so narrow that only four men could walk abreast. By some misapprehension the Governor of the district had left this impregnable site insufficiently guarded—probably because the arrival of the Macedonians was unexpected. Soon after, Alexander became seriously ill with a fever attributed to his having bathed in a cold mountain pool; the malady delayed his advance. At this time Parmenion warned Alexander that he had learned from a trustworthy source that his physician, Philippus, had been bribed by Darius to put poison in his evening drink. But Alexander had confidence in his medical adviser and whilst he drained his cup he handed the letter to Philippus and watched his expression. Philippus showed no trace of guilt; handing back the letter he remarked that his patient would be restored to health when he had taken the remedies prescribed. On recovery Alexander guided a brief campaign in the Cilician mountains in order to secure his flank.

BATTLE OF ISSUS, November, 333 B.C.

Meanwhile Darius had been waiting with his army in the plain of Sochi, in Syria. Unaware of the illness which had interrupted the Macedonian advance, the Persians supposed that Alexander had feared to meet them. In vain did Amyntas, a Macedonian exile, try to dissuade Darius from leaving Sochi. The Persians crossed by the Northern Anamic Pass just as Alexander had started through the Southern Pass and arrived at Myriandros. Thus, whether by choice or by chance, the Persians had cut across Alexander's communications and were stationed behind his rear; this would compel the Macedonians to fight with their faces toward their base. And the sick and wounded in hospital had been brutally murdered by the Persians at Issus.

At first incredulous, Alexander despatched a reconnoitring ship which confirmed the fact that the Persian army was waiting on the plain of Issus, which lay along a semi-circular bay and was divided by the Pinarius river. Alexander, obliged to retrace his steps through the Southern Pass, marched all day, rested at night and resumed progress at dawn. The troops, disturbed by the news that their line of retreat had been cut, grumbled loudly; accustomed to express their opinions, they complained that their officers had been careless of the lives of the common soldiers. Rumours among the rank and file did not disturb Alexander, but it was essential to discuss with his officers his future strategy. To the council of war he explained that the Macedonian Intelligence had been ignorant of the existence of the Northern Pass through which the Persians had travelled. Fortunately, the new position of Darius was less favourable for him than the plain of Sochi. The plain of Issus was too circumscribed for the manoeuvres of a great army; its right was bounded by the sea; its left, by the foothills of high mountains. In front, the Persians had the river Pinarius which on their left took a wide bend from north to south. There Alexander proposed to cross with his cavalry while the infantry would force a passage over the river. When he, with his horsemen, had reached the rear of the Persian left, the enemy would be obliged to fight a defensive operation on both front and rear. Alexander had a personal approach for every general, praising his accomplishments since the crossing of the Hellespont. His officers crowded round him, grasping his hand, fired with enthusiasm as they listened to his masterly exposition of the ordeal ahead.

Defective as had been the Macedonian Intelligence, that of the Persians had been even more at fault; they could have defended both the Northern and the Southern Passes. But on the critical day of battle Alexander's consummate strategy averted the threatened danger. The numbers of the respective armies are not known; but as many had been left in garrisons the Macedonians had fewer men than at the Granicus. The Persians had placed the Greek mercenaries in the centre; in front, the river bank had been strengthened with stakes to impede the troops who tried to cross. On their left, on the foothills, the Persians had stationed a lightly armed force so that if, as expected, Alexander attacked from his right, his advance would be delayed, even prevented. Close to the sea shore, on the Persian right, Nabarsanes, an able general, commanded a great mass of cavalry.

Alexander came forward cautiously, keeping his line in column until he had carefully examined the disposition of the enemy. Seeing the immense advantage of the Persian cavalry alignment he ordered the Thessalian horse to be transferred from their usual position near his Companions. This movement to his left was carried out with extreme caution; the men rode behind the phalanx so that their objective was not visible to the enemy. This manoeuvre diminished the grave threat to the left; the fine body of the Thessalians would stem the attack expected to come from Nabarsanes. When this rearrangement had been accomplished, Alexander dispersed the lightly armed foes on the foothills with the Agrianians, bowmen and a limited number of cavalry. Three hundred of the Companion cavalry were then despatched to a position where they could ward off any attack on their right.

After giving his men time for rest and food, Alexander addressed the troops, assuring them that the future of Asia depended that day upon their valour, endurance and perfect adherence to discipline and obedience to the orders of their respective commanders. They would be fighting Greek mercenaries, traitors to their country; but as free men, they would conquer the paid servants of a foreign master. His inspiring eloquence was greeted with shouts from the army that they longed to start battle at once.

The foothills having been cleared, Alexander rode on, without haste, with the heavy-armed Companion cavalry; when within bowshot, he gave the order to charge. With his usual lightning attack he drove impetuously into the Persian ranks; nothing ever withstood Alexander's Companion cavalry onslaught. On the Persian right, however, Nabarsanes succeeded in crossing the river; but, although he had forced the Macedonians back, he could not reach so far as the flank of the phalanx. Meanwhile, the infantry, attempting to cross, had been engaged in a desperate struggle with the Greek mercenaries on the bank. Alexander came to their rescue, pushing aside all opposition till he reached the flank of the mercenaries, then made straight for the chariot of Darius. Terrible slaughter ensued on both sides as the phalanx assisted Alexander and the Persian nobility stood fast to shield their King. Darius, fearing that he would be made a captive, threw aside his cloak, mounted a horse and fled. At once the troops in his vicinity scattered. On the right, when he saw the flight of Darius and consequent *débâcle*, Nabarsanes also retreated with his cavalry. Pursuit of the fleeing enemy was impossible because of the gathering darkness. Many escaped, some to Cilicia, some to southern Cappadocia, others reached Egypt; about 2,000 Greek mercenaries succeeded in linking up with Darius in the north. In a hollow by the roadside was found the royal chariot, with the mantle, bow and shield of the monarch of Asia; it had been wisely abandoned by the driver when he could not conduct it up the stony mountain track.

When the evening meal was set Alexander enquired why he heard the sobbing and wailing of women near his tent; he was told that the mother, wife and family of Darius were prisoners, mourning in the belief that Darius was slain. At once a messenger was sent to inform them that Darius was alive, and at the same time an imperative order was issued that all must be treated with the respect and the honour due to royalty.

Some writers tell that next day the King, with Hephaestion, paid a ceremonial visit to the family. Sisygambis, the mother of Darius, prostrated herself before Hephaestion, the taller of the two men, thinking that he was the King. Finding her error, she was afraid, but Alexander smilingly remarked that his companion was another Alexander. He fondled the young children and showed every mark of kindness. To the astonishment of the world of that time, and indeed of many future centuries, Alexander took no advantage of these captives. The wife of Darius was reputed to be the most beautiful woman in Persia, but Alexander refused to see her, respecting her position and desiring to avoid scandalous imputation. For this conduct Alexander was regarded by his contemporaries as the noblest of all conquerors. Later, the mother of Darius (Sisygambis) had much influence with Alexander; a sympathetic mother and son relationship developed between them.

The victory of Issus conferred on Alexander the reputation as of a god. Although most of the treasures had been sent in advance to Damascus, the magnificent Persian tents, the goblets, vases, ornaments, hangings, rugs and furnishings were to the Macedonians, accustomed to simple living, impressive and bewildering. As usual, Alexander gave liberally to his officers and friends; to his mother he sent a few precious and beautiful objects. For himself he reserved little, but chose a small golden casket, in which he preserved the copy of the *Iliad* which accompanied him in all his travels. Many treasures and suits of armour were sent to Athens to ornament the city; his gifts were coldly received.

SIEGE OF TYRE, JANUARY TO AUGUST, 332 B.C.

Much as he desired to turn east, Alexander decided that he must first ensure the loyalty of the Phoenician coast towns; thus the Persian fleet could find no harbours for supplies and repairs. If Tyre, the most powerful town, did not submit, a long siege would be required. Parmenion went to Syria with transport and baggage while Alexander marched down the coast. Many cities greeted him, bringing gifts; among the most important were Byblus and Sidon. Envoys also came from Tyre, but when Alexander asked permission to worship in the Temple of Heracles he was told that as no strangers were allowed to enter the new town, he should visit that in the old town.

Old Tyre stood on the mainland; new Tyre on an island, long and narrow, about half a mile from the coast. They were separated by a sea channel, shallow near the shore, eighteen feet deep near the island. New Tyre had two harbours: one looking south, toward Egypt; the other northeast, toward Sidon. New Tyre was encircled by a stout wall built of square stones and strong cement, its base being protected by rocks and boulders collected in loose heaps which prevented the close approach of siege engines. These defensive measures were believed to render Tyre impregnable. Alexander explained why so strong a fortress could not be left in the rear of his advancing army:

> Friends and allies, I see that an expedition to Egypt will not be safe for us so long as the Persians retain the

sovereignty of the sea; nor is it safe for other reasons, especially when considering the state of matters in Greece, to pursue Darius whilst leaving in our rear the city of Tyre in doubtful allegiance, and Egypt and Cyprus occupied by the Persians. . . . While we advance towards Babylon in pursuit of Darius the Persians would again conquer the sea districts, and transfer the war into Greece with a larger army. The Lacedaemonians are now without disguise waging war against us, and the city of Athens is restrained rather by fear than by goodwill towards us. But if Tyre were captured, the whole of Phoenicia would be in our possession, and the fleet of the Phoenicians, the most numerous, and the best in the Persian Navy, would in all probability come over to us. For the Phoenician sailors and marines will not put to sea, and incur danger when their cities are occupied by us. Then Cyprus will either yield to us without delay, or easily be captured on the arrival of a naval force. Then, navigating the sea with the ships from Macedonia, together with those of the Phoenicians, Cyprus coming with us, we shall acquire absolute sovereignty over the sea. Thus an expedition into Egypt must be successful. When Egypt has submitted, there will no longer be any anxiety about Greece and our own country, and we shall be able to pass on to Babylon in safety, having gained a high reputation by taking possession of all the maritime provinces and all the land on this side of the Euphrates.

Engineers, divers, chemical inventors, men of every rank displayed supreme bravery; throughout the siege the skill and ingenuity of the combatants were equally matched. Expecting the Phoenician allies and Carthage to come to their aid, the Tyrians watched the horizon; in vain. Alexander built a mole from the mainland to the island, 200 feet wide and strong enough to support the tall towers which would deliver stones and heavy missiles over the wall. On piles driven in deep were packed stones taken from old Tyre. Trees from adjacent forests formed the next layer; when these were bound with rushes torn from the swamp, the mole made rapid headway. The Tyrians sent divers to undermine its structure; Alexander provided his labourers with covering protection. At length there rolled along the completed mole two tall towers shielded by various devices to ward off fireballs thrown from the rampart. The Tyrians sent a warship with metal arms from which hung cauldrons containing sulphur, oil and other inflammable material; these were set alight when a strong wind blew towards the towers. Fanned by the wind the blaze could not be subdued. Thus in one hour the labour of many months was rendered useless; even part of the mole was cracked and swept away by the waves.

Historians tell us that Diades, the engineer, took Tyre with Alexander. While he constructed a new mole to carry a greater number of towers, Alexander set out to find allies with ships. The report of the victory at Issus having attracted many waverers to his cause, and the prestige of the Persians having declined since the refusal of coastal cities to admit their ships into the harbours, Alexander was confident of gaining friends in Asia Minor. His magnetic personality and convincing speech won over many who had decided to remain neutral until the future would show whether victory would lie with Persia or with Macedonia. He returned to Tyre with some 250 ships, some with three and four tiers of rowers, equipped by Lycia, Cyprus, Rhodes and Cilicia. Thus the Persian navy no longer endangered his flank or rear; it could not now join with Sparta to invade Macedonia when he advanced into Persia.

Whilst the new ships were being prepared for action Alexander spent ten days in the mountains behind old Tyre and forced the tribes to lead honest lives as his subjects. Thus he made safe a district which had never been free from robbers who raided the villages, terrified the inhabitants and plundered passers-by. Little is recorded of these numerous hill campaigns, full of danger for the King and his army.

The Tyrians were dismayed to see the number and the power of the newly fitted Macedonian navy, three times larger than their own, with many ships recognised to have come from former allies. Alexander offered to fight on sea, but Tyre refused the unequal combat. Mooring his ships along both sides of the mole, Alexander could keep watch on both the northern and the southern harbours. The mole approached nearer the island; siege engines rolled along its surface and endeavoured to breach the wall. Loose boulders and rocks which obstructed the battering rams, and stones thrown from the rampart were lifted up with cranes and carried out to the open sea. Tyre's divers severed the crane ropes; Alexander replaced them with iron chains.

As the peril of the battering rams became imminent, the Tyrians devised a plan to elude their assailants. As part of the Tyrian fleet was in the northern, and part in the southern harbour, they could not join forces while Alexander had his Cyprian vessels on the northern, and his Phoenician ships on the southern side of his mole. Toward noon Alexander was accustomed to stay in his tent and his crews went ashore to fetch provisions. The Tyrians in the northern harbour hid with a screen of masts their preparations to reach the open sea and attack the moored Cyprian fleet. But it happened that Alexander on that day was alert and realised that his Cyprian ships were being damaged. The mole was now so high that he was obliged to sail all round the island to reach the enemy. Watching from their wall, the Tyrians sent signals warning their sailors to return, but in the din of battle their cries were drowned. Many large Tyrian vessels were destroyed. Further schemes for escape were prevented by blocking both harbours.

The attack on the city wall, carried out with increasing vigour, caused damage which the defenders repaired. It was now July; after six months of hard endeavour success still seemed so far off that some of the army wondered whether Alexander would leave Tyre and pass on to Egypt. But Alexander never contemplated withdrawal. When at length a large breach was made in the wall he led the assault in person; the troops poured in after him, eager for revenge. They had often witnessed their captured comrades being tortured, then slain, on the top of the ramparts, their bodies thrown into the sea, thus deprived of burial rites. Even the King's heralds had been slaughtered, then pitched over into the water.

Terrible was the carnage; thousands were sold into slavery; but those who fled for refuge in the Temple of Heracles were pardoned and protected. We who have experienced the horrors of modern scientific warfare dare not pass judgment on the vengeance perpetrated after the fall of Tyre.

Sacrifices of thanksgiving were held in the temple; then followed the Hellenic games and festivities always arranged for the relaxation of troops after long periods of strenuous labour. Tyre long remained a ruin, but became an important fortress for the Macedonian advance. After years of tides and mud silting against the mole the island became a peninsula.

All the towns along the coast submitted except Gaza; its strong wall led its commander to believe that he could withstand a siege; Alexander sent for the mighty engines from Tyre, tracked out a weak spot in the wall and gained the fortress within two months. During the assault he received a severe wound in the shoulder which confirmed his augur's prediction of danger to him in person during this siege.

Experts say that coins dug up in Asia Minor bear the impress of Alexander as King, a proof that he was regarded as a King south of the Taurus range of mountains; but west of these hills the cities were free, and maintained their own government.

During the siege of Tyre a letter came from Darius offering Alexander all the region west of the Euphrates, 10,000 talents, and the hand of his daughter in marriage. Parmenion advised acceptance of these terms; but the King drily replied that he too would agree if he were Parmenion, but as he was Alexander, the offer was refused. Here one may quote the characteristic introductory and the closing sentences of his reply:

Your forefathers came into Macedonia and other parts of Greece and did us harm. . . . Now I, having been appointed leader of the Greeks and desiring to punish the Persians, have crossed into Asia. . . . My father was killed by conspirators whom your people instigated, as you have

boasted in your letters. . . . Now that I have conquered
in battle, first your generals and satraps, then you and
your army, and am by gift of the gods in possession of your
country, I am protecting those of your men who escaped
. . . to take refuge with me, and of their own accord
joined my army. As I am Lord of Asia, come to me; but
if you fear harsh treatment, send some of your friends to
receive pledges of safety from me. . . . Ask for your
mother, your wife, your children, and anything you
will. . . . Nothing will be denied you that is just. And
for the future . . . send to me as the King of Asia; do not
address me as an equal. . . . But if you dispute my right
to the kingdom, stay and fight for it; do not play the
runaway, for I shall march against you, wherever you
may be.

That is a straightforward letter from a confident young man.

EGYPT, WINTER, 332 TO 331 B.C. (FOUR MONTHS)

Late in 332 B.C. Alexander arrived in Egypt and was
greeted as a liberator. For two centuries the people had
groaned under the yoke of the Persians, who had shown
contempt for their religion, even violating their temples.
The civilisation of Egypt had existed over 7,000 years; its
immense buildings and inscriptions bear witness to the
strength of the nation and its respect for religion. Would that
we had any record of the thoughts of Alexander and his
army when they first saw the gigantic pyramids and the
mysterious Sphinx watching over the limitless expanse of the
plains. Thus had its impenetrable eyes gazed during long
centuries whilst generations of men lived and died, and
mighty monarchs with their armies came and passed.

At the head of the Nile delta the Macedonians crossed to
the capital, Memphis, then one of the largest cities in the
world, now only a ruin affording fruitful occupation for
modern excavators. There Alexander was crowned as
Pharaoh and captivated priests and people by sacrificing
to their sacred deity, Ptah, represented by the sacred bull,

Apis, in which the god was supposed to be incarnated. Such conduct was in marked contrast to that of the Persians, who had wounded the sacred bulls. Leaving the main army in Memphis, Alexander examined the mouth of the Nile. There he found two harbours protected from the open sea by the island of Pharos, and decided at once that this was an ideal position for a new town which would become a centre of commerce between Egypt, Arabia, India and the cities on the Mediterranean coast. Thus was born Alexandria, which became a large and prosperous town when Ptolemy was King of Egypt. Later, on the island of Pharos a great lighthouse was constructed which was regarded as one of the wonders of the world.

Strabo, the geographer whose works escaped destruction during the centuries when many valuable writings were lost, described the lay-out of Alexandria, with its two main avenues 100 feet wide, lined with colonnades. Every detail was considered under the personal supervision of Alexander: the market square with public offices, school, gymnasium, temple, theatre and roads wide enough for chariots with horses. Excavations have confirmed the grandeur of Alexander's conception and the achievement of his architect, the town-planner, Deinocrates.

Having concluded his military and civilian duties Alexander was free to give rein to the romantic and mystical aspects of his temperament. He was eager to visit the oasis of Siwah in which stood the Temple of Ammon, famed for the wisdom of its Oracle. The route through the Libyan desert was unmapped and arduous; only the devotion of his officers could have endured such an expedition without any military objective. Stories of miraculous guidance have been handed down, describing how the path was shown by snakes who glided before the company and how, in the darkness, when the direct track was missed, ravens flew near and croaked until the right trail was regained. At length the oasis was seen, a wondrous contrast to the desert over which they had made their weary journey; its palms, dates and rich verdure formed an ideal retreat for the small community who dwelt in the temple. The chief priest welcomed

Alexander, addressing him as "son of Ammon", the title usual for a Pharaoh. Alexander entered the inner shrine of the temple alone; no one heard his questions nor the answers he received. Callisthenes, the historian, although not present at the meeting, caused confusion in future years by stating that the priest had greeted the King as a "son of Zeus", thus labelling him as a god. An imaginary conversation repeated by Callisthenes also led to trouble when that flatterer fell deservedly out of favour with his King.

In the temple Alexander evidently had a prophetic revelation which influenced his whole future. He wrote to his mother that he could confide to no one what he had been told; but at their next meeting he would reveal to her alone the secret which had been divulged to him. As Fate decreed that his life was cut short, mother and son never met again. The information so sacred to Alexander will never be known; throughout the remainder of his life any slighting reference to that experience roused him to intense anger.

On returning to Memphis, Alexander instituted wise lines of government: peasants and officials were protected against extortion, having the right of direct appeal to the King. Civilian and military control were separated; as the former collected the taxes, the military were not tempted to interfere with finance. To ensure that no local trouble could develop into organised resistance against the central Government, Egyptians were left in their posts under Macedonian supervision. These arrangements pleased the people, because the oppressive Persian system of tax collection was replaced by a method more efficient and more just.

About this time Athens requested that the Greek prisoners taken at the Granicus should be returned, and as the envoys adopted a more conciliatory tone than usual, Alexander sent a favourable reply.

In spring, 331 B.C., Alexander began the march to the east which was to occupy him and his army for many a long year. None could have foreseen the many obstacles which were to crop up at every advance into new territory. Meanwhile Darius and his generals had been collecting an enormous army; all felt that victory would this time crown their efforts. In Athens also the failure of Alexander was confidently predicted; Demosthenes spoke openly of letters received from Persia prophesying the early downfall of this too self-assured young man; for how could his limited force withstand the great numbers which Persia had been collecting from every race and province of her vast empire?

During the summer of 331 B.C. Sparta had seized the opportunity given by the absence of Alexander and invaded Macedonia. But after severe fighting Antipater had defeated the large Spartan army; in the conflict, their King Agis had been slain. Sparta appealed to Alexander for merciful terms, to which he agreed on condition that the Lacedaemonians now joined the League of Corinth. This news from Pella relieved all anxiety regarding the security of the rear in Europe; the unification of Greece rendered safe the advance into Asia. It is said that Alexander remarked that the trouble with Sparta, in comparison with the fighting experienced in Asia, appeared like "a battle with mice".

BATTLE OF GAUGAMELA, 331 B.C.

Marching east with 40,000 men and 8,000 cavalry, Alexander reached Thapsacus in August, 331 B.C. A division had been sent ahead to construct a bridge over the Euphrates. Mazaeus, waiting on the opposite bank, retreated and reported to Darius that the encounter would not be long delayed. An eclipse of the moon on September 20th was regarded as an omen favourable to the Macedonians, promising victory before the month was over. From captured Persian sentinels Alexander learned that Darius was stationed on the left bank of the Tigris with an army much greater than that defeated at Issus. The crossing of so swift a river in the face of an opposing force being impossible, Alexander sought for a site where the current was fordable; during the difficult passage over the Tigris not one life was lost. After a day of rest the army proceeded on its eastward march.

It is a not a simple matter to explain to the lay reader the famous victory at Gaugamela; the manoeuvres of fighting armies are bewildering to follow. And yet it would be unfair to dismiss in a few lines the critical turning point of the

Asiatic campaign, the victory which, on October 1st, 331 B.C., changed the whole course of the world for many centuries. The sketch-plan on page 47 explains more clearly than can any enumeration in the text, the respective positions of the opposing armies and the arrangement of the many races who engaged in that desperate struggle for the mastery of Asia.

Some seven miles from the enemy, Alexander gave his men four days' rest for recuperation and thorough preparation. He left there the hospitals and heavy baggage so that the troops, having only their weapons to carry, would be more free for the ordeal ahead. The march began on the night of September 29th-30th, and, owing to the nature of the ground, occupied more time than had been expected.

The figures estimated for the Persian army cannot be vouched for; historians quote different numbers. But some prisoners stated that Darius had about a million soldiers, 40,000 cavalry, many scythed chariots and some elephants—animals especially dangerous because horses would not face them. So many Greek mercenaries had been lost at Issus that the Persians were short of infantry. Through the mist of the early morning, from the hills, Alexander carefully considered the vast army on the plain below, with cavalry and infantry arranged in deep squares. Seeing that his much smaller army would be outflanked, he decided on precautions to meet this disadvantage. Halting the onward march, he called a council of war and discussed the situation. Parmenion advised that the plan should be examined for traps; agreeing with this counsel, Alexander set out with a small contingent of infantry and Companion cavalry to reconnoitre the ground. Then he addressed his officers in a stirring speech, explaining that the existence of the army depended upon their perfect discipline throughout the day of battle. They would advance in complete silence, so that when the trumpets sounded, and the signal was given, their battle cry would convey even more terror than usual. Defeat or victory would be determined by the response of every individual to the orders of his commander.

A night of rest was ordered so that the men should be fresh and vigorous after a good breakfast in the morning. Late in the evening Parmenion visited the King in his tent and urged that an attack should be made during the night, when the Persians, having removed their armour and unsaddled their horses, would be taken by surprise and confused. But Alexander did not agree with this suggestion; it was better to keep the Persians on edge, suspecting an attack, sleeping badly in consequence; he added that he would not "steal a victory". He refused to consider the plan because such a victory would convey to the Persians no real sense of defeat.

Alexander then slept so peacefully that in the morning Parmenion went to awaken him after the troops had breakfasted. To Parmenion's reproaches he cheerfully replied that he felt victorious already, because at last they had caught up with the battle-shy Darius.

Documents found after the conflict showed the plans and composition of the Persian army. Darius was in the centre, surrounded by his kinsmen, nobility and loyal courtiers; Indians, Uxii and men from the Persian Gulf reinforced this position. In front of Darius were fifty chariots and fifteen elephants; further along, on both sides, stood a large number of scythed chariots. Part of the plain had been levelled to enable the chariots to be driven forward swiftly, unimpeded by obstacles or rough ground. To resist the Macedonian phalanx Greek mercenaries were stationed on each side, just behind Darius. Behind him also were Babylonians, Sitacenians, Indians, and troops from the Red Sea. In command of the left wing was Bessus, a relative of the Great King and satrap of Bactria, with a large contingent of horsemen from Bactria, Sogdiana, Saca and the Jaxartes allies; also on the left was the cavalry of Barsaentes, satrap of Arachosia. On the Persian right, under Pharasmanes, were horsemen from Parthia, Tapuria and Hyrcania; and behind, under Atropates, the Medes and troops from Syria and Transjordan; cavalry also came from Armenia and Cappadocia. The right wing, which was to play so important a part in the fray, was commanded by Mazaeus. Thus Mazaeus faced

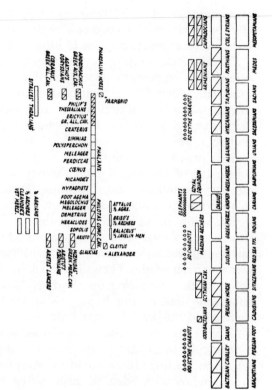

SKETCH OF THE OPPOSING ARMIES AT GAUGAMELA

From *Alexander*, by Lieutenant-Colonel Dodge, by kind permission of
Messrs. Houghton, Mifflin & Co.

Parmenion on the Macedonian left, and Bessus faced Alexander on the Macedonian right. Both Mazaeus and Bessus were experienced men of high fighting quality.

The Macedonian army was arranged so that on the right were the Companion cavalry under Philotas, and the Royal squadron under Cleitus, with Alexander. Then came in order the squadrons of Glaucus, Ariston, Sopolis, Heracleides, Demetrius, Meleager and Hegalochus; next these came the phalanx, light and heavy-armed. With Alexander, in front of the cavalry, were Agrianians, archers and javelin men. On the left of the cavalry came the Agema of the hypaspists and the battalions under Coenus, Perdiccas, Meleager, Polyperchon, Simmias and Craterus. Further left was Philip, commanding the Thessalian cavalry, a body which had proved itself a rival to the Companions. On the extreme left Parmenion was in command, with the Pharsalian horse, the best squadron of the Thessalian cavalry. Finding that the Companions were facing the chariots, Alexander threw out before the line of the hypaspists a force of Agrianians, archers and the javelin men of Balacrus.

As his army was outflanked on both sides Alexander for the first time in any battle stationed a strong reserve column behind both wings; these would be ready for any emergency if the enemy succeeded in penetrating the Macedonian front, because they could wheel to the right, to the left, or turn to face attack from the rear. The left reserve column consisted of the Thracian and half the allied horse, and the Greek mercenary cavalry under Andromachus. In the right reserve column were Greek mercenary horse under Menidas; Paeonian cavalry under Ariston; lancers, Agrianians, archers and veteran mercenaries under Cleander. Thus those most exposed to danger were Ariston and the Greek cavalry under Menidas. Well behind the army the Thracian infantry guarded the camp with the baggage, the prisoners and the family of Darius.

As no one could be spared from the front line, all depended upon the opening manoeuvres. The armies advanced slowly toward each other. Alexander deployed to the right in echelon, with Cleitus, light infantry, hypaspists and two battalions of the phalanx; all was conducted with precision and in silence. The Persians made a counter-move with some disorder on their left, where their line overlapped the Macedonian right. Scythian horsemen trotted out to attack the oblique move to the right, but Alexander ignored them, continuing his course. Darius, fearing that Alexander might arrive beyond the ground which had been levelled for the chariots, ordered these out; the Agrianians and the archers met them with stones and javelins, wounded the horses and frightened them by beating their shields with their spears, dragged drivers and riders from their seats and cut the harness; then, when the Macedonian infantry opened their ranks, the chariots passed through without doing any damage.

Meanwhile Darius had sent Bactrian and Scythian cavalry with orders to turn the Macedonian right wing; to meet this threat Alexander ordered Menidas to resist their charge. But as Menidas' small number was repulsed, the Paeonians were despatched to his assistance and together these fought with vigour and forced back the Bactrians and Scythians. Another company of Bactrians charged with such fury that those who had been driven off were able to re-form and fell upon Menidas and Ariston. Then Scythians, armoured from head to foot, with horses equally protected, hurled themselves on the Paeonians and the veterans, but though many were slain and wounded the Macedonians did not yield.

During this time of fierce combat Alexander watched and issued commands necessary for success. He had not yet engaged the Companion cavalry; the time for their use had not arrived; he pursued his steady course to the right, his keen eye judging every movement of the struggle. When within bowshot of the enemy he hastened his pace and ordered Aretas with his sarissophores—the last reserve horsemen—to assist Menidas and Ariston. Seeing this manoeuvre, the Persians detached cavalry to counter it, thus opening out a gap in their left wing. This provided the opportunity which Alexander had anticipated and for which he had been waiting. Without a moment's delay he gave the signal for the assault and at lightning speed turned obliquely to his left, charging at the head of the Companions with Cleitus and the hypaspists shouting their terrifying battle cry. This irresistible charge of the Companion cavalry broke through the Persian front rank, dispersing them; Perdiccas and Coenus at the same time rushed to the centre, concentrating on the group which surrounded Darius. The Scythians, chased by the sarissophores, the Paeonians and the Greek cavalry, could do little to stem the Macedonian onslaught. The Persian left wing crumpled up. Then came a scramble to hurry off the field when Darius, seeing his own charioteer transfixed with a spear, turned and fled. Bessus, powerless to arrest the fleeing crowd, sullenly joined in the retreat.

Alexander had begun to pursue the demoralised army when he received an urgent message from Parmenion, begging for help. Owing to the skill of Mazaeus the Macedonian left had been in serious trouble. He had attacked the Thessalian cavalry with such vigour that Craterus and the adjacent phalanx battalions had been obliged to go to their aid. The Parthian and the Indian cavalry had passed right through the Macedonian phalanx, but instead of attacking its rear, as they should have done, they went on to the camp, probably with the object of securing the family of Darius. The Thracians in charge of the camp were too lightly armed to guard it; many were killed and the camp was set on fire. Seeing this disaster, the reserve column turned round and drove off the Persians. It was at this time that Parmenion had sent his urgent call for help. Although Alexander is said to have exclaimed that Parmenion must have lost his head, with his Companion cavalry he at once turned and galloped as fast as possible to the Macedonian left. Caught between the Companion cavalry and the reserve column behind the phalanx, the Persians put up a desperate fight, but were annihilated. By the time Alexander reached the Persian right their line had broken. Mazaeus saw that further resistance was useless, but by skilful retreat many lives could be saved; Bessus, having formed the same conclusion, followed Darius. Alexander rode on through the clouds of dust raised by the fugitives until darkness fell.

It was essential to hasten after the panic-stricken army; only thus could the Persians be prevented from turning to re-form into an organised whole capable of strong resistance. Even after midnight Alexander's swift pursuit was continued over thirty-five miles, as far as the village of Arbela; but Darius had the advantage of a long start. Owing to the time lost when Alexander had returned to extricate Parmenion, the headlong race was not rewarded by the capture of Darius. Mazaeus escaped to Babylon; Bessus fled with Darius. The Persian losses at Gaugamela were heavy; many thousands were slain; some reports mention 40,000; others say 60,000—even 90,000! The Macedonians lost only 500. Thus, as at Issus, the victors lost few lives; the vanquished lost many.

Lieutenant-Colonel Dodge sums up his professional opinion of Gaugamela: "Never were dispositions better taken to resist the attacks of the enemy at all points; never on the field were openings more quickly seized; never was threatening disaster more skilfully retrieved . . . The world will never see more splendid tactics."

Gaugamela was the Waterloo of the Persian Empire; on that memorable day the world was altered for many centuries, for on that first of October, 331 B.C., Alexander of Macedon became Great King of Asia.

CHAPTER III

BABYLON TO HINDU-KUSH, OCTOBER, 331, TO NOVEMBER, 330 B.C.

*Welcome at Babylon—Persian Governor appointed—
Civil and military duties—Character of Macedonians
and Persians—Susa—Uxii tribe subdued—The
Persian Gates—Persepolis and Pasargadae—Darius
retires to Ecbatana and the Caspian Gates—Darius a
prisoner of Bessus—Alexander pursues Bessus—Finds
body of Darius—Alexander passes to Hyrcania
through Parthia—Appoints Persian Governors—
Bessus assumes title of King—Satibarsanes rouses
Aria to revolt—Submission of Aria—Alexandria-
in-Aria founded—Friendly country of Ariaspae—
Projects dawning for combination of East and West*

WHEN Darius fled from the field at Gaugamela he did not turn toward Babylon, for it was certain that Alexander would follow him there. With a small force he accompanied his relative, Bessus, to Ecbatana, the royal city in the high mountain region of Persia. One of his generals, Ariobarsanes, had escaped with some 40,000 men to the Persian Gates, a strong position where he expected to arrest the advancing Macedonian army. Mazaeus, who at Gaugamela had impressed Alexander by his competent leadership against Parmenion's left wing, had arrived in Babylon and warned the town of the imminent approach of the Macedonians. Alexander had traversed the 300 miles to Babylon with his usual speed, for he had anticipated stern resistance which might demand a prolonged siege. However, as Mazaeus convinced the authorities that it would be useless to attempt to hold the city, Alexander was met by a long procession bringing flowers and gifts to greet him.

The Persian rulers had not been welcome in Babylonia. As in Greece and in Egypt, Xerxes had aroused hatred by his disrespect for their religion and his destruction of sacred edifices. He had not even spared E-Sagila, an immense temple, one of the wonders of the world, which had been left intact by all previous conquerors.

But Alexander had already the reputation of one who was interested in the religious faiths of every nation, and soon became friendly with the priests of Babylon. He promised that their famous temple should be restored; but on his next visit, a short time before his death, he found that the ruins had been so extensive that the site had not been cleared. Hellenic games and festivities were instituted during a time of rest for the army; thanksgiving sacrifices were conducted according to the rites of Babylon. In gratitude to so unusual a victor, Alexander was given the title of King of Babylonia.

The thirty days spent in the town were all too brief for the innumerable tasks connected with military reorganisation and the civilian government. Enquiry into the effect of the Persian rule revealed to Alexander that the people of Babylonia had become as apathetic as had other provinces; if he instituted strict control under Macedonian authorities, the Babylonians would feel further humiliation and resentment, and would not assist the measures he desired to adopt to ensure their co-operation. He determined to arouse their latent energy, to infuse into a people once active and brave some of the Hellenic initiative; as they recovered self-respect and hope for the future they would take on responsibility under a capable Governor of their own race. This had been in the past a successful method of Greek colonisation. Therefore, having formed a high opinion of Mazaeus, his strongest adversary at Gaugamela, Alexander appointed him to be Viceroy of Babylon, an unexpected decision which gave much satisfaction to the people.

The kingdom of Babylonia had a chequered history dating

back many thousand years. In the south, near the Persian Gulf, the civilisation of the Chaldeans was almost as ancient as that of Egypt. Throughout the kingdom the land was fertile, owing to its excellent irrigation; the ruins of numerous cities, deeply buried in dust, are still being excavated. Babylonia was the cradle of humanity; for centuries its prosperity drew over it successive waves of conquerors, some of whom are recorded in the Old Testament. Nebuchadnezzar I reigned forty-three years, united the provinces of the kingdom and made Babylon its capital. With the advent of Cyrus the Great, in 538 B.C., Babylonia became a province of Persia.

Babylon was guarded by a wall 300 feet high and 70 feet wide, with high towers and 100 brazen gates opening on to the surrounding country. Recent archæological research does not confirm this number of the gates, nor the measurements of the towers and the wall. The town was divided by the Euphrates river; on one side stood the royal palace with its famous Hanging Gardens which legend tells were created by Queen Semiramis. On the eastern side of the city was the Temple of E-Sagila, which from 2150 B.C. remained a majestic monument until the coming of the ruthless Xerxes. To-day, Babylon is represented by mounds of earth which archæologists continue to examine; stones being obtainable only from the distant mountains of Armenia, the city was built of clay and brick, which do not endure. Thus this once mighty town is now reduced to a small village, Hillah.

The alluvial deposit from the rivers and the wisely cultivated soil produced every type of vegetable, fruit and cereal; thus the land was thickly populated, and a prosperous civilisation was the natural consequence. The Macedonian army was overcome by the luxury of this glamorous city; never had they seen such profusion; the immense statues and great edifices, the display of wealth and beauty in a land where they had expected to find only "barbarians" was a revelation which proved dangerous to the morale of many of the officers and men.

The history of culture in Babylonia from 7000 B.C. had brought about a high standard of general education. Their scientific experts were so learned that they could co-operate with the distinguished men who came from Greece with Alexander; knowledge of mathematics and astronomy was then so advanced that it stands comparison with that of modern days. Slaves were apprenticed to acquire knowledge of many trades, and the lives of the people were enriched with the common use of fine embroideries, rugs and carpets with exquisite patterns of flowers and strange animals, beautiful tapestry and every branch of artistic craft: carved and engraved precious stones, jewels, exquisitely wrought ornaments, cups, vases and other vessels of gold and silver for use in the home or the temple. Knowledge of dyes was then unequalled and has never been surpassed; infused from natural flowers, herbs and shrubs, they were superior to those of modern days because they did not fade in the sunlight as do colours of chemical manufacture. The Babylonians had also a range of good musical instruments: harps, cymbals, trumpets and pipes.

Alexander acquired some knowledge of the religion of the country. The Chaldean religion was noble; the poems to the Moon God are of high spiritual quality; in the northern regions the Sun God had more prominence. But even a superficial account of that subject would require a separate volume.

The nobility of Babylonia were ceremonious in manners, used to intrigue, of luxurious habits, often servile, as is usual with a people who have dwelt long under the rule of a foreign race. The Macedonians formed a striking contrast: proud, often arrogant in bearing, and hardy in mode of life until in later years many adopted extravagant habits in Persia. The Greeks with Alexander were of another type: alert, energetic, with much initiative; they included the philosophers, artists, poets, inventors, the companions suitable for a King who never forgot the value of the Muses. Precious books were continually being despatched to him from Greece; in this respect he resembled Napoleon, whose coach, as it sped from one end of Europe to another, was continually refilled with literature from Paris.

When in Egypt, Alexander had begun to understand that

the only possible foundation for an enduring and successful government in a foreign land was an attitude of friendly co-operation between the victor and the conquered race. The problem became more insistent as he advanced. Such a plan, new to the world at that time, he gradually and with caution put into practice. In the not distant future he declared his principle: "I have not come here to destroy nations; I have come here that those who are subdued by my arms shall have nought to complain of my victories." Satraps who had fiercely resisted him now approached him with confidence and acted as his willing helpers. Those whom he believed to be trustworthy he left in their positions of authority; but posts concerned with finance and military organisation were retained by Macedonians.

Preparations for the advance to the East entailed intricate planning for an army so far from Europe. Communications had to be safeguarded for armaments, supplies, and heavy transport. Even at this early date the King had begun to consider whether Persian recruits could be incorporated into his army formations. Who can believe the fluent writers of discreditable tales that in Babylon this King, overwhelmed with administrative legislation and military plans, spent his nights in drinking bouts and revels with the courtesans of Babylon? The credulous who believe such scandal over-estimate the physical limits of the body and brain.

Susa, the capital of the Persian Empire, was the next step on the journey. The weather was cooler; in the summer the heat would have made impossible a rapid march. A messenger had been sent from Susa to tell Alexander that he would meet no opposition; all the treasures would be found intact. These surpassed all expectations: furnishings, tapestries, precious stones, jewels, ingots of gold and silver. Silver was despatched to Macedonia to help Antipater; statues which had been conveyed from Athens by Xerxes were returned to Greece, to be erected on their original positions; the ingots were broken and turned into useful coinage to defray the salaries of the army and to aid commerce. Here, too, a palace was placed at the disposal of the family of Darius, who had accompanied the army during its advance in considerable discomfort. At last they obtained a home befitting their rank, and Alexander arranged that the younger members should have instruction in Greek culture and language.

Reinforcements, much needed, had come from Macedonia, and soldiers who desired to return home were encouraged to do so. The army required drastic reorganisation, for with a new type of country fresh methods of warfare would be necessary. The system of signalling was altered; torches were to be used in the dark hours of the night, whilst heavy volumes of smoke provided new means of sending messages by day from long distances. The cavalry squadrons were divided into two companies, each with a Companion at the head. Alexander had a gift for instructing novel methods of discipline to inexperienced recruits; he foresaw that even for his tried soldiers new formations and new rules of drill would be necessary when they entered into countries with contours to which they were unaccustomed, and when Persian recruits were gradually drafted into their ranks.

Persepolis, the next objective in the advance, stood high in the hills with no easy line of approach. Military experts agree that most historians minimise the immense difficulties which had to be surmounted on the road between Susa and Persepolis, where chains of hills rose in nine and ten terraces to snow-clad heights of about 14,000 feet. It is said that the passage to Persepolis was almost equivalent to a march over the Alps; and this adventure took place during the cold months of winter.

Of the untamed inhabitants who dwelt in the hills, the Uxii tribe were the most menacing, accustomed to exact payment from all who essayed to pass through their region. The Uxii of the plains agreed to submit to Alexander, but the mountain branch of the tribe refused to exempt him from the tribute paid by all travellers. Even the Kings of Persia were held up on the road to their own great town until they settled the amount demanded. As this practice would imperil the army communications and transport, it was imperative that the mountain Uxii should either submit or be enrolled as willing subjects.

Early in December, when Alexander received notice that he would be permitted to pass after payment of toll, he replied that the Uxii would obtain their due when they came down from their heights to the usual meeting place. Leaving part of his army at this chosen site, Alexander, with 4,000 men, was conducted by a native guide during the night through dense forests and over racing streams to the village homes of the mountain Uxii. Ptolemy and Craterus were stationed where they could intercept fleeing stragglers. The mountain tribe were still asleep when the Macedonians fell upon them; when at length the fighting members of the clan arrived on the scene they found their chief stronghold occupied. Thus, with a mere handful of troops, and within a few hours, Alexander had succeeded in a task which the Persian kings, for generations, with heavy forces at their disposal, had in vain attempted to accomplish. The territory was placed under a Susian satrap. Apparently Sisygambis, the mother of Darius, was influential later in obtaining mild terms of surrender for the Uxii: they were ordered to cease from demanding toll from passengers along the roads, to cultivate their land, and to pay to Alexander an annual tribute of horses, cattle and sheep.

Parmenion had in the meantime been advancing without opposition over the road which wound over the southern foothills to Persepolis. Alexander took with him a light force of the Companion cavalry, Agrianians, lancers, archers and horse bowmen; in five days they travelled 113 miles to the Persian Gates. He dared not proceed to Persepolis by the low road; had he taken that route his rear would have been insecure. Ariobarsanes had fled from Gaugamela with 40,000 men, and awaited the Macedonians at the end of the narrow defile known as the Persian Gates. A strong wall had been built to guard the entrance of this gorge which led to the plateau of Iran. When the Macedonians had advanced some way up its narrow path, Ariobarsanes hurled down on them heavy stones and rocks from his position on the top of the wall. As only three men could walk abreast, so constricted was the road below the wall, Alexander retired some miles to consider his plans. From prisoners he learned that he could be guided by night, through forests, by imperceptible tracks now deep in snow and ice, to a height where his army could form above and behind that of Ariobarsanes, firmly stationed on the wall's summit. Craterus was ordered to remain with the infantry in the defile and keep many camp fires burning for one or two nights until he received a signal that Alexander had reached the height behind the Persian force. During daylight an appearance of bustling activity would deceive the Persians into believing that the whole Macedonian army was still below the wall, busy with plans to scale it.

With a selected company of foot soldiers, cavalry, archers and Agrianians, all carrying three days' ration of food, Alexander set forth by night on the most arduous and perhaps the most dangerous mountaineering task he ever undertook. So rough and so slippery was the path that one false step would have been fatal. By the early morning he reached the summit, and during the day he rested, concealed in the forest. He then divided his forces, sending cavalry toward the plains with orders to build a bridge over the Araxes river and to cut off any retreating Persians. During a storm which raged all the second night, his army picked their way through forests, over ravines and precipices. The Persians on the wall felt secure as they counted the numerous camp fires below. Suddenly, at dawn, the trumpets sounded on the right of their camp; Craterus and his troops, relieved to hear the signal announcing Alexander's safe arrival, at once began to clamber up the wall. Ariobarsanes turned to meet Alexander on his rear, but Ptolemy, advancing from the side, checked this movement. Completely routed by unexpected attacks from three directions, Ariobarsanes fled, escaping with a mere handful of his army.

It was imperative to travel swiftly to Persepolis so that it could be reached before Ariobarsanes could arrange to defend the town or remove its treasures. A messenger reported that all the valuables would be secured if Alexander continued his rapid night march. The contingent which had been sent ahead to construct a bridge over the Araxes river had accomplished their task so well that Alexander was able to hasten on at full speed, covering forty miles in one night. His early arrival achieved its object; the town was not defended; its treasures—even greater than had been hoped —surpassed in number and value those collected in Susa. More were found at Pasargadae, an adjacent town where the tomb of Cyrus the Great had been erected in a finely timbered park. Many horses and dromedaries were required for the transport of the precious objects, which some historians say were equal to forty million of our currency. All were deposited in the care of Parmenion, who was entrusted to guard communications; later, they were confided to the unworthy Harpalus.

Thus, between March 334 and March 330 B.C., Alexander had gained practically all the land from Greece to the mountainous plateau of Iran. Winter quarters were given to the army for a few months; but the King, obliged to deal with the warlike Mardian clan, set out in about three weeks. During his short time in Persepolis he was fully engaged with civil and military duties, preparing for further advance and collecting information concerning the shortest route to Bactria; but in that wonderful city many of his Macedonians fell victim to Persian luxury; this led to trouble in the near future.

To this day travellers who venture so far into Asia are overcome by the splendour and the immensity of the ruins of Persepolis and Pasargadae. The great palaces in Persepolis were approached by a staircase of 106 steps, wide enough for ten horsemen to ride abreast. Above were the Gates of Xerxes, guarded by winged bulls of immense proportions, eighteen feet high. These led to two platforms; on the first was based the palace with a hundred columns round an immense hall; not one of those pillars now remains. Tradition tells that, against the advice of Parmenion, Alexander set alight the chief palace; by its destruction he intended to proclaim to the whole Greek world that he had avenged the burning of the beautiful buildings of Athens by Xerxes. The calumniators of Alexander went so far as to invent an Athenian courtesan, Thais, who incited this method of revenge, and even to this day some believe that the King, decked with flowers, headed the gay company which started the fire. Tarn and others have proved the unreliability of the sources of this sensational story. It is not disputed that on his second visit to Persepolis Alexander regretted the wreck of the palace.

After resting four months the Macedonians resumed their march in spring, 330 b.c. Darius had waited in Ecbatana, intending to retreat to the mountains if the Macedonians continued to advance; but, on reaching Ecbatana, Alexander found that the Persians had moved on to the Caspian Gates, where they hoped to make a successful stand. After Gaugamela Alexander had consulted with Sisygambis on what terms hostilities might be ended; but no message had come from Darius, who still believed that trouble might be stirred up in Greece, especially in Sparta. Although most of the Persian nobility remained loyal, some counselled Darius that, as it was useless to oppose Alexander, abdication was advisable. But Darius postponed decision until too late. Thereupon Artabazus and several other governors expressed regret that they could be of no further assistance and retired north to Tapuria. Slowly, without hope or confidence, the Persian army followed their King. Bessus, Viceroy of Bactria, had many adherents; he was a kinsman of Darius, and planned that if he betrayed him to Alexander he would be permitted to reign in Bactria, and later could claim the throne of Persia. One night, with several confederates, Bessus entered the tent of his King, bound him with ropes and conveyed him toward Bactria, intending to hold him as a hostage during negotiations with Alexander. The news of this evil coup soon spread to the army, with demoralising result.

When encamped at the junction of the roads leading to Hyrcania, Bactria and Aria, Alexander learned the story of the capture of Darius and the flight of Bessus with his prisoner toward Bactria. Wasting no time, Alexander set out to follow Bessus with a contingent of cavalry; they rode post-haste all night, and after a brief rest during the hottest hours of the day they resumed the race during the whole of the second night. About midday they learned that Bessus was still ahead; by this time men and horses were worn out. Alexander made enquiries whether there might be a shorter route by which he might catch up with the traitor. Over a waterless desert, he was told. Selecting a company of 500 horsemen noted for their strength and endurance, Alexander started off, ordering the rest of the cavalry to follow as fast as possible by the usual road. All that night the 500 rode with their King; many fell out, exhausted, on the way. Only about sixty are said to have remained with Alexander when he came upon the enemy at dawn, resting and sleeping, unguarded, taken completely by surprise. Without hesitation the King rushed upon the half-awakened troops, who fled in terror at the sight of Alexander in person, supposing that he was at the head of a large force. Bessus and his ignoble associates seized Darius, their helpless prisoner, stabbed him with their javelins and threw the corpse into a waggon whilst they hurried on with their panic-stricken crew. Alexander, following them, came upon a cart lying neglected by the wayside. In this humble vehicle lay the body of Darius; there he had been left to expire, alone, uncared for. Deeply touched by the pitiful sight of this once mighty Lord of Asia, deserted, murdered by his own kinsman and officers, Alexander removed his cloak and laid it gently over the corpse. The funeral was carried out with appropriate royal and military honours at Persepolis, and orders given that the family of Darius should be allotted a palace and be treated with the respect due to royalty.

Alexander's amazing race after Darius is summarised by Lieutenant-Colonel Dodge: "After a march of four hundred miles in eleven days, at the close of which but sixty of his men had been able to keep up beside him, it was he who always led the van, cheered on his men . . . and who stood the heat and thirst, the fatigue and danger, best of all. It was he who headed the weary handful in a charge on the Persian thousands . . . such things endear a leader to his men beyond the telling."

So much in history has been told of the defects of Darius III that his finer qualities have been forgotten. He was a model of the domestic virtues: as a husband and father he was faithful and affectionate; as a son, dutiful and devoted to his mother, Sisygambis; as a king, he upheld the traditions of the throne; his dignity, regard for truth, and kind treatment of his subjects retained their respect and obedience. Such a combination of the homely and the royal virtues was rare in a Great King of Asia. In times of peace he was an ideal monarch; in the troubled times of war he was incompetent, shrinking from responsibility, lacking in foresight, unable to make rapid decisions; as Alexander described him, he was "battle-shy".

When at Ecbatana, careful for the comfort of his army, Alexander gave permission to the Thessalian and Greek cavalry to return home, laden with gifts and money. But many of the Thessalians pleaded to be allowed to stay with the King and share his adventures in Asia. When the time came to leave Ecbatana, Alexander considered it unwise to proceed until his flank was protected; for this object he must enter Hyrcania and ensure its fidelity. This proposal was not welcomed by the troops, many of whom longed to turn homewards. However, Alexander persuaded them, as he always seemed able to do, with his enthusiasm, encouragement and tireless energy.

The plains of Parthia were crossed in the heat of July, and then this remarkable army scaled the heights, bitterly cold even in summer, of the chain of mountains which divides Parthia from Hyrcania. On the south side of the Hyrcanian (Caspian) Sea innumerable streams rendered the region marshy, with thick woods, but few villages. The climate was changeable, rainy from November to March, dry and hot in summer. The army was divided into three columns: Alexander selected for himself the most arduous western route; Craterus was to lead the eastern column and to gain Tapuria by persuasion or by force; the third column with the heavy baggage went to Zadracarta, the Hyrcanian capital. The army followed their indefatigable leader over unfordable rivers and marshes, cut their way through dense forests, and scaled snow-capped heights. Icy mountains and swift rivers by this time had no terrors for this stalwart company; they were taken as a matter of course, part of the day's routine. Few details of this campaign are available;

sometimes there was fighting, but many of the leading chieftains preferred to serve this surprising new King.

Alexander knew that those who had been faithful to Darius would become his adherents. One was Phratophernes, a friendly ally, to whom was confided the government of Hyrcania and Parthia. Neither Alexander nor his officers felt confidence in Nabarsanes, who also proffered allegiance. Artabazus, who had tried to persuade Darius that resistance was useless after Gaugamela, had in youth spent some time in Pella, where he had known Alexander and become acquainted with Occidental modes of thought. He now swore fealty to Alexander and brought with him his three sons; one was Ariobarsanes, the defender of the Persian Gates. Satibarsanes and Barsaentes had departed to their respective dominions, Aria and Drangiana, where they began preparations to join Bessus.

Alexander became interested in the potentially great future of Hyrcania, a country with fine forests, easily defensible hills and defiles, and important trading prospects on the Caspian Sea. Phratophernes was eager to co-operate, but Alexander did not live long enough to carry out their vision. In Zadracarta many former enemies offered to aid Alexander; it has been said that no conqueror understood as he did how to attach such men to his service. The Greek mercenaries who had escaped from Gaugamela were here interviewed and told that they must surrender without terms, as traitors to the League of Corinth. They were censured, pardoned, and gladly joined the Macedonian army. The hard-worked troops were given a time of repose in Zadracarta, and after the usual Hellenic games, sacrifices and thanksgiving, all started off again, taking the shorter northern road to Bactria, the kingdom of Bessus. When they arrived at Aria the Governor, Satibarsanes, offered allegiance to Alexander, who confirmed him in his position as Satrap of Aria, but took the precaution to leave in the province a small force under a Macedonian general.

Now came the news that Bessus had assumed the title of King, worn the diadem, the symbol of royalty, and collected troops to defend Bactria. Graver reports followed: Satibarsanes had broken his oath, slain most of the Macedonian force and their general; Barsaentes, another confederate of Bessus, was gathering an army in his provinces, Drangiana and Arachosia. Flank and rear being now insecure, the rapid march along the northern route to Bactria had to be abandoned; the army must turn back to quell the insurrection in Aria. For this purpose Alexander carried out another lightning drive, covering seventy-five miles in two days. Satibarsanes had arranged a mass meeting in his capital, Artacoana. When the great gathering were listening to inflammatory speeches, suddenly, to their amazement and consternation, without warning of his approach, Alexander appeared in their midst. Satibarsanes escaped over the hills to Bessus; his rebellious Arians were severely punished, but those who had remained undecided gladly took the oath of obedience to their new King. Aria was a province of importance because of its position near roads leading to Hyrcania, Parthia, Bactria and to the long Cophen (Kabul) valley through which ran the river of that name on its path to the Punjab. Therefore, about 100 miles from Artacoana, a new city was founded: Alexandria-in-Aria, which became a flourishing town, Herat.

The bitter experience of the Arian revolt proved to Alexander that it was essential to consolidate his position; his authority as King must be recognised in the provinces which aided Bessus. Therefore he had no choice; he must take the longer road to Bactria. This decision had at least the advantage that more was learned about the topography of the country and the nature of the inhabitants of Iran than could have been gained otherwise. When Drangiana was reached, its satrap, Barsaentes, fled to neighbouring territory but was returned to Alexander by his hosts and executed.

In the territory of the Ariaspae Alexander found a contented, prosperous, self-governing people engaged chiefly in agriculture; their civilisation was based somewhat along Hellenic lines. So delighted was Alexander to find such a veritable oasis in the surrounding desert, that he offered to confer more territory upon the people; but although grateful for his consideration they accepted little; they did not desire more responsibility and had simple tastes. More time was spent in this province than could well be spared; this happy interlude left friendly memories on both sides.

It was now late in 330 B.C., when snow and ice would prove formidable obstacles to the mountain march which lay ahead. But still more threatening clouds were accumulating in the psychological atmosphere. These were hardly noticed by Alexander, intent as he was with plans beyond the comprehension of his army. Many had begun to criticise the continual advance to the East, the object of which was to them inscrutable and debatable. During the time of comparative relaxation in the royal residence of Drangiana the tragedy of Philotas took place; this lamentable episode is described in Chapter V.

The eulogies of a military expert have frequently been quoted in previous chapters; here it is advisable to refer to the estimate of Droysen, a historian who had deeper insight into the psychology of the conqueror of Asia. Unless one has some understanding of the vast projects forming in the mind of Alexander one is sometimes apt to linger doubtingly, wondering if, after all, his critics had some justification for their interpretation of his motives. The minds of the majority move in a limited sphere without even a dim idea of the mental process or psychological drive which impels genius to action. But Alexander was so far in advance of his time that no one then could grasp the reasons which drove him on; perhaps not even he himself at that time could have explained why he felt impelled to undertake the mountain march towards India.

Droysen, commenting on the administration adopted for Babylon, says that one cannot know whether the measures adopted by Alexander were dictated by a clear understanding of the situation; but it is certain that they were the most judicious, and, in the circumstances, the only possible solution of a complicated problem. Babylonia's high level of civilisation leaned more to that of Arabia and India than to that of Greece. Further, if a Macedonian government had supplanted the rule of Persia, the support of the cities of Syria and the Mediterranean would not have been gained. The appointment of Mazaeus as Viceroy of Babylon had created a most favourable impression; would any other victor have chosen for such an important post his strongest opponent at Gaugamela? In later years Alexander followed the same plan whenever he found a reliable native to aid his administration. Thus he retained the respect, often even the affection, of many Persian and Indian subjects. Unfortunately, this attitude offended many of the Macedonian soldiers who could not become accustomed to the idea of friendship with defeated enemies, and later, when their King desired to show respect by adopting Persian court ceremonial, they complained that his character was deteriorating under the influence of Persian wealth and magnificence.

From these small beginnings arose the growing disaffection which came to a head during the following three years.

CHAPTER IV

HINDU-KUSH TO SOGDIANA, 330 TO 328 B.C.

Alexander explains his plans of campaign—Re-organisation of army—Alexandria-ad-Caucasum—Bessus flees to Sogdiana—The Oxus river—Bessus delivered to Alexander—Cyropolis and seven fortresses taken — Alexandria-the-Farthest — Alexander crosses the Jaxartes and subdues Scythians—Spitamenes regains Cyropolis and defeats Pharnuches—Alexander hastens after Spitamenes—Five flying columns reduce Sogdiana—Winter in Zariaspa (329-328)—Spitamenes slain by his allies—Envoys from far and near flock to honour Alexander

HAVING called the Assembly, Alexander explained that it was imperative to secure Bessus; he had assumed the title of King, and as Viceroy of Bactria and a kinsman of Darius, would have much support throughout Persia. True, the relationship of the King of Persia and his barons was not that of a monarch who could command their obedience, but they were morally bound to aid their King against foreign invaders. Until the capture of Bessus the Macedonians would be in constant danger; they might be forced to make an ignominious peace, even retreat to the West. So humiliating an end to their hitherto successful campaign could not be contemplated. Great difficulties would be encountered on the route to Bactria, for they would be obliged to march over trackless mountains peopled by stubborn tribes who would combine to resist any foreign army. In those desolate regions no towns existed, only small villages with a fortified citadel and a so-called palace, the residence of the local chieftain. But after having crossed the mountains they could relax in the fertile, highly civilised provinces of Bactria and Sogdiana.

Apparently Alexander was unaware of any objections to his plan; but dissentient critics, longing to return homeward, were uneasily questioning whither they were bound; their growing complaints precipitated a crisis which came to a head when the army had a time of repose in Drangiana. Before the ascent to the high hills, thorough reorganisation of the army was essential. For such climbing it was necessary to renew clothing and to provide footwear suitable for rough ground, snow and ice. The equipment was arranged to be light and less cumbersome to carry. Gaps in the ranks were filled with fresh Oriental recruits, an innovation not welcomed by the Macedonian troops. During these preparations Alexander founded a new city—Alexandria-ad-Caucasum its site, some twenty miles north of Kabul, was selected because it commanded three important roads leading to Bactria. The Governor appointed for this city was later dismissed as incapable. News came that with the assistance of Bessus, Satibarsanes had returned to Aria and fomented an insurrection. A strong contingent was despatched under Artabazus, a Persian, and in the ensuing battle Satibarsanes was slain. Under a new Governor, Stasanor, the province of Aria flourished. Only when satisfied that he had secured his rear did Alexander begin the march toward the great mountain range.

Persia has several varieties of climate. North of the wide central plateau the air is clear, cold and bracing; the majestic grandeur of its towering mountains, with pinnacles wreathed in clouds and snow, strikes every traveller with awe. South of this plateau lie the deserts and plains, sultry and enervating. In this southern region the excellent irrigation system in olden days produced a vegetation rich enough to support a prosperous and numerous population.

The Himalayas, "Snow-Abode" in Sanscrit, extend along the plateau in a series of mountain chains. Radiating from them on the east are the heights of the Hindu-Kush, called the Caucasus by the Greeks in the time of Alexander, and the

Parapamisus by the Persians; to-day these are part of Afghanistan. The western arm of the Himalayas passes along Central Asia, and is separated from the eastern Himalayas by the river Indus running its lengthy descent to the sea on the west coast of India. North of this mountain chain Turkestan stretches as far as the Caspian Sea; in that province are many streams, rivers, and marshes; its climate resembles that of the West Indies. From the western system of the Himalayas spring two great rivers: the Oxus, flowing through Turkestan in a north-westerly direction, and the Helmund, running southward through Afghanistan. Bactria lies north of the Parapamisus heights; still further north is Sogdiana; in both these provinces bitter fighting was to occur during the following two years.

Bessus believed that he was safe for the winter in his kingdom; little did he realise the persistent and intrepid nature of his pursuer. No one in Bactria dreamed that any army would be so foolhardy as to attempt the passage of these frowning heights while covered with snow and ice. Realising that Bessus would expect that the lower, easier path to Bactria would be chosen by any foe so venturesome as to cross the Hindu-Kush during the cold season of the year, Alexander decided to take the higher, supposedly impassable route, and thus turn the position of his unsuspecting enemy who at Tashkurgan was ready with a considerable force, together with two Sogdian barons, Oxyartes and Spitamenes.

While awaiting the approach of the Macedonians Bessus laid waste the northern slope of the mountains, so that neither food nor protection would be available for the invaders. Bessus hoped that Alexander would be attracted to pass on to India, leaving Bactria behind; if this choice were taken, Bessus intended to attack the Macedonian rear. With the combined forces of Bactria, Sogdiana and the Scythian territory he believed that at last he could dispose of the hitherto unconquered Western army. But Alexander's strategy had thwarted that design. When he heard of Alexander's close approach to Drapsaca, Bessus had so rude an awakening from this dream that he fled precipitately north to Sogdiana, where he could rely on the aid of Oxyartes, Spitamenes and other barons. Deprived of their leader, the Bactrian cavalry submitted with apparent relief to the Macedonians, who passed into Bactra-Zariaspa, the capital. The province of Bactria was known as the "Garden of Asia"; its irrigation was so thorough that even underground channels had been constructed from the Polytimetus and the Oxus rivers.

Travelling along part of the Cophen valley, the Macedonian army crossed by the Khawak pass, 11,600 feet high, and eventually reached Drapsaca (now Inderaub). The ground was practically barren; as even wood for firing was hard to obtain from the sparse, scrubby bushes which pushed lean twigs through the snow, the troops suffered from both cold and hunger. On the southern side the snow had been deep for twelve miles, but on the northern descent the army had travelled forty miles of deep snow. This crossing of the Hindu-Kush in winter is dismissed by most writers in a few cursory sentences; but, said Lieutenant-Colonel Dodge, a professional soldier, do they realise that this was a phenomenal achievement without parallel in history? Hannibal crossed the Alps, but that lesser military success was accomplished after he had studied the methods of his great predecessor and from them drawn inspiration.

The campaigning season 330 to 328 B.C. confuses the lay reader with its many to-and-fro lightning moves over deserts, plains, hills, to towns and fortresses, and over unfordable rivers. Little geography was then known; all the more remarkable was Alexander's unerring instinct in finding his route over strange territory, and his selection of suitable sites for founding new cities. So far as can be computed, the marching distance amounted to some 3,900 miles; a figure sufficiently approximate to give some idea of the arduous labour of the army under their indomitable leader. When reading the names of the places traversed during the two years' campaign one feels as bewildered as when watching from the window of an express train a rapidly receding landscape. Therefore only the incidents which throw light on Alexander's character can be briefly dealt with in this chapter.

Early in 329 B.C. Alexander started to follow Bessus into Sogdiana. Only with the aid of a map of classical geography is it possible to follow his involved route over Bactria and Sogdiana. On leaving Zariaspa the army passed over forty miles of desert, where many suffered from thirst and the intense heat of the spring season. On arriving at the Oxus river, deep and with a swiftly running current, they found that during his retreat Bessus had destroyed all means of crossing. But Alexander quickly improvised a method by which the whole army were able to disembark on the opposite bank in five days; firm animal skins, packed with hay and sewn together, provided safe carriage for wooden rafts. Thus no time was lost, and on shore no precious minute was wasted; the march was at once resumed.

By this time Bessus had become somewhat of a problem to his supporters; after the death of Darius his leadership had been so weak that his allies regarded him as a handicap. Alexander received messages from Spitamenes, Oxyartes and other barons, who offered to deliver up Bessus when troops were sent to fetch him. Under Ptolemy, some 6,000 soldiers, including the shield-bearing guards, lancers and infantry, marched to the meeting-place. The chieftains, reluctant, when it came to the point, to hand over their former colleague, left the district, but after some delay Bessus was taken prisoner, stripped and questioned. When the report of his interrogation was read aloud by a herald, the troops expressed satisfaction that justice had been done. Bessus had a fair trial and was executed after mutilation of the nose and ears—the usual Persian punishment for a regicide—had been carried out. This is said to be the only instance of torture having been ordered by Alexander.

After replacing the horses lost in Asia, Alexander marched on to Maracanda, the capital and royal summer residence of Sogdiana. Situated in a fertile valley, it had natural barriers against invaders—deserts on the west, and high mountain ranges on the east, north and south. The Macedonians were now in a threatened position, for the Scythian nomads and some Indian princes had agreed to assist Bactria and Sogdiana. As he proceeded north toward the Jaxartes river Alexander learned that the Scythians had massed their forces to resist any attempt to cross, and that enemies might also be expected from Hyrcania and Parthia. A battle took place during which Alexander was seriously wounded in the leg; as a bone was splintered (? the fibula) he was obliged to supervise operations from a litter.

Cyropolis, the next objective, had a stone wall, said to have been constructed by Cyrus the Great, and was guarded by seven adjacent fortresses which gave protection against Scythian nomads and brigands. On his way Alexander secured Gaza, which had only an earthen wall, and on the following day two neighbouring fortresses. Then, as expected, the other fortresses surrendered without resistance. Thus five towns had been taken in two days—quick work even for Alexander's lightning methods. Now attention was turned to the strongly fortified Cyropolis with its large garrison. While Craterus kept the enemy on the alert in front, Alexander studied the wall and found that a tributary of the Jaxartes had dried up, leaving a channel which provided a tunnel through which his soldiers could creep into the town. Craterus redoubled his efforts with his siege engines, so that the garrison were dismayed on learning that with a small force Alexander had penetrated within, and opened the gates for the entrance of his army. Thus once again were displayed the resource and ingenuity of a commander who neglected no opportunity to carry out in person a minute examination of the details which could make or mar success. But before the final surrender of Cyropolis Alexander and Craterus were seriously wounded; Alexander, hit on the head by a sling stone, found his vision impaired for a time; Craterus was injured by an arrow. Leaving good garrisons in Cyropolis and its chain of fortresses, Alexander returned to supervise the new city rising on the Jaxartes river, and named it Alexandria-the-Farthest, to mark the proposed northern limit of the empire. It is now Chodjend.

As Alexander had the mistaken impression that the

Sogdians desired to be on friendly terms, he called a conference of their prominent barons and proposed that they
should together discuss their future relationship. But his
suggestion was coldly received. The Sogdians had expected
that when they had delivered up Bessus the Western King
would return to Europe. Not unnaturally they now suspected
treachery; they would all be assassinated according to the
usual practice of victorious conquerors. The whole country
rose in revolt and Spitamenes regained Cyropolis with its
seven fortresses.

The Scythian nomads, hearing of this success, increased
their activity on the north bank of the Jaxartes, fired over
arrows and rode swiftly away, as was their custom, beyond
the reach of the Macedonian weapons. With insulting ges-
tures they called out over the narrower stretches of the
water that at last the Macedonians would discover how the
sturdy men of the hills differed from the effete Persians of the
plains. Their continued jeers exasperated not only the army,
but also Alexander himself. Although aware of his dangerous
position, he decided that before he could deal with Spitamenes, he must subdue the Scythians.

It is said that Alexander did not sleep one night as he
watched in front of him the Scythian fires across the river
and knew that behind him Sogdiana was seething with
insurrection. He was far from his base, and ahead stretched
deserts and mountains peopled with strong enemies. To the
troops the King betrayed no trace of anxiety as they crossed
the Jaxartes; their passage was protected by the missiles
from the siege engines and catapults. The slingers and
archers were so efficient that the infantry and the cavalry
crossed with little interference. At first the Macedonians
were so outnumbered that the Scythian riders were able to
circle close, shoot their arrows, and swiftly make off; but
when Alexander led his cavalry in close formation, they
were obliged to abandon their customary method of warfare.
Chased over the plains, 1,000 were slain, 150 captured.
During the pursuit, many of the army, overcome with thirst,
drank impure water from a marsh. Suffering from dysentery,
Alexander rode on and became so weak that his physician

feared for his life, but his strong constitution and his will power triumphed over the malady. His augurs had predicted victory after grave personal trouble.

Turning to the problem of Spitamenes, Alexander despatched a force under Pharnuches, whose tact had often won over reluctant natives. He expected that this interpreter would arrange favourable terms with the Sogdian chieftain. But Spitamenes met him with an army. Now Pharnuches was not a military leader; too adventurous, he followed Spitamenes to the plains; there the Sogdian turned and took the offensive. The Macedonian officers realised the gravity of their situation, but hesitated to offer suggestions. Seeking shelter, all hurried to the river Polytimetus. Losing their way, the army became a confused, straggling, leaderless crowd; many were slain; many were taken to be slaves. No such disaster had ever befallen the hitherto invincible Macedonian army.

Deep was the sense of humiliation and disgrace when the news of this defeat reached the soldiers at work on the new city near the Jaxartes. Again they realised how all depended upon the genius of a King who always seized the correct moment to take control and even at the eleventh hour turned disaster into victory. Elated by his success, Spitamenes attacked Maracanda. But Alexander, ashamed of the calamity at the Polytimetus, marched 135 miles (some say 170) in three days and arrived at Maracanda on the fourth day. Hearing that Alexander was approaching in person, Spitamenes fled. Such was the reputation of the King who never relinquished a plan which he had begun, and never lost a battle. To prevent further Sogdian revolts Alexander turned back, buried the dead with military honours, and traversed the whole country, spreading desolation in his wake. Yet it is said that Caesar, when he conquered Gaul, wrought even greater devastation. At whatever cost he must conquer this most stubborn and most skilful foe, who had delayed the advance into India for many months. By the summer of 328 B.C. Alexander possessed only half of Sogdiana and Spitamenes was still at large.

Near the Oxus river rose a spring of petroleum; such a

phenomenon had never before been seen. The augurs said that it predicted victory, but only after heavy labour. While Craterus watched the frontier of Bactria, five flying columns, under Alexander, Ptolemy, Artabazus, Coenus and Perdiccas, swept circuitously from Bactra-Zariaspa and converged to meet in Maracanda; the "Garden of Asia" was thus reduced to a desert. The destruction carried out had been a deplorable military necessity; to Hephaestion was deputed the task of restoring Sogdiana, of providing food for the starving and building cities for the homeless. To prevent incursions from the Daān tribes a chain of forts was erected along the frontier of Bactria; four looked south, two looked west. Spitamenes fled to the far north, for refuge with the Massagetan clan. After two years of almost continuous warfare the army retired to Bactra-Zariaspa for winter (329-328).

Spitamenes continued to cause anxiety by brief incursions into Bactria and Sogdiana; with promises of booty he induced the Massagetan tribes to accompany him. But he was driven back by Coenus on every occasion. His allies lost heart, and when they heard that Alexander intended to deal with them in person they decided to surrender; as Spitamenes refused to agree they cut off his head and sent it to Alexander. One story tells that this terrible deed was carried out by the wife of Spitamenes, that she brought the head to the tent of the King, who recoiled in horror.

Alexander had so deeply admired the courage of this enemy that he sent his orphaned daughter to Susa to be educated—with the family of Darius and other Persian ladies—in the Greek language and Hellenic culture. Later, he gave her in marriage to Seleucus, one of his finest generals, and she became the mother of Antiochus I.

During the winter ambassadors came from many countries. One welcome visitor arrived from the Scythian King of the plains, who apologised for the behaviour of his mountain subjects; they had acted without his authority. In proof of his sincerity, he offered the hand of his daughter in marriage if Alexander would deign to consider the proposal;

if not, perhaps highly placed Macedonians would wed the daughters of prominent Scythian chieftains. Alexander courteously replied that at present he did not desire to marry, but if any of his officers entertained this plan he would welcome their decision. He returned all the Scythian prisoners, a gesture which gained for him a high reputation. After an exchange of gifts the Scythian King offered to provide troops—a welcome suggestion when recruits were required for the depleted Macedonian ranks. Earlier in the winter reinforcements had come from the western provinces; without that additional personnel the Sogdian revolts could not have been quelled.

Pharasmanes, King of the Chorasmians, arrived with 1,500 horsemen to beg the aid of Alexander against enemies near his kingdom by the Caspian Sea; he would provision the whole Macedonian army and guide them over the mountains. Alexander explained that his immediate objective was India, but on his return he would gladly aid Pharasmanes. Atropates, satrap of Media, sent 100 Saca girls famous for riding and shooting, but Alexander sent them home lest they should be violated by the soldiers. With the passage of time, one can understand how eagerly sensational writers elaborated this story into a romance—the visit of the Queen of the Amazons desiring to have a son by Alexander!

History tells us that documents believed to have been composed about this time reveal that Alexander had learned from shepherds, nomads and merchants that geographers were mistaken; the Caspian or Hyrcanian Sea had no direct connection with the Ocean. Destiny did not permit him to live long enough to fulfil his promise to Pharasmanes to explore that northern sea. He now mapped the limits of his empire: the Oxus and the Jaxartes should mark the northern, the Tigris and the Euphrates, the western boundary; thence to the south and east, the great rivers, the Indus and the Hydaspes, would complete the territory which he wished to unite with the bond of Hellenism.

Did the great Ocean lie near the eastern border of India? This question, never to be solved in his short life, continued to haunt his imagination.

Administrative duties occupied much time; Alexander received the Viceroys of Parthia, Aria and other provinces. Messengers were sent to depose Autophradates, Viceroy of Tapuria, and add his territory to that of the Governor of Parthia; Stasanor was despatched to Drangiana, Atropates to Media. Fresh troops, urgently required, were ordered to come from Macedonia. The death of Mazaeus in Babylon made it necessary to appoint a suitable successor. During the few leisure hours left from these multifarious tasks Alexander studied maps and prepared for the advance into the Punjab.

It is clear that the King could have had little time for the drinking habits which some believe he developed at this stage of the campaign. The water supply being suspected, it was replaced by the wine of the country, a stronger beverage than that to which the Macedonians were accustomed. With his practical common sense Alexander would know the folly of consuming drink which interfered with a vigilant state of the brain. The commander of a great army must always be on the alert; danger is never far away.

No doubt the King had become more irritable and "prone to wrath"; it is probable that he would be impatient when the "adulators", the poets who strove to outrival each other with flattering verses, presumed to criticise or to offer advice. When gnawed by anxiety which he dared not admit to any subordinate, the King might be buttressed up, so to speak, by hearing praises of his exploits. Years of warfare, combined with ever-growing responsibilities, must have robbed him of the joyous exuberance of spirit which characterised him when he crossed the Hellespont. How restricted the canvas of Troy in comparison with his vast empire and authority over millions of human beings! No longer could Achilles be his model; his thought was reaching toward a higher plane. He had far outstripped that hero of his youth and had passed on to emulate Heracles, the god from whom he was descended. Nor could he find relief from mental tension by discussion with any confidant; no one could have understood the gigantic planning activities simmering in his mind.

Droysen said that at critical periods of world progress a spiritual upheaval is required to lift it to a higher level, and then it is that Destiny, Providence, or God—call it which you prefer—produces the man who is born to accomplish the almost superhuman task. Arrian, writing soon after Christ, regarded Alexander as such a man. But no exponent of analytical psychology then existed who could have explained to his often bewildered but devoted followers that their King was driven onward by a subconscious urge, a dream to fuse the nations, to bring harmony where there was discord, and, as Heracles had taught, to live for the benefit of his subjects. We get hints from Aristobulus, who tells how the King loved to introduce topics for interesting debate during the evening meal when there happened to be no cause for alarm. But Alexander did not talk nor write about his projects, as did Napoleon.

The winter ahead had gloom enough in store.

CHAPTER V

THREE TRAGEDIES

*Reports of conspiracy against Alexander—Execution
of Philotas and his father Parmenion—Proskynesis is
adopted at Court—Cleitus inveighs against the King,
who kills him in anger—Alexander is inconsolable—
Conspiracy of the royal pages—Callisthenes involved—
The professional Sophists*

UNLIKE Napoleon who, during his years of exile in
St. Helena, provided for posterity his own point of view,
Alexander was so over-occupied in his brief life that we shall
never know his version of the deeds for which he has been
criticised and misrepresented.

When in Drangiana in 330 B.C. Alexander was informed of
a conspiracy against his life which involved his old friend
Philotas. Rumours of unkind comment by Philotas and
members of his family had reached the King when in Egypt,
but with his usual confidence in the friends of his youth he
had dismissed such statements as incredible. In that respect
the Alexander of 330 B.C. was still the man who crossed the
Hellespont. Although aware that even some of his friendly
officers disapproved of the continued advance into Iran, he
paid little attention to such opinions. When an army is not
engaged in active warfare the time is ripe for whispering
complaints. For the morale of any community it is essential
to keep its members engaged with work, competitions or
festivities; otherwise their idle minds indulge in gossip and
grumbling about their superiors.

Alexander was profoundly shocked when he heard of dis-
loyalty on the part of Philotas, the distinguished and

popular head of the Companion cavalry. A certain Dimnos had confided to a friend that a number of important officers had decided to replace Alexander within a few days. Lest the danger were real, the story was passed on to Philotas, who visited the King every day in his tent. One of the royal pages thought it his duty to warn his King. Alexander invited Philotas with others to dinner, and from observation of his manner considered that there was definite ground for suspicion. Alexander consulted several generals, who convinced him that the matter was so vital for the discipline of the army as well as for his personal safety that a full investigation should be carried out at once. Philotas was arrested next day and questioned; he admitted that he had heard of a plot against the King, but had not wished to cause him anxiety about what was probably a baseless rumour. Dimnos committed suicide, a deed which the Military Council regarded as a confession of guilt.

Philotas had been leading such a life of pomp and ostentation that Parmenion, his father, had often rebuked him for his extravagance, telling him that he lived in greater luxury than his King. Proofs came that he had boasted in public that the credit of the Asiatic victories belonged more to him and his family than to Alexander; such remarks had injured discipline and fomented discontent in many quarters. To the War Council Alexander made a formal accusation, then retired so that Philotas could speak freely in his own defence; this ensured that he had a fair trial by his peers, as was the correct procedure. Further evidence incriminated Parmenion; a suspicious letter implied that the old man was aware of the attempt to replace Alexander by a less ambitious leader.

There are, of course, several versions of the trial; some writers say that confession was extracted from Philotas under torture, Alexander listening concealed behind a screen. Cleitarchus and Curtius relate this tale with their usual embroidery; but Tarn has traced the unreliable sources from which they drew their information. Other authors declare that throughout the examination of the alleged conspiracy Alexander maintained an attitude of dignity and took trouble to secure a true verdict. Arrian, relying on the

Memoirs of Aristobulus and Ptolemy, which were written independently, reminds readers that they tell how presumptuous Philotas had been even in Egypt, but make no mention of torture applied to extract confession. As the trial proceeded, further evidence of wild talk against Alexander was brought before the examining Council; it was also recalled that after Philip's death Philotas had advocated the claim of Amyntas, a son of a former Macedonian King. After weighing the testimony of many witnesses the Military Council concluded that Philotas was guilty. When his avowal of complicity and knowledge of conspiracy was read aloud to the army, they clamoured for punishment of both father and son. The King ordered messengers to ride to Ecbatana and ensure the death of Parmenion before he could learn that Philotas had been slain by the javelins of the Companions; those entrusted to carry out this terrible deed travelled on dromedaries and in eleven days covered 860 miles.

Several young men, supposed to be accomplices of Philotas, were tried, exonerated from all reproach, reinstated in their high positions and later justified the confidence placed in their integrity. This fact points to evidence against Philotas and his father which is not on record. Both Ptolemy and Aristobulus believed in their guilt and stated that their execution did not impair the happy relationship between the King and his generals. But even admirers of Alexander blame him for giving Parmenion no opportunity to plead his cause before a court. Did Alexander know more than has transpired in the available historical reports? If he had waited, what might have happened? It is improbable that he would have convicted Parmenion, with his long record of faithful service, unless he had reason to believe that it was dangerous to leave him in Ecbatana. Beloved by the army, Parmenion might have become a centre of rebellion on the line of communications. The condition could not be judged with the cool detachment of a civilian; history abounds with examples of the irreconcilability of the opinions of the man on the spot and the official far off, at home.

Although controversy on the subject will ever continue, there can now be no more than conjecture as to the right or wrong of Alexander's stern measures. Napoleon justified the execution of the Duke of Enghien as necessary to prevent future attempts against his life. As loyalty to old friends was so marked a characteristic of Alexander, it is hard to believe that he would have destroyed Parmenion without serious proof. A long list of his officers never came under suspicion: Ptolemy, Seleucus, Perdiccas, Craterus, Coenus, Hephaestion, Leonnatus, Eumenes, Nearchus; even Antipater, of whom Olympias was always complaining, never for a moment incurred reproof. Strabo, the geographer, not always favourable to Alexander, said that in this matter Alexander had acted justly, because both father and son had been involved in the plot. In any case, the King regarded the conspiracy so seriously that he never again entrusted the position of head of the Companion cavalry to one man only.

A second tragedy arose from the adoption at Court of the Persian ceremonial approach to their King, *proskynesis*. Alexander considered that as Great King of Asia he would not maintain his position of authority with the Persian nobility if in their presence he permitted the Macedonians to address him with their usual blunt camaraderie. The subject had been fully discussed with several of his officers and it was believed that Callisthenes also agreed that at public functions it would be advisable that all should follow the Persian custom. Before his monarch a Persian prostrated himself, covered his mouth with his hand, and as he rose the King advanced to salute him with a kiss. *Proskynesis* was natural to the Oriental; to the Macedonians it appeared a humiliating procedure.

There has been much dispute concerning the introduction of *proskynesis*; some consider it a proof of "corruption by Persian luxury", others an example of Alexander's good sense of values; how could he make any distinction between the two nations when both were present at a Court reception? Throughout history it is acknowledged that kings, queens and nobles have more authority when their position is

evidenced by costly clothing, jewels and distinguished bearing and manner. Even representatives of the British Empire
in the East have known the importance of gorgeous trappings
and adherence to strict etiquette, and native races have not
respected high officials who received them with homely
speech and garments.

The question came up when an important banquet was
arranged at Nautaca with Persians and Medes of high rank
among the guests. After the feast a debate was held on the
subject of *proskynesis*. Anasarchus led off in favour of its
observance. Callisthenes, who had often boasted that the
fame of Alexander would depend upon his narrative of the
campaign, then contradicted all that had been said by
Anasarchus. This came as somewhat of a surprise because
Callisthenes had already described how the waves had
performed *proskynesis* at Mount Climax to enable the army
to pass along the sea shore. But at Nautaca, as a master of
Rhetoric, he adduced all the arguments against *proskynesis*.
The custom, he said, was repugnant to the free men of the
West; although followed by the Orientals for centuries, for
Greeks and Macedonians it implied that they were bowing
to a god, and for a god one required the accessories of a
temple and songs of praise. In the past Greek visitors had
refused to adopt this ritual. How could Anasarchus advocate
honours paid only to a god when Heracles, the son of Zeus,
had not been addressed as a god during his lifetime? On his
return home, would Alexander exact *proskynesis* from his
countrymen?

The audience listened to this eloquence in silence. In the
circumstances it was embarrassing, for although it voiced the
feelings of many Macedonians it was not calculated to please
the King nor those officers who had decided to support the
principle of making no distinction between the nations at
the royal receptions. Then the Persians and the Medes, as
they rose from prostration, received the King's kiss of
greeting, and the Macedonians followed the example. When
a friend whispered to Alexander that Callisthenes had
omitted the formal approach, the King tactfully continued
to converse with Hephaestion. But Callisthenes was unwise

enough to draw attention with the blunt remark: "So I go the poorer by a kiss!" No notice was taken at the time of this comment; but it displeased many and was the beginning of a strained relationship with the King and his army.

In 328 B.C. Artabazus, over ninety years of age, asked that his post as Viceroy of Bactria should be taken over by a younger man; Amyntas was appointed as his successor. To celebrate the occasion a banquet was held, it is said, in Maracanda (Samarkand); important Greek, Macedonian and other guests were invited, among them Cleitus, the foster-brother of Alexander. Cleitus was preparing the sacrifice due to Dionysus, and as he hurried to the hall, some of the sheep followed him; this was pronounced by the augurs to be a serious omen. During the meal many of the company drank too deeply the heady wine of Iran, and Cleitus became conspicuously boisterous. Excited conversation took place when the poet-flatterers vied in adulation of Alexander, whom they compared with Heracles, the son of Zeus. Cleitus interrupted their fulsome praises, and exclaimed that the victories in Asia had been accomplished by the valour of the soldiers rather than by any feat of the King. In spite of loud expostulation from those who knew that the success of the campaign was due to Alexander's military genius, Cleitus refused to desist from shrill recrimination, discourteous and unsuitable before the King and a company of guests. He went so far as to chant from Euripides:

Alas, in Greece how ill things ordered are!
When trophies rise for victories in war,
Men count the praise not theirs who did the deed,
But give alone to him who led the mead.

Several officers tried in vain to stem this flow of abuse, born of wine. All records agree that Alexander maintained composure and long sat silent under the torrent of angry language. Discussion grew heated when some belittled Philip, saying that in history his name would be known only in connection with that of his son. Losing all control, Cleitus exalted Philip as warrior and statesman, and shouted that Parmenion and Philotas were fortunate not to have lived to see Persians placed in authority. All writers agree that Alexander turned to a Greek seated beside him and remarked: "Does it not seem to you that Greeks in comparison with Macedonians are like demigods among wild animals?" Cleitus may have heard this aside; raising his arm he called out: "This was the arm which saved you at the Granicus! Don't invite free men to your table. Any man could speak to Philip, but we must crawl on our knees when we approach you. Go to the barbarians whom you prefer to Macedonians." Aristobulus, who was present, tells us that Ptolemy and other officers, ashamed, and seeing that the King was becoming angered, seized Cleitus and led him outside. But Cleitus, hearing his name called, returned by another door, crying, "Here is Cleitus, Alexander!" Goaded beyond endurance, Alexander snatched a weapon and flung it at the drunken man, who staggered and fell dead at his feet.

After any accident how many can recall distinctly the incidents which preceded the disaster? Every barrister, cross-examining a witness, takes advantage of this fact. There can be little doubt that many of the young men present on that fatal evening were half-intoxicated; it is to the discredit of Alexander that he had not at an early hour arrested the foolish flattery of his achievements which had so enraged Cleitus. To permit such talk was unworthy of a great King; doubtless he, too, must have taken too much of the strong wine of the country.

Every version of this calamity tells that when he beheld Cleitus lifeless at his feet, in stunned, horrified silence, Alexander drew out the blade and turned it on himself; had not his officers intervened, a second death would have occurred. Without a word he fled to his tent and there lay prostrate, without food or change of clothing for three days and nights. Lamenting, inconsolable, he cried piteously that thus he had rewarded the loving care of Lanice, his foster-mother, the sister of Cleitus; she had lost two sons in the war, and now her own brother had been slain by the hand of his King.

His friends became alarmed, not only for his sanity, but for their own safety. What might happen if they were left without his guidance, far from home, with enemies on all sides? They remonstrated with him, pointing out that the fault lay with Cleitus; indeed, both Aristobulus and Ptolemy in their Memoirs say that Cleitus had been so insolent that he had deserved his fate. His officers protested that such excessive grief was unworthy of so great a King; the head of a great empire could no longer neglect his duties. Alexander remaining inconsolable, the philosopher Anasarchus explained that Dionysus had been affronted and had taken this revenge for the faulty performance of the sacrifice due to him. Callisthenes also reproached the King; so mighty a sovereign was above the law.

Alexander at length resumed his duties, but the tragedy left an ineffaceable mark; he felt so humiliated that his character became profoundly altered. Moderation and self-control he had steadfastly striven to acquire; that he had failed, with such lamentable result, was a source of self-reproach which bit deep into his soul. Eventually, the terrible lesson made him a better man. Even some fervent admirers of Alexander believe that his introduction of *proskynesis* was an early sign of megalomania, but this is contradicted by the fact that the King dismissed its observance by Greeks and Macedonians. Apparently, until Cleitus' outburst of plain-speaking, he had not realised the strength of their objection.

Arrian, the wise historian, relates the tragic story and concludes that many a conqueror had done wrong, but every one of them, even when aware that he was in error, had made excuses for his evil deeds. Alexander alone, of all these eminent men, had shown remorse and repentance for the sin he had committed.

Some time later the army had a term of rest. But for Alexander it was full of anxiety, for Spitamenes was still at large. Nor could he share his fears with anyone; he must appear as the confident victor of Asia when he entertained ambassadors and representatives from many nations who sought his advice and alliance. Then occurred the tragedy of the conspiracy of the royal pages in which Callisthenes was involved. These pages were selected young men of noble birth who waited upon the King: they took messages, brought his horse, watched him in his tent at night and were responsible for his safety whilst he slept. They studied military methods and those of good character and ability could rise to high positions in the army. The royal pages had no idle time; as Alexander never spared himself, his subordinates were often overworked. One day, when hunting a boar, a page named Hermolaus rushed forward to throw his spear, thus depriving the King of his right to be the first to attack. The offence was pardonable if due to thoughtlessness, but in this case Hermolaus was considered to have committed a grave fault and he was punished according to the usual custom. He talked angrily about the tyranny of his treatment, and how in Greece it was considered a virtuous deed to slay a tyrant. Apparently Callisthenes had expressed sympathy with the complaint of the excited youth, and although it is improbable that he had implied that Alexander was one of the tyrants so resented by the Greeks, Hermolaus and several other pages conspired to kill their King when they were entrusted to guard him in his tent at night. A woman soothsayer, so the story goes, warned Alexander to avert danger by remaining late at the dinner meal. Finding the pages still awaiting his return the King thanked them and rewarded them with a gift; this did not deter them from their design to carry out their plan on the following night. The plot becoming known to other pages, Ptolemy was informed. When arrested, the pages admitted their conspiracy, but blamed Callisthenes as having instigated them to rid the world of a tyrant who had adopted Persian customs.

Alexander ordered a full investigation. After a fair trial the pages were condemned and Callisthenes was imprisoned; Ptolemy and Aristobulus, acquainted with all the evidence, were convinced of his guilt. As a Greek, Callisthenes could not appear before a Macedonian tribunal; the correct legal procedure was to send him to Corinth. But this was so difficult to arrange that he was conveyed with the army into India. Some say that he died in prison there; others that he was condemned by an Indian court. The discrepancy between the records of Prolemy and Aristobulus regarding the mode of his death may be due to their incessant work during the campaign in the Punjab, where men lived daily with danger and death. Callisthenes had not been a favourite; at the evening meal his presence cast a gloom as he sat silent, grimly criticising the ebullience of the youthful military circle. Memoirs written many years later might well be inexact regarding the absence of one who had never been a congenial companion.

But the death of Callisthenes had an evil aftermath. When one looks back along a lifetime one often sees how an apparently unimportant incident precipitated a series of events which at the time were unpredictable. A tiny spark can set on fire an immense forest. When the news of his death reached Athens, much resentment was felt by the friends of Callisthenes; unaware of all the facts, they talked of Alexander as a tyrant who had deteriorated in Persia. Thus the conspiracy of the pages injured Alexander's reputation for many centuries. But, if the pages had not received misleading instruction concerning the merit of slaying a tyrant, it seems improbable that on their own initiative they would have planned to kill their King. Alexander could not have retained an instructor of youth whose training in Rhetoric had wielded so much influence over inexperienced and immature minds.

The Greek word "sophia", which orginally signified skill and wisdom, had degenerated to indicate mere clever twisting of truth by trained oratory. In Greece a class of professional Sophists had aroused distrust because of their ability to teach their students how to conduct arguments to uphold right or wrong. Speech had great power when printing was unknown and books were few. Direct, truthful, accurate, Alexander had no use for the plausible oratory taught by the professional Sophists. For this reason he had decided that the retention of Callisthenes would have imperilled the security of the expedition into India.

CHAPTER VI

THE ROCKS TO THE HYDASPES, WINTER 328 TO MAY 326 B.C.

Pacification of Sogdiana—Capture of the Sogdian Rock—Marriage with Roxane—Capture of the Chorienes Rock—Preparations for campaign in the Punjab—Mountain crossing to Alexandria-ad-Caucasum—Army divided into two columns: Alexander travels along the north side, Hephaestion and Perdiccas the south side, of the Cophen valley—The mountain tribes—Massaga—Aornos Rock, late winter or early spring 326 B.C.—King Porus and the battle of the Hydaspes, March to May, 326 B.C.

THE DEATH of Spitamenes had as its immediate result the pacification of Sogdiana. Having ordered measures to restore the well-being of the people and the fertility of the ruined countryside, Alexander spent much of the winter at Nautaca, busily engaged with preparations for the journey south to the Punjab. Before starting on that enterprise he weighed up the consequences which might result from the fact that as several prominent barons had not yet made formal submission, their rock fortresses could endanger his rear.

The expedition to the Sogdian Rock began probably in the late winter of 328. This formidable fortress stood upon a rock so steep and so high that it was reputed to be impregnable. Oxyartes had sent his wife and family there and had laid in sufficient stores to withstand a prolonged siege. When Alexander arrived at the rock, desirous to avoid bloodshed, his heralds requested permission to visit the fortress. To this suggestion came the jeering reply that only men with wings could reach their citadel and camp. This challenge stimulated the King and his army to make the attempt by night; volunteers were called for and prizes offered to those who gained the summit by dawn. Three hundred responded, and in the darkness, using stakes of iron, strong ropes and tent pegs pushed into crevices, this brave company arrived above the camp with a loss of only thirty men. Huge blocks of ice had added to the danger of their mountaineering feat. In the morning, when the heralds shouted to the garrison to look above, the Sogdians stared, incredulous, amazed to see Macedonians waving flags on the summit of the supposedly insurmountable rock. Alexander explained that this miracle had been accomplished by soldiers with wings. Believing that the "winged soldiers" had a strong force behind them, the Sogdians, without further parley, surrendered to their resourceful conqueror, and on finding how clement were his terms they induced neighbouring clans to follow their example.

Here Alexander met Roxane, the daughter of Oxyartes, and was deeply impressed by her beauty and charm. As it was his invariable rule to treat captive women with respect, Alexander proposed honourable marriage; his offer was joyfully accepted by the Princess and her father. Some maintain that this marriage was merely a matter of policy, but I find it hard to believe that a man who cared so much for Homer and the Greek drama, which depicted so many noble women, would have entered into a loveless marriage at this stage of his career. Some sympathetic attraction Roxane must have possessed; for Alexander had met many beautiful Persian women of high rank and passed them by, coldly indifferent. Many of the army objected that their King should have chosen a "barbarian" for his bride, but his Oriental allies rejoiced when the marriage ceremony was conducted with the rites of the country. History tells us little about Roxane. She bore a son after Alexander's death; both were destroyed by the ambitious Cassander; they obstructed his path to the coveted throne.

Apparently it was soon after his marriage that Alexander proceeded to the Rock of Chorienes. Its site is disputed, but the campaign involved arduous climbing in snowy weather. To overcome its natural defences demanded great valour and ingenuity. The circumference of the rock measured seven miles; at one end was a defile about two miles long, too narrow for more than one man to pass along. The steep rock was encircled by a deep ravine with a mountain torrent. Alexander surveyed the position and drew up plans for the capture of the fortress. From felled pine trees ladders were hastily constructed on which troops descended to the bottom of the ravine; under covered galleries their work was concealed from the garrison above. Piles driven into the river supported a heavy weight of wooden and osier hurdles; on these were thrown thick layers of earth. Alexander, Leonnatus, Ptolemy and Perdiccas supervised the labour by day and by night; but even with the aid of the whole company, working in shifts, only thirty feet could be securely erected in one day. At first the defenders watched this mighty effort with amusement, but as the days passed it dawned on them that they could not inflict any injury on the attacking force, hidden and protected by their shields; on the contrary, it was they who began to suffer from the Macedonian missiles. Most ominous of all, the mound of earth was steadily rising, and nothing could be devised to prevent its approach.

Chorienes made an overture; he asked permission to consult Oxyartes. When this friend arrived he spoke in such high terms of Alexander that Chorienes surrendered and became a loyal ally. After being entertained in the royal tent, Chorienes conducted his former enemy round the rock fortress. Alexander admired the military precautions, congratulated the baron on his methods of government and restored to him all his territory. Chorienes, delighted, offered to provision the whole Macedonian army for two months, as he had laid in an abundant store of food. This unexpected gift was most welcome to the troops after their heavy exertion in bitter weather.

At last the way was clear for the long postponed journey to the Punjab. Alexander proposed to claim the land as far as the Indus, which had been reached by Darius I. Whilst preparations were in progress, he returned to Bactria to institute a government pleasing to the people; the province must be independent, free to make its own laws. Authorities who had proved unworthy were superseded by reliable men.

Little was known about the geography of the land which lay beyond the great rivers which rose in the mountains of Iran. It was supposed that the earth was surrounded by an immense ocean which turned from the far north toward the eastern border of India; after traversing the Punjab Alexander thought that he would be near that encircling ocean. Eratosthenes tells us that "those who made the expedition with Alexander acquired only cursory information about everything, but Alexander made accurate investigations; the men best acquainted with the country described it for him". Confirming this evidence, Strabo states that "Alexander discovered India". In his Geography, of which most has been preserved, Strabo gives maps of the limit of the world and the calculations of its surface made by Eratosthenes.

The troops looked forward with interest to this new adventure, having heard tales about wonderful birds, animals and plants, also of princes, rajahs, resplendent towns and treasures. But the King knew that they would be strongly opposed by the mountain tribes on the northern side of the Cophen river. However, he could rely on aid from Taxiles, who reigned over the land extending from the Indus as far as the Hydaspes river. Taxiles and his father had decided to assist rather than oppose Alexander, for they feared the encroachments of their powerful neighbour, King Porus, whose dominion lay south of the Hydaspes.

Late in the spring or early summer of 327 B.C. Alexander set out from Bactria with his Queen and an immense gathering, taking the usual Bamyam route. On reaching Alexandria-ad-Caucasum he found that it had been so misgoverned that he appointed a new satrap. The number of the company is disputed: some estimate 120,000, others 135,000. The Europeans were few in comparison with the recruits from Persia, Greece, Egypt, Cyprus, Phoenicia, and even from the once defiant Scythians, Arians, Sogdians and wild trans-Oxian tribes. More than military members followed Alexander—engineers, mineralogists, builders of boats and bridges, architects, astronomers, surveyors, geographers, sinkers of wells, zoologists and botanists, priests and augurs. The Arts also contributed representatives for a King who loved poetry, the drama, music and song. For the transport, the provisioning and equipment of this throng many technicians and artisans were needed; add to these the wives, children and attendants for the tents, the number might well approximate 135,000.

The Cophen (Kabul) valley, 250 miles long, leads to the Khyber Pass and to Gandhara, the mountain district between the Indus and the Kunar rivers. Through the gorges rush tributary streams; at the end of these defiles dwelt brave clans ready to resist every foreign invader.

The army was divided into two columns: Perdiccas and Hephaestion, accompanied by Taxiles, went along the southern bank of the Cophen to construct a bridge to be ready for the King when he could rejoin them. Alexander took the main column and hoped to gain the alliance of the people on the northern bank. For river crossings boats were built from local timber; they could be taken apart, carried about and joined together when required. Along the Kunar, Swat and Bunar valleys the terrain was rough, the climate changeable, the inhabitants fierce and stubborn warriors.

The Five River country is seen on both ancient and modern maps; one must trace up the Indus from its delta to its source in order to find where the rivers enter it. During the centuries annual floodings have carved new channels; the delta of today has moved many miles distant from that explored by Alexander. The names of towns have been changed or modified, but can be identified on a modern map by following up the course of the rivers. Owing to the dispute about these rivers to-day, I mention here the old and the new names of the tributaries: the Hydaspes is now the Jhelum; the Hydraotes, the Ravi; the

Acesines, the Chenab. The Hyphasis, which the army refused to cross, is now the Beas, which joins the Sutlej on its way to the Indus.

The King sent heralds to the local chieftains, princes and rajahs, requesting them to meet him on the northern bank of the Cophen; refusal to acknowledge his sovereignty would imply the use of force, but agreement would ensure his protection, even extension of their territories. But, as the British found, many centuries later, the men of the North-West Frontier enjoy warfare for its own sake; trained from boyhood to the excitement of danger, they go to battle often unaware on which side they fight. Thus the campaign lasted much longer than Alexander had expected. An effective method was to block the entrance to the defiles with a fortress; imprisoned in their own valleys the people were compelled, sooner or later, to submit and thereafter gained his protection. Some who took no notice of the first summons to attend the King hastened later with plausible excuses for delay. No threatening clan, no town commanding important roads could be left to endanger flank or rear; but only the main battles and sieges can be mentioned here.

Arigaion, abandoned and burned by its inhabitants as they fled, was rebuilt because it overlooked two valleys; friendly natives settled in it. Some of the remarkable cattle in its district were sent to Macedonia to improve the home stock.

The Assaceni, prosperous and strong, prepared to defend their land; it stretched from the Indus almost to Kashmir. In the valley of the Swat stood their capital, Massaga; its Prince had a large army which included 7,000 Indian mercenaries. To draw the Massagans to a position where his swift tactics would have the advantage, Alexander feigned a retreat. His ruse succeeded, and at the selected site the Macedonians turned and charged. Hastening after them Alexander was wounded in the leg; calling for his horse he drew out the arrow and did not stop to quench the blood. But soon he was obliged to retire for rest till morning. Probably it was on this occasion that he jested ruefully: "They call me a son of Zeus! But this is not the ichor of the gods; it is mortal blood."

As no headway was gained on the following day, a siege tower was erected close to the rampart. Still no success—a novel experience for the Macedonians. Protected by their shields the soldiers dashed over a bridge hastily constructed from the tower to the wall; it broke under their weight. Next day both sides fought on with increasing ferocity until, suddenly, the Massagan Prince was slain by an arrow. Having admired the bravery of the defenders, Alexander sent his heralds with mild conditions of surrender which were gladly accepted—the family of the Prince were to be delivered as hostages, and the Indian mercenaries were to join the Macedonian army.

The Indian mercenaries withdrew to a camp on the hill to discuss their position; thereafter history varies with the writers. Droysen states that the mercenaries, fearing that they might be obliged to fight against their own kindred, decided to steal off in the night and cross the Indus. It is not known how Alexander learned of this plan which, if successful, would have constituted a serious menace to his next objectives, Ora and Bazira. Further parley being useless, a contingent was sent to check the attempt to escape; in the fierce struggle all the Indians were slain. This "Massacre of Massaga" has been cited as an example of Alexander's cruelty; but other writers are of Droysen's opinion. Alexander's Intelligence was rarely at fault; if he had knowledge of a plot to circumvent the surrender terms, his precaution to prevent the flight of the mercenaries was correct. The tragic slaughter could not have been foreseen; in the darkness the army was beyond normal control. As Alexander was always a strict observer of his promises and had greatly admired the prowess of the Massagan defence, it is difficult to believe that he would have committed a grave breach of an agreement which he had himself drawn up.

After heavy fighting the two Assacenian towns, Ora and Bazira, capitulated; Ora had received reinforcements from Abisares of Kashmir. When the inhabitants of Bazira heard that Alexander was near, many fled to the great Rock of

Refuge, Aornos. Alexander turned south to join Hephaestion and Perdiccas on the Indus. A lesser general would have pursued the fugitives to the north, but reference to the map will explain to the reader that it was wiser strategy to retain the army in the south.

The mountain campaign had been strenuous; ice, snow and wind storms had added to the strain. But in the Swat region the troops enjoyed a restful interlude at Nysa, a beautiful country lying in a fold of the Himalayas. Travellers arriving in that delightful valley feel that they have reached the peace of Arcady. Nysa claimed descent from Dionysus because the plants associated with his name abounded in profusion there; enchanted, the Macedonians picked grapes and ivy which they had not seen since they had left their homes—so long ago. Admiring the institutions, the methods of government and the industries of the people of this dominion, Alexander conferred independence upon its ruler.

The time had come to turn to serious grips with those who had fled from the upper Swat district to the Rock of Aornos. Now that its site has been identified by Sir Aurel Stein, historians recognise that its capture was a necessary strategic operation undertaken to protect the rear of the army. Yet for many centuries historians had maintained that the King attacked this formidable fortress from an unworthy motive; that, "avid of glory", he desired to prove that he could accomplish a task which had baffled all previous heroes.

Sir Aurel made two surveys of the North-West Frontier. On his first visit he failed to trace any rock resembling that described by ancient writers. Fifteen years later his quest was successful: Aornos is part of the Pīr-sar massif. In his fascinating book are full details of his discovery, which was based on a study of the relationship of Indian modern names with those of ancient Greek nomenclature. His illustrations show the great mountains of that region, many snow-capped, with icy crests glistening like crystal, some covered with fir and cedar trees, others barren, showing only cliffs, precipices, rocks and gorges. But the valleys were gay with flowers, green meadows, birch and rhododendron.

Taking with him Arrian's history of Alexander's Indian expedition, Sir Aurel followed the journey of the conqueror through the Swat region; able to identify Bazira, but not Ora, he understood why Alexander was obliged to possess these towns before advancing to the Indus. The Pir-sar massif stands on the west bank of the Indus, 7,000 feet above sea level and 5,000 feet above the river which makes a wide bend from north to south, then curves to the west as it rounds the base of the massif. The two flat-topped ridges of Pir-sar meet at Una-sar; at one end is the famous Aornos Rock, separated from the plateau by the deep ravine of Burimar.

From the summit of Pir-sar is a wide panoramic view of distant mountains, of the plain and the river. To storm such a natural fortress demanded masterly organisation and stubborn tenacity; the longer Sir Aurel examined the ground the more he admired the courage of the King and his army. The plateau is one and a half miles long by 300 yards wide; it has a fertile soil, a spring of pure water, much timber and abundant crops.

For the assault on Aornos Alexander drew up careful plans. Craterus was sent to Embolina (a village not yet identified) to gather supplies for a siege which might last a month. To ensure a reserve of water in the event of a thaw, snow was shovelled into a pit and covered with earth and boards. Conducted by a native guide by a secret path, Ptolemy reached a height from which he could threaten the fortress; there he lit a beacon as a signal of his arrival. Next day Alexander began to climb by another route, but the ascent was so steep that the defenders threw him back, then fell on Ptolemy's camp. A letter was sent to Ptolemy at night, with instructions that they must attack from two directions early in the morning. After fierce fighting their combined forces marched along the ridge, but just as they imagined that they had reached the plateau they found the unsuspected obstacle, the Burimar ravine, 600 feet deep.

Darkness was falling when Sir Aurel Stein, over 2,000 years later, had the same experience; when close to the plateau he found himself slipping downhill. Thrilled, he consulted his copy of Arrian to find how Alexander had coped with the problem. Every man had brought 100 stakes from rapidly felled trees and on these a mound had been raised to the level required for the siege engines and the catapults. With encouragement and praise, and above all by personal example, Alexander roused his soldiers to heroic exertions which were at length crowned by success. Thanksgiving services were duly carried out, the fortress strengthened, and an Indian appointed Governor of Aornos.

Reports came that with 2,000 men and fifteen elephants the brother of the slain Prince of Massaga had taken the fortress of Dyrta. As Alexander hurried to Dyrta friendly natives told him that its inhabitants had fled over the Indus to Kashmir, and deserters said that their leader had been killed by his own men when they heard of the approach of Alexander; it was useless to oppose such a King. Alexander secured the elephants; knowledge of their habits proved useful in the future.

Alexander now linked up with Hephaestion and Perdiccas, who had met with little opposition on their way along the southern side of the Cophen. The Indus was crossed at Attock. Elated by their successes in the north, the soldiers told their comrades the story of Aornos; Heracles, the son of Zeus, had delivered Prometheus from his chains, but had failed to take Aornos. On their triumphant journey to the plains, the army would leave behind the vast Himalayan panorama, unique in the world, with ridge upon ridge of snowy mountains, the noise of many waterfalls, the roar of rushing rivers and torrents, the vibrant shrieking of winds over snow and whistling over rocks. On the foothills this formidable scenery was replaced by luxuriant vegetation, brilliant flowers and immense trees covered with blossom— pink, red, white and gold—a welcome contrast to the bitter cold and the barren scenery of the north.

News of the victory of Aornos having spread far and wide, ambassadors came from many Indian princes who sought the friendship of the new King of Asia. One of the most important was Taxiles, who had already given valuable information about the people on the north bank of the

Cophen, and had aided Hephaestion and Perdiccas along the south side. Taxila, the capital of the country ruled by Taxiles and his father, was situated in a valley between the Indus and the Hydaspes; its remains have been recently examined by Sir John Marshall. In antiquity, trade routes met there from eastern India, Bactria, Kashmir and Central Asia. The surrounding country was beautiful, the soil fertile and the climate invigorating, being 1,700 to 1,800 feet above sea level; there was in consequence a numerous population.

On the approach to Taxila the Macedonians met the Indian ascetics who sat immobile, naked, solitary, lost in meditation, indifferent alike to the burning rays of the sun and the icy cold of the night. The effect of this impact is dealt with later (p. 225). Clad in the gorgeous raiment of their country, Taxiles and his father offered formal allegiance to the King and placed their capital at his disposal. An interchange of rich gifts followed; Taxiles gave 700 horsemen, thirty elephants, 2,000 sheep, 3,000 animals for sacrifice, and coinage. To Taxiles Alexander presented money, Persian tapestries and engraved Hellenic vases of gold and silver. These tales of the Indian journey have the glamour of a dream world.

From Taxila Alexander sent a message to King Porus, suggesting that they should meet at his frontier; Porus replied that he would be ready to meet Alexander, but only in battle. Porus was no friend of Taxiles nor of the "kingless peoples" (the Arattas), who dwelt beyond his other frontier. He drew up his highly disciplined army on the south bank of the river Hydaspes, ready to meet the Macedonians. Cutting short the festivities at Taxila Alexander sent orders to Coenus to bring to the Hydaspes all the vehicles, boats and army equipment which could be transferred from the Indus. As they left Taxila the rains set in which were to play so important a part in the near future. Now was to come the hardest and most costly struggle of the campaign; formidable because the enemy forces were under a capable King; no previous armies encountered in Asia had been efficiently trained to work as one unit under one able leader.

The Hydaspes could be forded in winter when there was

ice; but in the rainy season it was impassable, swollen with melting snows and floods to about half a mile wide. Porus' army had excellently equipped infantry, cavalry, chariots and some 200 elephants. Alexander had left his fifteen elephants behind; as horses were afraid of them, they were worse than useless. Consternation filled the Macedonian army at the sight of the 200 massive elephants drawn up on the southern bank of the Hydaspes, where they stood like an immense grey tower. What could the Macedonian cavalry do in a contest with such enormous beasts? But Alexander's men were confident that he would find a solution. Nothing daunted, Alexander set about to find, and did find that solution. Although Abisares had sent a message that he was loyal, and denied having aided the Massagans, Alexander had no confidence in his sincerity. As reinforcements for Porus might arrive at any time from Kashmir, the Macedonian attack could not be long delayed.

Alexander planned to keep Porus constantly on the alert; by day and by night the Indians must be maintained in a continual state of fear and uncertainty as to where and when the Macedonians would attempt to cross. A report was spread that they intended to wait till after the rainy season; with the subsidence of the floods a fording would be more simple. The camp was stocked with provisions and stores to confirm the rumour. Night after night it was arranged that noises, shouting, even battle cries were heard at varying points along the bank; boats were put out, collections of troops hurried here and there; sometimes the cavalry drew up as if preparing for action. Porus, expecting surprise attacks, sent men to the positions where there were most noise and signs of aggressive preparations on the north bank. Thus almost every night the Indians were compelled to hurry here and there, ready to oppose any attempted passage of the river. Alexander remained on the alert, watching the effect of his feint attacks. Finding that after so much uproar and apparent activity, nothing ever happened, and the piling up of stores continued in the Macedonian camp, Porus relaxed his vigilance and believed that his foe awaited the subsidence of the floods.

But every night Alexander, under cover of darkness, was exploring the banks for a suitable fording site. At last, some seventeen miles upstream, where the river made a bend to the west, he found an island so thickly wooded that the crossing of troops and boats would be concealed. These features, which are mentioned by Arrian, have been identified within recent years. All the way to the main camp sentries were posted along the bank so as to ensure safe communications with Craterus. On the night selected, Craterus showed signs of increased activity which induced Porus to think that the crossing might be expected to come opposite his great army. Thus Alexander was able to reach the island unobserved. He took with him 13,000 men by a route well inland, roofed by many trees; the sodden earth had not given rise to the cloud of dust which in dry weather would have betrayed the march. At night there came a tempest; the sounds of human movement were drowned by Nature's deafening roar of thunder and the heavy downpour of tropical rain. Although the storm raged all night preparations had been so complete that the army reached the island in safety and began to disembark, but found that what had been supposed to be the opposite bank had become another island, the swirling torrent of the flood having forced a path through the earth. A strong current had still to be traversed before the army could gain the southern bank; many had to march over with breast and shoulders level with the water. It is said that it was on this occasion that Alexander exclaimed: "Oh Athens, if you knew to what hardships you drove me in my desire to win your praise!" First to step on shore, he waited to assist those who followed him.

Owing to the delay caused by this unexpected obstacle, the light of dawn had revealed to Porus' outposts that some troops had crossed the river. They hastened to report this strange occurrence. Porus questioned whether this could be the arrival of the first reinforcements espected from Abisares; as the chief camp on the north bank had been active all night it seemed impossible that any Macedonians could have made the passage over. However, he sent out a reconnoitring force of 2,000 men with 120 chariots. Alexander scrutinised this company with care; when certain that it consisted of only a limited number of men, he ordered a vigorous attack to be pressed. Porus' son was slain; 400 horsemen fell; all the chariots were captured or destroyed. From the few who escaped to report the result of the encounter Porus learned the terrible truth that Alexander had reached the southern bank of the Hydaspes during the stormy night.

There are differing accounts of the numbers of the opposing armies; it is said that Alexander had 14,000 to 30,000 or 40,000 of the enemy. He had 5,000 to Porus' 4,000 horse, but he had no elephants. Then, by his foresight, he had gained the advantage that he had the site selected by himself, near the river, with reserve battalions stationed along the northern bank. The Indians were drawn up on the southern bank, opposite the camp of Craterus, which they dared not regard as negligible whilst it continued to keep up an appearance of busy preparations to cross. Deciding that he must first engage Alexander, whose line stood at a right angle to the river, Porus was compelled to wheel round his immense army to face his foe. Had he taken the offensive, he might have destroyed the Macedonian force early in the day; but as Porus hesitated, Alexander saw that he was to be given the advantage of the offensive. On his right he had Seleucus, the Agema and other brigades under Antigonus, 6,000 hypaspists, and Tauron with the light infantry. Between the fording site and the camp of Craterus were several thousand mercenary troops under Meleager, Gorgias and Attalus. All had strict orders not to move until they received a signal that Porus' left was in disorder. Thus, if by any mischance Alexander was obliged to retreat, his flank and rear were securely protected. The presence of these battalions had the further advantage that they effectually prevented any Indian attempt to cross to the northern bank.

When Porus wheeled round his immense army to face Alexander he had on both wings 2,000 cavalry; in the centre 200 elephants placed about 100 feet apart; between them foot soldiers and behind them a mass of infantry; on their backs sat drivers in well-protected towers. It is said that the

Indian line extended to about three to four miles, whilst the Macedonian line was about a quarter of that length. Although Alexander preferred to lead off from the right, with the Companion cavalry, this preliminary movement was conditioned by the fact that, as both he and Porus were well aware, no horses would face elephants unless accustomed and trained to meet them. Therefore the King designed to avoid the elephants, leaving them to be dealt with by the infantry. By taking an oblique course to the right Alexander induced Porus to turn so that the Indian cavalry would meet the Companions. As the Indian left swerved, Alexander despatched Coenus with a contingent of horse to ride, concealed by rising ground, to the rear of Porus' left. Ignorant of this manoeuvre, Porus, watching Alexander, believed that he saw the entire Macedonian cavalry and considered it to be so small a force that he could readily dispose of it, and therefore he attacked it with confidence. The Dāān archers kept the Indians on the alert whilst Alexander rode toward their flank, thus attracting his foe too far from his supporting infantry. Then Coenus began his pressure on their rear. Taken completely by surprise, Porus' cavalry had to fight in two directions, against Alexander in front, and against Coenus behind them. Whilst they were thus confused, Alexander made his usual lightning charge on the weakened point with such vigour that the Indian horse were forced to retire to the elephants, seeking, as Arrian expressed it, "a friendly wall for refuge". The elephants of the left centre were then driven towards Alexander, frightened his horses, and were supported by the Indian cavalry as it rallied.

Now came the opportunity of the Macedonian infantry to prove their mettle, and most bravely did they do so. With sharp pointed lances they struck the great animals, opened out their ranks when the beasts advanced, then rushed under interlocked shields to prod the hides of the distracted creatures until at last, maddened with terror and pain, the elephants turned back, trumpeting, trampled on their own soldiers and inflicted more damage on the Indians than on the Macedonians. Meanwhile, as Alexander charged the retreating cavalry, a ferocious struggle ensued.

Not a foot of ground did the Macedonians cede, for their training enabled them to fall back, rally and re-form. Coenus, on his return, charged the Indian infantry, who fled for safety to the elephants. Porus sent out forty fresh elephants to attack the phalanx, but the javelin men and the archers kept them at bay. After eight hours of this sanguinary conflict, Craterus received the signal to cross and relieve the troops who had fought all day after the night spent in fording the river. The Indians, disorganised, fled to the open country and the woods.

Porus had never fought against such formidable weapons as were possessed by this enemy; nor had he ever met with such masterly tactics, nor encountered any foes led by a military genius. But he was an indomitable King; unlike Darius, brave as a lion, seated on his elephant, he was everywhere on the battlefield, directing and encouraging his men. The toll of slain and wounded was heavy; Porus lost his two sons, his relative Spitakes and most of the leaders of his cavalry and his infantry. An accurate estimate does not exist; it is said that the Indian killed numbered 20,000, including 3,000 cavalry. In comparison, the Macedonian figures were small—230 cavalry and 700 infantry.

Throughout the day Alexander had watched with growing admiration the heroic attitude of Porus. Toward the end of the long conflict he realised that the Indian King was seeking death on the field and determined to save the life of so noble an opponent. A messenger was despatched to implore Porus to surrender; in vain. Then Alexander rode out to follow him, but his beloved horse, Bucephalus, worn out with age and the toil of that long day, fell dead beneath him. He had faithfully served his King all over Asia, but the Hydaspes battle was his death knell. Alexander sent Taxiles to tell Porus that he desired to meet him as a friend; but the Indian, recognising in Taxiles a former enemy, spurned him off and tried to strike him; Taxiles fled. After several messengers had approached Porus without result one at length persuaded him to dismount from his elephant. Weary, Porus alighted and demanded a draught of water before meeting his victor; then his friend, Meroes, led him to Alexander.

The story of the meeting of these two great men illustrates the chivalrous character of both victor and vanquished. When told that Porus was being escorted to his presence Alexander rode out, with a few of the Companions, to greet him. Impressed by the dignity, the handsome stature and the mien of this brave King, he asked him what treatment he wished to receive. "Treat me as a king", was the reply. Delighted with this response, Alexander smilingly said: "For my own sake I would treat you as a king, but for your sake, tell me what is pleasing to you". To which Porus answered that all was comprised in that request. Still more impressed, Alexander ever after treated him as a king and as a friend. During the following year Porus' knowledge of the country proved invaluable when Alexander's advance led him to many brief but severe encounters with the Arattas, the "kingless peoples".

Porus has been described as an intrepid "old man". But was he indeed an elderly man? The account of the Hydaspes battle comes from the Memoirs of Ptolemy; to a young man under thirty the man of forty or fifty appears quite old. The vigorous assistance rendered by Porus in the next stage of Alexander's journey was surely more than could have been contributed by one who was truly "old".

Many readers of the Victorian time, when peace was believed to be perpetual, regarded the Indian expedition as a hideous series of episodes of slaughter. But the modern generation knows how hard it is to bring about any understanding or reconciliation between nations with different customs, traditions and religions, and how it happens that when war begins, the opponents fight on till one is too exhausted to continue the struggle. The Macedonians conducted war on the heroic lines depicted by Homer. However arduous the task demanded, their King could rely upon the obedience of every man in his army; they kept to time, carried out orders with disciplined precision, and fought to the death with never a thought of surrender. The beautiful verse of the *Iliad* sheds a glow over the stark realities of war; its descriptions of the glittering armour and the plumed helmets of the combatants transform into poetry the facts of injuries and death; comparatively little is told of wounds, which may have healed rapidly, not being contaminated by soil manured for centuries.

The consequences of the battle of the Hydaspes were as important and far-reaching as those of Gaugamela. Just as the victory of Gaugamela had opened up the whole of Central Asia, so the victory at the Hydaspes gained the greater part of Northern India and the Punjab. Chandra-gupta, the Indian King, to whom Seleucus, after the death of Alexander, was obliged to yield up much of the Punjab, said that so high had been the reputation of the Macedonian conqueror that he could, had he so desired, have acquired and ruled over the whole of Northern India.

But circumstances unforeseen were to bring about another ending to the Indian expedition.

CHAPTER VII

THE INDUS TO THE MALLIAN
CAMPAIGN

*Alexander founds Bucephala and Nicea—Discusses
terms of government with Indians—Assacenian
revolt—Timber floated down the river to Craterus—
Porus brings reinforcements—Crossing of the Hydraotes
—Capture of Sangala—Army refuse to cross the
Hyphasis—Return to Nicea—Crossing of the Hydaspes
and the Acesines—The Mallian campaign—Alexander
severely wounded—Submission of the Mallians and
the Oxydracae*

AFTER the victory on the Hydaspes the fallen were buried
with the highest funeral honours. The Greeks attached great
importance to the correct disposal of the dead, for they
believed that until this was carried out the departed soul had
no peace. Several Greek tragedies were based upon the
theme of the agony of Antigone when forbidden to bury the
corpse of her brother. Therefore Alexander always ensured
honourable burial of the slain, whether friend or foe.

Two cities were founded: Bucephala, in memory of the
beloved horse, who had died on the field of battle; and
about two miles away, a second city, Nicea, on the site of
victory. For a time Alexander took up his quarters there; it
was a convenient meeting place for the Indians with whom
plans had to be considered for future civilian, legal and
military administration. He had no intention to deal with
them on the lines which had been suitable for Persia; he did
not desire to annex Indian territory, but must secure co-
operation to enable him to pass down the Indus to the great

Ocean. The civilisation of India had attained a high level of culture and its people had not lost their martial vigour and independent spirit; the Indians had for many centuries followed their own ways of life, under their own kings, princes, rajahs and chieftains. They had also a religion of rare spiritual enlightenment which could not be altered nor modified to combine with that of Greece; the teaching of the Upanishads could not harmonise with the Pagan deities.

From the Indian Viceroy of Aornos came the unwelcome news that the Assaceni had slain the Macedonian Governor; their rebellion was believed to have been incited by Abisares of Kashmir. As this unexpected rising threatened his communications Alexander ordered the satraps of the adjacent regions to quench the trouble before it assumed dangerous proportions. But it was obvious that the time had come for a definite understanding with Abisares. Leaving Craterus to fortify the two new cities Alexander set out north-east, accompanied by Taxiles and Porus, and soon reached the Glaucian territory on the foothills of the mountain frontier of Kashmir. The Glaucians offered no resistance; their country was thickly populated, having thirty-seven towns and villages containing 5,000 to 10,000 inhabitants who were content to be placed under the rule of Porus. As soon as Abisares learned that Alexander was in his vicinity he despatched envoys to explain that ill-health was responsible for his inability to come in person to proffer his allegiance, and in proof of his sincerity his messengers brought a gift of forty elephants. His apologies were accepted, for Alexander had not time to spare on a mountain campaign against Abisares.

Forest trees were felled, and the timber floated down the river to Craterus with instructions to build a fleet on which the army could sail to the sea. The Thracian cavalry, who had been waiting in Hyrcania and Parthia, were now summoned to join the army.

The river Acesines, rapid and dangerous, was examined for a crossing place where the waters broadened out and the flow was less violent; but in spite of all precautions considerable damage occurred. Coenus was placed in charge, and

Porus was sent home to collect troops and elephants. First, action must be taken against "the guilty or cowardly' Porus, a label coined to distinguish him from his uncle, "the faithful" Porus. This worthless prince had fled to the Gandaridae, near the Hyphasis, but as an expedition to follow him would occupy too much time, the task was deputed to Hephaestion while Alexander passed on to the lands of the Arattas, the "kingless peoples", who clung to their oligarchic rule and bitterly resented any democratic form of government.

Of these "kingless peoples" Porus warned Alexander that the Cathaeans were so dangerous that only Western weapons could prevail against them; they had never experienced defeat. Sangala, their strongly fortified town, was stationed on a hill with a commanding view over the surrounding country. Behind this hill stood their stronghold, also on an eminence and protected on one side by a long shallow lake. The Cathaeans were drawn up behind three rows of large waggons, a novel device which at once told Alexander that their high military reputation was well merited; the waggons both concealed and protected the soldiers. Immediate attack was ordered. Alexander went forward with his horsemen on both wings, the heavy infantry in the centre, the lighter armed between and behind them. From the first rank of the waggons the Cathaeans disputed his progress so successfully that Alexander was obliged to dismount. The front row was readily overcome, but the destruction of the second line demanded prolonged fighting, the path being obstructed by the debris of the preceding vehicles; for such close work the shorter spears of the hypaspists had more deadly effect than the long lances of the hoplites. The Cathaeans retired to their city, which Alexander surrounded, and posted troops on the far side of the lake to prevent attempts to escape during the darkness. On the second night those who groped from the ramparts to cross the lake found their path cumbered up with intact waggons and upright boar spears.

Porus arrived with 5,000 soldiers and many elephants, a welcome reinforcement; great breaches were made with the

battering rams and siege towers, and the catapults brought
about the final collapse of Sangala. The death toll was heavy;
many Macedonian officers of high rank were among the slain.

Eumenes, the Greek secretary, was now sent in advance
to persuade the people that all who submitted would receive
generous treatment; but the fate of Sangala did not dispose
them to have faith in such promises. Other tribes, however,
began to regard Alexander as a benefactor, and this
method of friendly discussion proved so successful that soon
no more fighting was required; at every stage Alexander
received a warm welcome.

The army now had an adventure which has the magic of
the Oriental tales we read in childhood. When they reached
the royal residence of Sopeithes, an important prince, they
found the gates closed; no sign of life was visible, and on
the ramparts no vestige of a defending force could be seen.
Yet it was known that the Prince was in the palace. Suddenly
the doors were thrown apart and between them there issued
a resplendent regal train, with a fanfare of loud trumpets;
at its head rode the Rajah, clad in brilliant silken garments,
and wearing a turban studded with precious jewels. Presenting homage to Alexander he offered rich gifts and a
pack of hounds. He was confirmed in his dominion and his
territory was enlarged.

THE HYPHASIS

The army marched to the Hyphasis, and there they
refused to advance further. Both officers and men had begun
to fear that they would never see their homes again; they
would be obliged to follow their King, whose energy
appeared to be inexhaustible, over the Hyphasis into other
countries—for how many more years? Alexander desired
to cross this river, for he had heard that the soil was fertile,
and that its inhabitants, engaged in agriculture under the
government of an aristocracy, had an excellent political
constitution. When made aware of the attitude of the army
Alexander decided to call a council to consider his next step.
In every country added to his empire he had maintained the

right of the people to be free in thought, speech and action; he could not with justice have refused the same liberty to his own officers and troops. Their refusal to proceed was no rebellion, no mutiny, only the natural result of depression accentuated by three weeks of heavy tropical rain in a sultry climate.

At the council meeting Alexander urged the army to speak without reserve; he would welcome free discussion. He began in his usual direct, frank fashion: "I call you together to take counsel whether I may persuade you to accompany me further, or you may persuade me not to proceed." The versions of his long address not only vary, but contain so many contradictions that some biographers condense this period of the campaign into a brief summary. The long list of towns and countries said to have been enumerated in the speech were not in geographical order, and among the provinces mentioned as acquired were Cappadocia and Paphlagonia, which had been by-passed during the first rush to capture Darius.

The veterans of the army were determined not to be swayed by the eloquence of their King; that had happened too often before. They had selected a certain Coenus to explain their views. There is doubt as to the identity of this Coenus; the general of that name had remained behind, an invalid, near the Acesines. Although the report of Coenus' reply is not authentic, it apparently made an impression upon the King. He thanked Alexander for his assurance that he would employ no compulsion, only persuasion. All agreed that they had received generous gifts and ample reward for their labour; not one of them would ever forget the victories and the trials which they had shared with their King. But the time had come when they wished to return to their homes, wives and children. Their numbers had been reduced by age, disease and wounds during their march of 21,000 miles; their spirits and their energy had been depressed by three weeks of torrential rains. The old army should be replaced by fresh recruits from Macedonia, young and vigorous. And was it not advisable that Alexander also should return with his trophies to adorn his native city?

Would not his mother welcome her son after so long an absence? Coenus concluded with the wise saying of the Hellenes, that no man dare forget, when enjoying the height of his prosperity, that he must exercise moderation; the turns of Fortune were sudden, unpredictable, and unavoidable by mortal man.

During the speech of the King the soldiers had been silent, many in tears, but their attitude expressed that they would not, could not, go across the Hyphasis into India. Napoleon used to feign wrath to strike fear and thus exact obedience. Possibly Alexander had recourse to the same disguise to conceal his deep emotion. Some say that he called the army again next day and angrily stated that he would go on and many would be glad to accompany him. But not one man responded. Profoundly disappointed, the King retired to his tent, and there, Nearchus tells us, he remained in anger, hoping that the army would reconsider the point at issue. Probably he occupied the three days of solitude with maps and reports from those who knew the country.

The story that Alexander wished to reach the Ganges has been disproved—the river was not known at that time—instead, the King believed that the eastern border of India and the great Ocean lay not far beyond the Hyphasis. A modern traveller finds it hard to understand how little was known by people of that century about the conditions of their neighbours. But inland journeys were full of danger from bandits, wild animals, deserts, floods and famine. Apparently even the friendly King Porus had not known that south of the Hyphasis stretched a great desert with few wells, and subject to sandstorms which darkened the sky at midday as if night had fallen and buried under its deposit the bodies of those who ventured over it. Rumours of this obstacle may have reached the King; he must also have realised that his army personnel were now too few to overcome resistance such as he had encountered in the Punjab.

After consideration Alexander announced that he would consult the omens; the augurs had always been correct. The verdict was not propitious; so ominous indeed that it provided the King with ample reason for his decision to return homewards. The troops gave way to tumultuous rejoicing; they hurried to the tent of their King, exclaiming that although he had never been conquered even by the strongest foes, he had allowed his own soldiers to vanquish him—this proved his surpassing virtue and goodness. Twelve high altars were built to mark the turning point of the campaign over Asia. Games and songs refreshed the weary men; thanksgiving sacrifices were duly carried out.

No doubt Alexander was aware that this had been a wise settlement of the problem; had he penetrated far into India what would have become of his empire in the West? But still the unsolved problem of the Ocean continued to haunt his mind—did it lie quite near? Droysen thought that Alexander might have succeeded, as nothing seemed impossible for his extraordinary genius to achieve, but the enormous extent of India would have absorbed more garrisons than he could have spared. Of all the great company who started homewards, Alexander was perhaps the only man who grieved to turn back from the north bank of the Hyphasis.

As usual, he wasted no time in vain regrets, but diverted his whole attention to the task ahead. As far as is known, he confided to few his intention to travel home by another route. A sea path should be found from the mouth of the Indus to the Persian Gulf; when navigable, this would form the southern limit of his empire. That this plan had been confided to Aristobulus proves how much reliance he placed on the honour and intelligence of that Greek.

Four months had passed since the victory on the Hydaspes; with the coming of spring the appearance of the river had entirely altered. The troops rejoiced in the beauty of its banks, crowded with reminiscences of the great battle, now covered with brilliant verdure, flowers and rich vegetation. Paths wound attractively through the woods of the foothills; quaint boats and waggons provided constant novelty. The two towns, Nicea and Bucephala, needed repair; the floods had damaged their mud foundations. Soon there came news of the death of Coenus, the general who had been left to recuperate near the Acesines; the funeral rites occupied time and detained Alexander in Nicea.

Indian princes and rajahs were invited to discuss details of future relationship and tribute. Alexander stipulated that their meeting was not to be that of a conqueror with defeated subjects; its object was to confer benefit on both nations, to institute friendly intercourse and arrange for commerce between the east and the west. Alexander promised that the Indians should be free to govern their own territories as they preferred; but to ensure safe passage to the sea, the whole course of the Indus river must be under Macedonian control and supervision. As the valley of the Indus must be guarded, plans would be drawn up with neighbouring and distant rulers, whose alliance must be guaranteed. The peace brought about in the Five River country would be lasting if the regulations which they had together drawn up were strictly observed. Their territories being enlarged, Porus and Taxiles were now friendly, having equal power. To Sopeithes and Abisares also more land had been apportioned; they would keep each other in check if one became too ambitious. For even Abisares, long so antagonistic, had vowed allegiance when he heard from many quarters that the conduct of Alexander appeared to be that of a man half divine. With this group of strong, independent rulers the eastern border of the empire was safely assured. The amount of tribute to be paid was agreed on without controversy.

Negotiations having been satisfactorily concluded, preparations for the fleet were begun. Experienced sailors had been summoned from Phoenicia, Egypt, Cyprus, the Greek islands and the coast of Asia Minor to man the ships destined to explore a sea route to Persia from the Indus. During the winter months the long mountain path through the Punjab was often impassable for merchandise conveyed by caravans, horses and camels. One may be certain that the King had made every possible enquiry before he left Nicea. Friendly natives had warned him that he would meet strong opposition along the descent of the Indus, and these reports were confirmed by reconnoitring parties.

The quickly assembled fleet consisted, it is said, of eighty galleys manned by thirty rowers, smaller ships, transport craft for food and for horses, native boats, amounting in all some say to 1,000, others 2,000 vessels. Nearchus, the Cretan, was placed in command. With Alexander were the hypaspists, the Agrianians, the Agema of the Companions with the shield-bearing guards. The army marched in three columns, Craterus on the right side of the river, Hephaestion on the left, with elephants; after him came the princes and Philip, Viceroy of the land between Bactria and the Indus. Sacrifices were offered; standing on the prow of his galley Alexander poured from a golden goblet the libations to the rivers: the Hydaspes, the Acesines and the Indus, also to the Ocean, the sea gods and his ancestral gods. Then the trumpets sounded the signal for departure and the unique assembly set forth on the venture which they expected to be a triumphant return to their homes in the West. No foreboding troubled these courageous travellers, certain that their King could conquer every obstacle on land or sea.

Arrangements for the embarkation had been carefully drawn up to avoid danger to the smaller craft from the eddying after-current set up when the heavier vessels moved off. Arrian's vivid narrative conveys some of the thrill which must have stirred the heart of every member in that gathering. The sonorous thud of the beating oars, the shouts of the boatswains directing the rhythmic strokes of the rowers and the cries of the sailors together raised so loud a noise that rocks, cliffs, ravines and forests resounded with the clamour and its echoes. From huts and villages the natives hurried to gaze on this strange, unprecedented procession, and for miles along the shore they sang and danced with exclamations of astonishment contributing to the general excitement. To them the most amazing feature of this wondrous crowd was the presence of the horses on the ships; such passengers had never before been seen.

At the junction of the Hydaspes and the Acesines the troops were awed by the noise of their turbulent waters. They had been warned that the tumult of sound would be audible from afar, but they had not expected so thunderous a roar. The two rivers seemed to struggle for mastery as they hurled over their meeting place into a narrow gorge, eddying in whirlpools till the falling water subsided in a broader expanse. Rowers and pilots fought with superhuman energy to guide their vessels to safety; the smaller craft suffered less than the longer ships.

Whilst Nearchus was repairing the damage, Alexander went inland to secure the submission of the Sibae tribe who were preparing to join the two Arattas peoples—the Malli and the Oxydracae; Porus and other Indian friends had warned Alexander that these tribes would unite to resist him. The territory of the Malli extended north of the junction of the Hydraotes (Ravi) and Acesines (Chenab); that of the Oxydracae lay on the east and reached as far as the country of the Cathaeans. Alexander planned to make a swift attack on the chief towns of the Malli and thus prevent their union with the Oxydracae. He divided the army into three detachments: Hephaestion was sent to the junction of the rivers, five days in advance, ready to deal with fugitives escaping from the towns; Ptolemy set out three days later to intercept those who fled westward; Craterus and Nearchus remained on the right bank of the Acesines. But those carefully considered plans did not work out as expected

So far have the rivers changed their beds that it is not now possible to follow the course taken in this momentous campaign. The Malli expected the Macedonians to approach from the junction of the two great rivers; the only other route lay across a desert so extensive that it was regarded as affording complete protection against all invaders. To take the Malli by surprise it was necessary to cross this desert at high speed and reach the town while its inhabitants were asleep.

In mid-November Alexander started out with archers, Agrianians, hypaspists and cavalry; all filled their waterbottles from a fresh stream, a necessary precaution before a long desert march. Hastening all that day and the next night they covered forty-five miles in twenty-four hours. The Malli, only half awake when roused by their assailants, retreated to their city and surrendered when the infantry came up. Meanwhile Perdiccas had reached his objective, only to find that the inhabitants had fled east over the Hydraotes and linked up with the Oxydracae, the combination which Alexander had hoped to prevent.

Turning back, the King found that the Mallians had sought refuge in their citadel on the northern bank of the river. With his cavalry Alexander plunged into the river and was the first to arrive on the opposite shore. With supreme audacity he chased the retreating enemy, but when the Indians realised that the pursuing force consisted of only a small contingent, they turned to face it. This suited Alexander well, being a master of rapid changes; wheeling his cavalry into a column, he rode round and round the Indians, seizing every opportunity to charge on weakened points. His disciplined cavalry could swiftly retire, re-form and attack; the foes, unaccustomed to such methods, were at the mercy of his tactics and fled precipitately when the infantry appeared.

After this encounter the troops were permitted several hours of repose; it was too late in the day to press on further. But early in the morning Alexander resolved to storm the citadel. This was surrounded by many high towers from which thousands of projectiles could be launched upon any invaders. Part of the wall was undermined and one gate forced open, but to reach the fortress it was necessary to scale the wall. When the soldiers tried to place ladders against the rampart, so heavy a rain of arrows fell that even the bravest quailed. Some delay occurred in bringing up the scaling ladders; Alexander, impatient, seeing that the troops were not displaying their usual dash and vigour in the assault, seized a ladder and with his shield and sword began to mount it, closely followed by Peucestas and Leonnatus. Under their combined weight the ladder broke; but without a moment's hesitation Alexander leapt clear and landed on the summit of the wall. Horrified, the hypaspists on the ground below shouted to their King to jump down into their outstretched arms; in vain; Alexander sprang down into the fort.

Recognised by his glittering armour and his plumes, the King was the target for innumerable darts and missiles thrown from the high towers. Standing with his back against the wall, fighting every man who dared approach, he slew several, including the leader of the enemy force. With his shield he protected his body from the arrows coming from every direction. When four of his foes had fallen the Indians retired, but the missiles from the towers became more dangerous. By his side stood Peucestas, Leonnatus and Abreas, a corporal; presently, Abreas fell, pierced by an arrow. Then, suddenly, another arrow hit Alexander in the chest and penetrated to the lung. Blood flowed profusely from the wound, mingled with his breath; still he tried to fight on, but fell unconscious. Though also wounded and bleeding, Peucestas and Leonnatus stood over their King, guarding his body until some of the soldiers, maddened with rage and fear, with stakes and pegs clambered up the wall, and others forced a way through gates and breaches which they had hammered open. Terrified at the sight of Alexander, prostrate and bleeding, their ferocity knew no bounds; the slaughter was merciless. Alexander was carried out, still unconscious, on the shield of Ilium.

When consciousness returned Alexander begged the surgeon to widen the wound with a sword and extricate the arrowhead. Only after much effort could this be done, the flanges being firmly fixed in the flesh. The operation caused so much pain and loss of blood that the patient fainted again. All that night his friends remained by his side in agony of mind, and outside his tent the soldiers waited in groups till dawn, weeping, hungry for news. For a week the King lay between life and death; only after that apparently interminable interval did his surgeon pronounce that he was out of danger.

Rumours and consternation had spread to both camps; the army believed that their intrepid King had been slain. Then who could take his place? And who could find the way home without his knowledge of the route? Would not all the warrior tribes in the territories through which they must travel fall upon them with redoubled fury, having no longer to contend with the mighty King? When convalescent, Alexander understood that by some method it was necessary to allay the fears of the troops, but nothing could be done until the surgeon decided that the patient could be moved without danger. Then Alexander was conveyed to a tent on a ship; by waving his sound arm he could relieve the anxiety of the men lining the banks and prove that he was on the way to recovery. But when his boat arrived at the river junction where the main camp had been stationed, the troops believed that the tent concealed his dead body. When told of this rumour Alexander ordered that he should be carried on a litter to the shore; there he insisted on mounting a horse, then walked to an adjacent tent. His soldiers pressed round him, weeping with joy, throwing over him flowers and garlands and kissing his garments as he slowly passed them.

The brave action on the fortress had created so profound an impression that the Malli clan sent messengers to explain their delay in reporting the submission of their people. Their neighbours, the Oxydracae, an equally powerful "kingless" tribe, had been preparing to resist with their large army, but when they heard the details of his valorous deed they too decided that it would be prudent to offer allegiance; they despatched messengers with gifts and promised to pay an annual tribute and send hostages to this western King whom they now regarded as belonging to the race of the Immortals. Alexander replied that if they sent to him 1,000 of their nobility, these could choose whether they would remain as hostages, or join the Companions and lend assistance against the hostile tribes who were expected to contest his journey to the mouth of the Indus. The thousand arrived with 500 war chariots; so delighted was Alexander to receive such a mark of confidence that he advised the nobles to return home, but gratefully retained the war chariots.

Nearchus has told in his Memoirs that Alexander was reproached for his temerity in mounting the wall of the Malli fortress. Several of his officers, including Craterus, regarded by Alexander as the best, the most respected and popular of his generals, remonstrated with their King for having risked his life from sheer inability to stand aside; he ought to have left such a foolhardy deed to soldiers who could not replace him as their leader. Nearchus tells us that Alexander listened in silence to this advice, looking somewhat ashamed, aware that the criticism was justified. An elderly Boeotian seated near him at the meal quoted Aeschylus: heroes did brave deeds but must be prepared to suffer in consequence. After so many rebukes Alexander was comforted to hear this kind remark; the Boeotian later became an honoured friend. This incident throws light upon the happy relationship which existed between the King and his officers, and provides a striking proof of the liberty of speech allowed; such would not have been possible in the presence of an Oriental monarch.

The greater part of the army now marched on to the region where the Four Rivers fell into the Indus, and there awaited the arrival of Perdiccas who, with the troops under his command, had travelled along the bank and gained the willing submission of all the tribes. The site being suitable for a centre of commerce, a dock was constructed and a new Alexandria founded which later developed into a flourishing town. Philip was placed in command and his position as Viceroy was extended to this limit. Oxyartes, the father of Roxane, now hastened to pay a visit, and to him was confided the satrapy of the Paramasidae.

All the threads having thus been gathered together, it was hoped and expected that the next part of their journey would be accomplished in comparative peace.

But Fate had further trials in store for this brave team.

CHAPTER VIII

THE LOWER INDUS TO OPIS

February 325 B.C., descent of the lower Indus—
Musicanus confirmed as Governor—Brahman re-
sistance—Musicanus breaks faith—Pattala—Indus
delta explored, July 325 B.C.; Nearchus appointed
Admiral of the Fleet—Gedrosian Desert—Adventures
of the fleet—Reunion in Carmania—Return to Susa—
Peucestas appointed Governor—Harpalus and the
treasures—Weddings of Macedonians with Persians—
Funeral of Calanus—Persians incorporated into the
army—Alexander pays all army debts—Mutiny at
Opis—Reconciliation with the army—10,000 veterans
return home

IN February 325 began the descent of the lower Indus. Alexander sailed down the river while Craterus marched along its bank to the region now known as Sind. No opposition was encountered on the way to their meeting place, where two cities were founded. The climate and the people were unlike those of the upper Indus; the land was very fertile; its extensive market gardens were covered with vines, maize and tropical vegetation. Here Craterus started on the homeward path, through Drangiana and Arachosia, taking with him the invalids and the heavy transport.

The majority of the chieftains welcomed Alexander, but no message came from Musicanus. As so often happened, this Prince was astounded when he learned that Alexander was near his border; much alarmed, he hastened to greet him with gifts. The King accepted his apology, praised his dominion, confirmed him as its Governor, but prudently left a garrison and a fortress. Prince Oxycanus, on the other side of the Indus, had also made no move to gain the favour of the new King. As his capital commanded roads to Gandhara and Iran, it could not be left behind; it surrendered after a three days' siege, during which the Prince lost his life. When the Brahmans—also Arattas people—instigated trouble among neighbouring tribes, their chief town was taken when a subterranean passage had been dug under its wall. Believing that he had seen the last of the Macedonians, Musicanus broke his pledge of fealty. Betrayal of trust Alexander never forgave; turning back, he ordered the execution of Musicanus and the Brahman leaders of the rebellion.

When Moeris, the last independent prince of this region, proffered allegiance, Alexander became master of the whole valley of the Indus; his gigantic plan could now mature. At Pattala he found a deserted town; its inhabitants had fled on hearing of his approach; their experience with previous invaders had left bitter memories. But they returned when prisoners were despatched to the surrounding country to assure them that they would be welcomed as friends in Pattala. Experts in the sinking of wells visited the district and taught the peasants how to irrigate their land and attract new colonists; this advice was deeply appreciated.

Although the campaign in the Indus valley had occupied many more months than had been expected, Alexander refused to hurry over the exploration of both arms of the Indus delta. As the river has moved far from its original bed it is not certain which branch was first examined. It is difficult for us to realise what a heroic adventure it was to navigate these frail vessels on that uncharted stretch of water without native guides to warn the oarsmen of dangerous rocks and currents; after several ships had been damaged, Alexander went ashore to procure Indian pilots.

The spirits of the sailors rose to a high pitch of exaltation when the first fresh wind from the Ocean brushed their faces. Soon the rising tide caused alarm; its waves lifted the ships to the bank where some remained stuck in the mud until released by the outgoing current. But when the rowers had learned the management of their oars the great Ocean was soon reached, and from its broad expanse the sailors looked back on the outline of the coast whence they had come. Sacrifices and thanksgiving were offered to the gods; and after libations had been poured to Poseidon, the Nereids and silver-footed Thetis, the King threw the golden goblet into the sea.

Having travelled unopposed along the bank of the Indus, Peithon arrived at Pattala and reported that new cities were springing up, with colonists settling contentedly in them. The second branch of the delta was found to broaden into a lake containing sea fishes, proof that it communicated with the Ocean. As this arm had no strong tidal current, Alexander decided that here was the site suitable for the harbour whence he proposed to send a naval expedition from the mouth of the Indus to the Persian Gulf.

Now the serious problem of the selection of the Admiral for the Fleet demanded consideration. Alexander could not be spared; he alone could guide the troops over the Gedrosian desert and retain the confidence of the men during what might be a terrible ordeal. As the crews were obliged to land frequently for provisions, the ships must sail close to the shore, where they would find depots with special markings to ensure safe collection. The Admiral must possess exceptional qualities; he must be of equable temper, resourceful in the event of storms or other disasters, experienced in the handling of subordinates, energetic, keen to explore and undaunted by the perils of a probably long voyage. Many names were passed in review, but all, for one reason or another, were discarded. Then Nearchus begged to be permitted to undertake the task: "With the help of God", he said, he would conduct the ships to Persia. Alexander knew that in Nearchus he had the right man, but hesitated to expose his old friend to so dangerous an adventure. But the sailors were delighted when they heard that Nearchus would be in charge; that selection ensured success.

The enterprise was all the more difficult because the ships had been designed by men who had no knowledge of the requirements of an ocean voyage. Nearchus had no instruments; he steered by the sun, the stars and the dim outline of the uncharted coast. Seasonal winds delayed his departure. He weighed anchor on September 21st, but was again delayed by a storm which damaged three ships.

Alexander was the first to set out and soon encountered strong resistance from the Oreitian tribe who surrendered when he over-ran their territory. Accompanied by Ptolemy, Leonnatus, archers, horse-bowmen and the Agema of the Companion cavalry Alexander marched close to the shore so that stores could be deposited for the landing crews. The Oreitians revolted as soon as he had passed, and killed Apollophanes, the newly appointed Viceroy. Thus the regular despatch of provisions to the desert was interrupted, with grievous result. Here should be mentioned a further blow: the caravans arranged to meet the advancing army with consignments from Carmania failed, for some unknown reason, to materialise. Hence during the desert march hunger became a menace, and when the soldiers, desperate, broke into waggons labelled for other destinations, Alexander, sympathising, turned a blind eye to such breaches of discipline. Early in the march the army came to the Taloi range of mountains, an unexpected obstacle which obliged them to march some 200 miles inland.

The Phoenician merchants were delighted to find myrrh, spices and the frankincense so highly valued and in great demand by the Greeks for religious and funeral rites. But all too soon vegetation ceased; only sand stretched as far as eye could reach. How recount the horrors of that terrible desert? First, perhaps, the shifting sand: often men and animals sank knee-keep in the dunes; at other times sudden gusts of wind blew it into clouds which hid the sky and filled eyes, mouth and throat with gritty particles. Without warning, gales would overthrow the tents in which weary men were sleeping. By day the heat was so intense that it became necessary to travel by night, when the cold was so severe that it cut the flesh as if with ice. Hordes of mosquitoes and flies added to the misery of the journey.

The crowning nightmare was the shortage of water; long distances separated the positions where springs and wells were usually mapped along the desert expanse. Once the native guides lost not only their tracks but also their sense of direction, and could not find a trace of a stream. In this perilous stage of the sixty days' march Alexander came to the rescue; with five of the Companion cavalry he set out in the direction which he considered led to the coast; there they dug with their swords until they reached a deep underground source of fresh water. On some nights the troops lay down to rest beside a dried-up river bed showing only a trickle of moisture, and yet, a few hours later, they were awakened by a flood from a cloudburst in the distant hills, which swept away tents and heavy transport, drowning men, women, children and every animal encountered in its path. Sickness followed when thirsty men drank to excess from impure pools. Discipline slackened; distracted by hunger, thirst and fatigue, baggage attendants slew the beasts of burden to provide food. Stragglers unable to keep pace with the main company found at dawn that they had been left behind during the night; unable to make contact with those who had gone forward, they lay down and died, exhausted and unnoticed.

Throughout the long march Alexander proved himself a true captain of his army, sharing all their hardships: hunger, thirst and exhaustion. His horse he had refused to ride, preferring to accompany his troops on foot. From Aristotle he had learned how to administer simple remedies for wounds and common maladies; this knowledge endeared him to his troops and their families when suffering from pain or fever. Once several grateful soldiers collected water in a helmet and carried it to their King; but Alexander poured it on the sand, quietly remarking that all must share alike.

After sixty days in the desert the infantry and cavalry arrived in Carmania in fair condition; the chief sufferers were the non-combatants, stragglers, transport and baggage attendants with their families. Some arrived at the town of the Governor of Gedrosia in a pitiable state—ragged, thin, their horses mere skeletons. Although the route over the Gedrosian desert had been necessary in order to ensure the provisioning of the fleet, this famous march has been criticised as undertaken from the desire to surpass Queen Semiramis, said by legend to have started with 100,000 men and reached Babylon with only twenty.

To return to Nearchus. Fortunately this brave Cretan wrote Memoirs from which historians have obtained a vivid narrative. Soon after the departure of the King, Nearchus found himself in serious trouble. Violent winds detained him in the new Alexandria harbour for some weeks, and when he set sail a storm again forced further delay. Although the rebelling Oreitians tried to prevent the sailors landing to repair their damaged ships, Nearchus gained his object after fighting. On November 21st the fleet reached the coast of the Ichtyopages, where the pitiless desert began. The natives of that desolate region ate dried fish beaten into powder and dwelt in huts built of large fish bones. Another tribe used flints and lived just as men of the Stone Age. But one of their most horrifying adventures was an encounter with a school of whales; these enormous creatures threw great waterspouts, astonishing and menacing to the crews, ignorant of the origin of this strange phenomenon. Nearchus ordered the sailors to blow their trumpets and row noisily, shouting as if on a field of battle; the monsters retreated.

In such adverse circumstances Nearchus drew up reports on the coast outline, bays, inlets and sites promising for harbours. Although many of his records were lost, the botanical, zoological and other scientific observations proved to be of permanent value. As conditions on the voyage deteriorated, the crews were on the point of mutiny when they recognised the vegetation of the Carmanian coast and knew that their sufferings would soon be ended. Nearchus conducted the fleet to Harmozia, on the mouth of the river Anamis, and made enquiries about the position of the army. Marching inland, he caught sight of a man in Macedonian uniform; all wept when they discovered that he was a Greek who had left the King some five days' march ahead. Nearchus was led to the Governor of the district and together they mapped out the route to the camp. Whilst Nearchus returned to moor and protect his ships, the Governor hastened to break the glad news to Alexander.

Days passed; doubting the reliability of the Governor, Alexander placed him in custody. Having ensured the safety of the fleet, Nearchus, with Archais and five officers, set out to find the camp. On the way they met messengers whom Alexander had despatched to seek the fleet, but his emissaries did not recognise Nearchus when they passed strangers, emaciated, unkempt, with ragged clothing, straggling beards and dishevelled hair. Archais suggested that these men might help them to find the Macedonians. Overcome with joy when they learned that the apparent beggars, whom they had scarcely noticed, were the very men for whom they were searching, the soldiers told how Alexander had been tortured with anxiety; his countenance had betrayed his distress when, after a lapse of several days, he had received no confirmation of the Governor's report. With cries of delight the soldiers conducted Nearchus and his officers to the tent of his King.

Fortunately his narrative of his meeting with Alexander was preserved for posterity; it reads like an epic poem. At first Alexander did not recognise the friend of his boyhood. Overcome with emotion he wept, continuing to hold the hand of Nearchus, but unable to utter a word. Believing that the men before him were the sole survivors of the naval expedition, he strove for self-control; when he could regain his voice he expressed his relief to find that Nearchus and Archais were safe. Again words failed; then, hesitatingly, he asked them to tell him how the ships and their crews perished. To which Nearchus answered that the fleet, all except four vessels, were now securely moored at the mouth of the river. Overjoyed, Alexander shed more tears, and swore by the Zeus of the Hellenes and the Libyan Ammon that this good tidings had given him more happiness than the conquest of the whole of Asia.

There followed a time of relaxation, with thanksgivings to the gods for so wondrous a victory over the sea. Then the question arose: who should lead the fleet to Susa? Nearchus implored the King to permit him to complete the task he had begun; understanding and sympathising with this point of view, Alexander consented, but with reluctance, lest his friend should be exposed to further danger. If storms damaged the frail vessels no ports were available for shelter and repairs. Before this second voyage Alexander proposed that Nearchus should recount his victory to the assembled army. With the King, Nearchus, garlanded with flowers, the hero of the day, led a triumphal procession through Carmania, surrounded by a crowd of spectators, singing and dancing, delirious with enthusiasm. Although similar festivities have marked the climax of heroic victories from that distant century to the present day, Alexander's detractors have called that natural form of rejoicing a "Dionysiac orgy" and the "Carmanian revels". But Arrian and other sound historians have dismissed that description as unreliable and incredible.

Alexander travelled through Carmania, which he had not seen for five years. Craterus joined him, bringing troops and transport to replace the desert losses. Reinforcements also came from Aria, Drangiana and Hyrcania, whose Governors had been loyal and efficient during the long absence of their King; from other allies came camels, horses and cattle. The morale of the troops rose higher every day as they passed over this fertile country. But Alexander realised that it was indeed time for his return to supervise his empire. Grievous abuses had taken place; satraps whom he had trusted had oppressed the people, hired mercenaries for their personal disputes, taken bribes, stolen and plundered temple treasures. Prompt and severe punishment was meted out to the evil-doers; trustworthy Macedonians replaced them. Governors who had employed mercenaries were commanded to release every soldier who was not enrolled in the army of the King. Three defaulting satraps were summoned from Media, and after a fair trial were executed. One satrap, accused of neglect to deliver food for a garrison, brought gifts in the hope of propitiating the wrath of the King; his bribes were thrown to his horses. But the people knew that Alexander would not permit oppression by officials; they could appeal to the King direct, certain that their complaints would be investigated and justice carried out.

A generation which has found how psychiatric treatment succeeds with some criminals will disapprove of the execution of many guilty satraps. But such was the custom of that practical age. Had Alexander hesitated to punish the guilty, the structure of his empire would have been jeopardised. More brutal sentences were carried out when Rome was all-powerful, and under the banner of Christianity torture and other cruelties were inflicted on those whom the Church regarded as heretics.

At Pasargadae the tomb of Cyrus the Great was found pillaged: the coffin opened, the corpse thrown out, the golden casing and treasures vanished; the thieves were never traced. Aristobulus was commissioned to restore the monument in its noble park enclosure. On his first visit Alexander had been deeply impressed by the tomb and had ordered the Persian epitaph to be copied below in Greek. It ran thus: "Oh, mortal, I am Cyrus, Founder of the Persian Monarchy and Sovereign of Asia. Grudge me not therefore this monument."

Peucestas was appointed Governor; a wise choice, for he had many Persian friends, spoke their language and preferred their costume in that climate. But the Macedonian soldiers grumbled that their King was too appreciative of a nation whom he had defeated. In connection with the subject of Persian garments Plutarch's remarks are of interest: "Alexander preferred Persian raiment because it was more simple. Eratosthenes recorded that he wore a composite dress adapted from both the Macedonian and the Persian fashion. As a philosopher what he wore was a matter of indifference, but as sovereign of both nations and benevolent King, he strove to acquire the goodwill of the conquered by showing respect for their apparel." He never wore the Persian trousers.

Oriental satraps had betrayed his trust, but could Alexander have dreamed that Harpalus, an old school friend, would be equally guilty? Early in the campaign his reliability had been suspected by some, but the King had dismissed the rumour and given him charge of the treasures at Ecbatana. There Harpalus had lived in luxury and introduced two Athenian courtesans whom the people were obliged to treat as queens. When he heard of the severe methods being taken with wrong-doers, Harpalus fled with most of the treasures. At first Athens refused to admit him, but he gained entrance by bribery. But the authorities, fearing that his presence would be resented by Alexander, ordered him to leave the city and deposit the valuables on the Acropolis for collection by Alexander at some future date. Harpalus departed, but took with him as many precious objects as could be conveyed. Nemesis pursued the thief; at Cyrene he was killed by one of his fellow-robbers.

From the East came the news that Abisares had died; his son was appointed to succeed. The Viceroy Philip had been assassinated; the criminals were punished and he was replaced by Taxiles and a Thracian.

Some months were spent in Susa during spring 324. There Hephaestion joined the King, having travelled by the coast, and Nearchus arrived with the fleet. Important visitors came to attend the celebration of the marriages which Alexander arranged in pursuance of his plan to fuse the nations and form a permanent bond between Macedonia and Persia. As his generals apparently raised no objections to this plan, it cannot have seemed so strange in that century as it does to-day. A noble banquet was prepared in a magnificent tent, and sleeping rooms with costly adorn-ments for the newly wed. Alexander took for his second wife Barsine, the eldest daughter of Darius; to Hephaestion was assigned her younger sister, Drypetis; to Nearchus, Ptolemy, Perdiccas and other generals were given high-born Persian ladies. Seleucus married the orphaned daughter of Spita-menes; it will be remembered that on the death of that baron she was sent to Susa for education in the Greek language and Hellenic culture. At the same time 10,000 of the troops were married to the concubines who had accompanied them through Asia. After the ceremonies Greek actors and singers entertained the guests, and competitive games and athletics were enjoyed for five days.

While in Susa, Calanus, the ascetic who had followed the army all the long road from his Indian home, begged that a pyre might be erected on which he could be burned according to the custom of his country. Suffering, he explained, was endangering the serenity of his soul, and his religious attitude to life was strained by the restrictions of old age. Only after much persuasion did Alexander reluctantly agree to this request. For the sad event the highest military honours were arranged; the cavalry and infantry attended in full-dress uniform; even the horses and the elephants were gorgeously equipped. Calanus, carried on a litter, bade farewell to all the generals, but to Alexander he said: "We shall meet ere long in Babylon." His words were recalled by many when Alexander died in Babylon. Then Calanus climbed the pyre, knelt down and chanted an Indian prayer while the trumpets sounded and the fire was set alight. When the flames had devoured the man whom Alexander had regarded as a friend, and with whom he had held much converse on sacred subjects, he turned to those near him, quietly saying, "That seer has vanquished more powerful enemies than I." To the discerning psychologist this simple remark reveals much of the character of the Great King of Asia.

For some time Alexander had been deliberating the reorganisation of his army. The time had come when it was necessary to enlist Persian recruits into the Macedonian ranks; they would receive strict training and later would be drafted into the existing battle formations. Alert, eager to prove their worth, in their attractive fresh uniforms the young Persians created a favourable impression when reviewed by the King and generals. But the Macedonian veterans, war-weary, looked on with disdain and labelled them the "dancing boys". Alexander, aware of the prevailing discontent and hoping to bring about a healthier atmosphere, offered to pay all the debts of the army. As the men grumbled that the King wished to discover those who had been too lavish in expenditure, he arranged that no names need be known when he settled the large sum. Gifts were bestowed upon those distinguished for special acts of valour. Golden

crowns were given to Peucestas and Leonnatus, who had
saved the life of their King at the Malli fortress; to Hephaestion, the builder of cities; to Nearchus, who had surmounted the perils of the Ocean; and to Onesicritus, the
pilot of the fleet on the Indus.

From Susa, Alexander sailed to the Persian Gulf, then
passed up the Tigris, examining the country on both banks.
The rivers had been rendered unnavigable with weirs and
obstacles arranged by the Persians to hinder the approach of
enemies from the sea. Now such barriers, no longer required,
were cleared away.

On reaching Opis Alexander called a meeting and
addressed his army in a stirring speech. A mind of his
calibre never realises how ignorant men dwell on imagined
grievances, repeating from mouth to mouth small incidents
which assume gigantic proportions. Why, they complained,
had their marriages been celebrated with Persian rites?
Why did the King and Peucestas wear Persian garments?
Why should the army include commanders from Bactria,
Sogdiana, Hyrcania, Parthia and other conquered races?
They would not obey such officers.

Thus it happened that Alexander's speech on the plain
near Opis did not arouse the spirit which he had expected.
First, he explained that he realised how many must long to
return home; for such men safe escort to Macedonia would be
provided, together with gifts and money sufficient to secure
them for life. The disabled, the sick and the infirm would
have a warm welcome at home, where their example would
inspire the young men of Macedonia to come to Persia. As
Asia was now at peace, 10,000 men could be spared. Suddenly
he was interrupted by angry shouts from a group who
incited their neighbours to join in a pandemonium of
protest. The King, they called out, preferred young Persians
and was tired of his old Macedonians; as they were no longer
wanted, they would all go home, and the King had better
go to his father Ammon. As usual, this profane mention of
the god Ammon roused Alexander to furious anger. In any
case such insolent insubordination could not be tolerated,
especially in a foreign country. As the violence and noise

increased, some even drew their swords as if to attack their King. Leaping from the platform Alexander strode into the throng with blazing eyes, took several by the shoulder and pushed them towards his bodyguards. Pointing out thirteen of the ringleaders he ordered them to be branded as mutineers and put to death as traitors.

At once the clamour ceased. All sat silent, awaiting with fear the next words of the King. Standing in the midst of the guards of his person, the hypaspists and officers, with a mien and a voice of thunder he addressed the trembling multitude. How much of the long oration cited by Arrian is authentic one cannot tell. He began by describing how these men had been shepherds, clad in skins, on the rugged hills of Macedonia; Philip had given them clothing and houses to live in, and had disciplined them to become the finest army in the world. Alexander had completed the work begun by his father. To cross the Hellespont he had been obliged to borrow money, and then had led them across the world— Asia Minor, Egypt, Syria, Persia and the Punjab. The victories, the mountain ranges and rivers crossed, the towns and provinces captured, were passed in review. What had he gained for himself except a purple robe and the diadem, a linen fillet round his head, the symbol of royalty? No treasures had he retained for himself; all had been distributed to his army. Most of the soldiers lived more luxuriously than their King, who so often was obliged to remain awake to guard them whilst they slept. He had shared all their sufferings and wounds; the front of his body was covered with scars caused by every type of missile—javelins, darts, arrows, stones. He had paid all their debts and bestowed precious gifts on the brave who had merited them. All who had lost their lives had been buried with the highest honours. Now he offered to send home the disabled and the sick; but they misconstrued his kind intentions. The concluding sentences, Tarn states, are characteristic of a Macedonian. Their direct, brief phrases stunned his audience: "And now, as you all want to go, go, every one of you, and tell those at home that you deserted your King, who had led you across the world, and left him to the care of the strangers whom he had conquered.

No doubt your words will win you the praise of men and the blessing of Heaven. GO!"

Abruptly he left the platform, strode from the hall and made his way to his palace. Without uttering a sound the army had listened to the hammering denunciation in that scornful, passionate peroration. Stricken to the heart, dazed, the men returned to their camp to discuss their future. What could they do, leaderless, helpless, dismissed, so far from home? They were as lost as in a trackless desert; they could never find the road to Macedonia.

Meanwhile, full of wrath, Alexander considered his next step. He had seized the reins and mastered the threatening crisis. Had he temporised for a moment the empire might have broken up. Well did he, like Napoleon, understand the danger of a furious mob, beyond control, at the mercy of ungoverned animal instincts of violence. He might have been attacked, even slain, as had happened to several of his best Viceroys. Just as in the thick of fierce struggle on the battlefield he had always known when and how to intervene, so too he had on this vital occasion checked a rebellion which would have ruined all his plans for the empire. He decided to form a complete Persian army, and sent a message to the troops that they were free to leave whenever they liked; they heard the sentence of dismissal with despair. So the rumours were true! Their King was selecting a Persian army; already the palace was surrounded by Persian sentinels. Then—they were no longer wanted!

In deep depression they hastened to the palace, threw their weapons on the ground and implored the guards to let them see their King. No notice was taken. Urgent requests were sent, begging forgiveness and mercy; they would wait by the doors of the palace day and night until they had seen Alexander. Two unhappy days passed before the doors were thrown apart and Alexander stood, silent, before the dejected company. He could not speak; his eyes filled with tears when he saw their misery. Then Calinus, an elderly officer chosen as spokesman, came forward to apologise for the noisy outburst which had drawn deserved rebuke. But, he added, what had caused their deepest sorrow was the fact that their King had addressed the Persians as his kinsmen, the title which gave them the right to embrace him. Profoundly touched by this humility, Alexander stretched out his arms impulsively, exclaiming with more tears: "But you are all my kinsmen!" and advanced to embrace Calinus. Delirious with relief, the soldiers pressed forward to exchange the kiss of reconciliation; others, crowding near the King, kissed the hem of his garments. Then, singing with joy, they returned to tell their comrades the outcome of the interview. Relieved from anxiety they knew that all would be well now that there was understanding between them and their beloved leader.

Alexander, too, must have been thankful that he had handled wisely a situation which might have had most serious results in the heart of Persia. For after years of continuous warfare many men become demoralised, ready to commit any crime in hot blood.

Soon after the King and his army had been reconciled it was decided that those who desired to return home should be taken to Macedonia by Craterus, the general who had long been the second in command. He was very popular; under his escort the soldiers felt that they would be secure. With his usual meticulous care for detail Alexander arranged that the Oriental wives should be left in Persia lest their presence in Macedonia might lead to dissension in the home. He promised that the children born in Persia would be brought up as Macedonians; the boys would have military training, and when they arrived at an age when they could express their preference, they would be left free to decide whether to remain in Persia or to join their fathers in Macedonia. This offer was received with acclamation.

When the day came for their departure many of the 10,000 veterans wept during the farewell ceremony. Nor could Alexander witness the leave-taking without deep emotion; he thanked the men for their valour and their services during the long years in Asia; never, he said, would he forget the toils and dangers which they had shared together. To all he gave rich gifts and a talent of gold to relieve them of financial anxiety for the rest of their lives. Craterus and

Polyperchon conducted the old soldiers safely on the long road to Macedonia where they were welcomed as heroes.

Antipater was summoned to Persia while for a time his duties in Macedonia were taken over by Craterus. Alexander had become anxious about the growing tension between Olympias and Antipater; although devoted to his mother, he knew too well that her impulsive temper made her unsuitable to intervene in public affairs. Much of her correspondence consisted of complaints against Antipater, who also wrote with increasing bitterness about her continual interference with his authority. Alexander sighed one day as he remarked to Hephaestion that Antipater did not understand that one word from a mother outweighed all his letters. But never did he imply, by word or deed, that he had any fault to find with the manner in which Antipater had acted when Regent of Macedonia; of special value had been his military success over Sparta.

CHAPTER IX

THE LAST YEAR, JUNE 324 TO JUNE 323 B.C.

Alexander orders repatriation of the Exiles and requests the honour of deification—Feast of Reconciliation and prayer of Opis—Festivities at Ecbatana—Death of Hephaestion—Cossaean campaign—Entry into Babylon —Predictions of disaster—Alexander investigates the irrigation system near Babylon—He reviews the new army brought by Peucestas—Illness and death of Alexander

DURING the last year of his life Alexander displayed energy and enthusiasm as in youth. One of his most severe modern critics even goes so far as to say that the King then became more great and more wonderful than ever. Many Governors had grown accustomed to think of him as killed in the mountains of the Punjab, or lost in the grim desert of the Makrene in southern Gedrosia, leaving them free to enjoy leisure at the expense of the populace whom they taxed. And now he had swept down, disturbing them all, full of initiative and resource, determined to arouse all to work hard for the benefit of the community. From far and near came envoys to honour the greatest King of Asia since the time of Cyrus the Great; his name resounded throughout the world.

It is not astonishing to learn from Arrian, who wrote soon after Christ, that he had to study over forty authors who had been attracted to write about the hero whose adventures had surpassed those of any mortal. His career supplied material for romance and exaggeration, for worship and for denunciation, according to the temperament of the writer. And as so many enjoy the belittling of great men, it is not surprising that a contradictory picture of Alexander remained popular for many centuries.

Thus, for example, even recent writers tells us that at this stage of his career Alexander lost mental balance, believing that he was not a man, but a god; they have therefore labelled him a megalomaniac. So strange a misrepresentation demands scrutiny of the evidence, and fortunately we have in Tarn's history of Alexander a complete investigation of the reasons which impelled him to request the honour of deification. He had in view an important political object: for the good of the country it was essential to issue a decree for the repatriation of the Exiles, a large body of unemployed and discontented men, dangerous because their excellent fighting qualities made them sought after as mercenaries by foreign masters. Many Persian satraps had retained such men for their personal use in warfare with their neighbours. On his return from India Alexander had ordered all troops to be disbanded except those under the control of the King; this sensible measure had created a number of idle men, said to be about 20,000. Although some of these, banished by Antipater, had no friendly regard for Macedonia, Alexander was determined that all must return to their homes in Europe.

Before this regulation could come into force a complicated legal problem had to be considered. How many critics were aware of two facts: first, that Greek cities resented interference by any king with their right to manage their own affairs, and secondly, the attitude of the thinkers of that century to the relationship of men and gods? Alexander could not order a city to receive back its exiles while every Greek city clung to its unassailable right to conduct its own policy. A king could interfere with its independence only if he had the title of a god. But with that title Alexander could order the repatriation of the Exiles. The majority of the Greek cities raised no objection to his proposal, but Athens did not favour it because compliance entailed the surrender of the island of Samos, which it had colonised.

At a meeting of the Assembly Demosthenes was overruled when he argued against Alexander's request. Some voted from fear of the power of Alexander, knowing nothing of his veneration for their beautiful city, its culture and all the other virtues which it represented, but aware of the antagonism of the Peripatetic school which had never forgiven nor forgotten the death of Callisthenes.

In that century men of great achievements were revered as above average humanity; for were not some of them descended from the gods, if not in truth gods dwelling in human bodies? The pagan deities received observance of the outward ceremonies of religion, but the intellectual spirits believed that above all the very human and erring gods and goddesses there reigned a supreme God. Alexander never discouraged his unlettered soldiers from their belief that he was a god, but to his associates and intimates he often made amusing and sarcastic remarks about his supposed divine origin; always he spoke of Philip as his father and discouraged those of his suite who indulged in gross flatteries. More than once he is reported to have said that such ideas were dangerous for the soul (p. 219).

Whilst many Orientals despised the body, the Greeks regarded it as sacred; the athletic and beautiful human body was a manifestation of the spirit. In the Orient, however, it had long been the custom to revere a monarch as if he were a divinity. Deification did not in that age convey any suggestion of blasphemy. It was a dignity conferred on the Pharaohs. In later centuries even insignificant and corrupt Roman Emperors claimed divine descent as a means of wielding power over their subjects. Isocrates had told Philip that if he defeated Darius he would "be as a god". The idea had been familiar to Alexander from boyhood, when Aristotle had taught him the duties of a monarch, and later had written a special treatise on the subject for his royal pupil. In his book on Politics Aristotle considers at length how men of surpassing excellence are as "gods among men". Thus it is clear that Alexander's request for deification was not a sign of megalomania nor of loss of mental balance; on the contrary, it was a proof of his political sound sense and his acquaintance with the thoughts of eminent Greek authorities.

The Greeks regarded the Hellenes as the crown of civilisation and therefore the masters of the world; hence Aristotle had advised Alexander to treat conquered foes as slaves; they were barbarians (foreign speakers). In the peaceful life of the Polis Aristotle found the ideal atmosphere for research and teaching; Alexander, King of many nations, lived in a wider sphere, governing millions of men of different races. But both men realised that to rule with wisdom during times of peace was more difficult than to win victories in war. Association with Oriental friends had taught Alexander that although the East would learn much from the West, the East also had much of cultural and spiritual value to contribute to the West.

About the time of the departure of the veterans to Macedonia an important meeting took place at Opis. The significance of this "Feast of Reconciliation" has been the subject of much controversy among historians; to understand its purpose one must know something of the psychology of Alexander. He had long believed that he had a mission; probably it was at Siwah that he had received confirmation of the intuitional force which impelled him along his phenomenal career. Many great military leaders have felt that sense as of a divine authority driving them toward a goal which seemed to contradict all arguments of common sense. Who could have foreseen the success of Joan of Arc, an illiterate peasant girl inspired by "Voices"? And even in this mechanistic age one encounters a mystic in most unexpected places. One eminent soldier and administrator told me that in the solitude of the jungle and the desert he had found that the best thing which this world could offer was the certitude there obtained of direct communion with God.

A vision of the brotherhood of mankind had been with Alexander since he had come under the spell of Egypt with its monuments of past splendour and reverence for the gods. Who can say whether men of genius are not driven by some mysterious and as yet inexplicable force of the spirit when they are impelled to follow a path without apparent reason?

In some cases these dreams of future promise arrive suddenly, irradiating as if by a flash of lightning the monotony óf the daily routine. At Siwah Alexander certainly received a message which sustained him throughout long years of war and suffering and enabled him to surmount obstacles which would have deterred most of the bravest men.

At the Feast of Reconciliation at Opis 9,000 guests assembled: Macedonians, Persians and other prominent men from many nations. Information about the banquet and the holy ceremony has come from the learned scholar Eratosthenes, who had met eye-witnesses of the unique gathering. In the centre of every table stood a large vessel of wine from which each guest would draw his portion when a trumpet sounded the signal for the libation and told those outside the main tent when to take wine from their central cup. On the chief table stood an immense *krater* which, recently found at Susa, has been identified as having belonged to Darius. The sacred ceremony was begun by Greeks and Magi; as these did not worship the same gods, the offering was to a god who transcended all national creeds; this was in accordance with Alexander's religious belief.

It is said, on good authority, that Alexander was the first to declare that God was not only the ruler but also the father of all men. At Opis he prayed that blessings might rest on the representatives of the many races present, that there would be equal partnership between Macedonians and Persians and that concord (*homonoia*) should unite the whole world. He did not agree, he added, with those who counselled him to treat the Greeks as friends, but other nations as barbarians, thus dividing mankind into two groups. He preferred to divide humanity into good men and bad men; for surely all must see that many Greeks were unworthy of respect, while many barbarians were refined and good, and had excellent political institutions.

His speech was not understood by the majority; its ideas were then so novel as to sound revolutionary and impracticable. Ptolemy heard the Prayer, but as he wrote his Memoirs in old age, after his long reign over Egypt, he could not reproduce the enthusiasm which must have animated the assembly who joined in the solemn act of worship and sacred hymn.

Sceptics have suggested that the Prayer for universal concord was only an expression of Alexander's desire that the East should remain quiet while he embarked on a campaign in the West for world dominion. But he had shown no sign of "intoxication by success" when he spoke at Opis; he had deliberately chosen a seat as the equal of his guests when he made the declaration of his mission to become the "Reconciler of the World". This remarkable phrase has received much attention from historians; Tarn's fifteen closely printed pages should be studied by all who wish to understand it.[1]

On his return from the East heavy duties awaited the King. With rare conscientiousness he carried out his self-imposed tasks; in his tent from morn to night he pronounced judgment on innumerable complaints brought by the humblest subjects concerning their sufferings under extortionate officials who oppressed the poor and misappropriated public funds. Deciding that a tour of inspection of his kingdom had become imperative, he began his journey about the end of August, 324 B.C. Sad events, prophesied by augurs, were soon to follow, which were unforeseen and unpredictable by the normal reasoning faculty. As precognition in this scientific age is often regarded as mere superstition, these omens are mentioned without comment in the following pages.

At Ecbatana, the royal summer residence of the Medes, Alexander organised an important festival for the army, friends and guests who hastened from all parts of the empire to congratulate him on his achievements. Competitions, games, banquets, dramatic and musical entertainments took place every day; thanksgiving services and every form of rejoicing occupied the days and nights for a week. But in the midst of these happy celebrations anxiety haunted the King; Hephaestion was ill and was not responding to treatment. When Alexander was presiding over the Stadium

[1] Volume II, Appendix 25.

games a messenger brought news that his friend had taken a sudden turn for the worse; hurrying to the bedside Alexander arrived only to find that Hephaestion had died. Stricken to the heart, he lay by the body of his beloved confidant, overwhelmed with grief, inconsolable; it is said that for three days and nights he refused to eat or drink.

The Anglo-Saxon dislikes such display of mourning, but it was usual in ancient Greece. The Greeks valued the virtue of "the Mean" precisely because they knew the devastating result of deep feeling with loss of self-restraint; but they were not ashamed to admit the existence of overpowering emotion. Achilles could not be comforted when Patroclus was slain. When the Oracle was consulted as to whether Hephaestion could be honoured as a god, the reply was that he should be remembered as a hero. A magnificent memorial was designed for the tomb; its size and the expense entailed were so great that it was never completed. At first the elaborate monument to the memory of Hephaestion appears to indicate a degree of mental instability, but when one considers the magnificence of the gifts exchanged by the King and the Oriental princes, one can understand how Alexander would consider no expenditure too vast in such a connection.

To alleviate his suffering, Alexander turned to work. As the supervision of his empire could no longer be delayed, he resolved to go to Babylon, destined to be his future capital; its situation and its harbour made it a suitable centre for land and sea communications. Toward the end of 324 B.C. he left Ecbatana and on the way decided that it was urgent to deal with the Cossaean tribe who, as brigand nomads, had for many years rendered unsafe the road to Babylon. They were as great a menace as had been the Uxii clan whom the King had trained to peaceful ways of life so many years before. During the winter months the Cossaeans retired to their mountain fastnesses, believing themselves then secure. But we, who have followed Alexander's methods, know how mistaken was their confidence. With Ptolemy, the King chased the robbers from their lairs; in forty days he reduced them to submission, instructed them in the rudiments of agriculture, ordered them to build villages, and persuaded them to give up their precarious means of existence by plundering passers-by. This useful campaign has been misrepresented as a method of consoling his grief over the loss of Hephaestion; critics dismiss it thus: "He was a hunter of men".

After the bracing climate of Ecbatana the atmosphere of Babylon was sultry and fatiguing. On the road, bringing garlands and gifts, envoys came from distant parts of the empire, from Greek cities, Ethiopia, Libya and Italy. Reports of embassies from Rome and from Jerusalem have been proved to be fictitious; Rome was then of little account, and Alexander had never visited the capital of Palestine.

Already the King was pondering over vast projects for the improvement of the empire and exploration of sea and land. Archais was despatched to make a preliminary survey of the coast of Arabia and report concerning possible inlets for harbours, docks, and sites for new cities. Nearchus was summoned to sail up to Babylon and organise a fleet. Boats and ships were built on the coast of Phoenicia, and divided into parts suitable for transporting overland to the Euphrates, where they could be reassembled and made ready to sail to the sea.

Still other designs engaged his mind. Before entering the Punjab Alexander had promised Pharasmanes that he contemplated exploration of the Caspian Sea as soon as he could spare time on his return to Persia. Then he intended to discover whether the Caspian Sea had any communication with the Great Ocean which was believed to encircle the Habitable World. Ships were ordered to be constructed on the shore of the Caspian Sea, to be ready for the day when he could undertake an examination and determine its limits. These plans prove that Alexander was in full possession of his reason, active and swift as ever in framing his objectives and arranging for their success in practice.

In preparation for the maturing of these plans the army formations were modified. Persians had been incorporated into all ranks and held positions of authority; these recruits could be trusted, for all were eager to prove their worth and to win the praise of their King. The troops did not regard this new blood with pleasure; but it was necessary because the Oriental subjects were to be counted in millions; in comparison, the Macedonians were few in number. This reconstruction of the army gave much satisfaction to the Persians; it proved that the fusion of the nations proposed at Opis was not the eloquence of a politician seeking applause, but a reality on which the King had set his heart. When disciplined and trained in the thorough Macedonian methods, the new army would attain a high pitch of excellence and should be able to overcome every obstacle on mountain, river or sea.

But Destiny had other designs for the near future. Predictions of disaster were not lacking. Arrian relates several of the sinister shadows which preceded the arrival of the King in Babylon. As he approached the city he was met by Chaldean seers, who drew him apart from his escort and besought him not to enter Babylon, where they feared that evil might befall him. Alexander answered with a quotation from Euripides to the effect that the best diviner was he who prophesied the good. The augurs then begged him to face the east when he marched into the town. With this request Alexander was willing to comply, but when he found that the road was too marshy for the army transport he was obliged to alter his route and travel in from the east, the forbidden direction. He had little confidence in the warning of the Magi, suspecting that they feared lest, by taking the eastern approach, he would find that they had not obeyed his order to rebuild the temple of E-Sagila. Later, when in Babylon, he set several thousand soldiers to work on the debris. Although some of the necessary clearance occupied his men for months, the task was not completed till long after his death.

A still graver prediction is recorded by Aristobulus. A certain Governor, aware that he deserved rebuke for neglect of duty, asked his brother Pythagoras, an augur, to consult the omens about his future. Pythagoras inquired of whom the Governor stood in awe, and was told that Hephaestion had good reason to reproach him. Pythagoras answered that Hephaestion was already a doomed man.

And within a few days Hephaestion succumbed to his fatal
illness. Later, the Governor admitted that he also feared the
wrath of Alexander; the augur said that he had dark fore-
bodings for the future of the King. Devoted to his King,
the Governor passed on this information. When in Babylon
Alexander asked Pythagoras why he had sent so alarming a
report to his brother; Pythagoras did not conceal what he
had read in the omens, and urged the King to be careful to
avoid danger. Alexander thanked Pythagoras for his frank
response and held him in high esteem for his sincerity.

Few in modern times believe in good or evil predictions,
but in those distant days men of the highest intellectual
attainments had confidence in the augurs. In my native
land the second sight of many Highlanders is regarded as
mysterious and inexplicable, but its veracity is not disputed.
As so many of the warnings of the augurs during the Asiatic
campaign had been correct, it is possible that Alexander
had been impressed by Pythagoras; some writers say that
he began to feel that he was no longer under the special
protection of the gods.

Among the visitors who travelled to Babylon to request
the assistance of the all-powerful King of Asia were people
from Macedonia, Thrace and Illyria who brought complaints about Antipater. Unfortunately, Antipater sent his
eldest son, Cassander, to plead his version of the disagreement; he could not have chosen a worse advocate. Cassander maintained that there was not a vestige of truth in
accusations against his father; Alexander answered that
unless the complainants believed that they had a good cause
they would not have undertaken so long a journey. Cassander
insinuated that the plaintiffs had other motives; their false
allegations provided them with an excuse for interesting
travel. Alexander, irritated, replied that such an explanation
savoured of sophistry; the Sophists could prove anything,
true or false; he had had much experience of their unhealthy
rhetoric and preferred to go direct to the core of a subject.
However, as he respected Antipater, he promised to consider
the point at issue.

The upshot of the problem is not recorded in history, but the result of the discussion lay in the not far distant future. Cassander hated and, no doubt, also envied Alexander; the two men were not in sympathy. In Macedonia, Cassander was of importance; in Persia, he was regarded as of little account and of uncouth manners. Selfish and ambitious, he had no insight into the visions of Alexander; for him the splendour of the Court and its obsequious etiquette were matters for laughter and criticism. After the death of Alexander he had his revenge.

Whilst the fleet was being prepared Alexander examined the Persian Gulf and its islands. The head of the Gulf then lay considerably north of its present site; the earthy deposit carried down by the Euphrates, Tigris and Karum has shifted the original estuary of the rivers. Every hundred years the muddy layer is said to extend three miles further into the Persian Gulf. Alexander devoted time to this investigation, seeking positions suitable for new colonies, harbours and landing places along the Arabian coast. Just as he had discovered a new route between the Indus and Persia, he hoped to trace a path of communication from Babylon to the Mediterranean cities. An immense volume of trade would develop when ships and caravans conveyed goods from Babylon and Arabia to the western pillars of the Mediterranean. The coast of Arabia must be explored; it possessed many of the products in great demand by Greece: frankincense, myrrh and other spices. But the captain of the reconnoitring ship reported that Arabia appeared to be of great extent; owing to the forbidding aspect of the natives, he considered it dangerous to proceed further.

The rich soil south of Babylon depended upon the efficiency of the system of irrigation. When the snow melted on the Armenian mountains in the spring, the Euphrates overflowed; the excess of water was drawn off into canals, of which the most important was the Pallacopas. This broadened into a lake and thence reached a marshy district extending to the Arabian boundary. The Governor of the region had employed 10,000 men for three months; the expense was heavy, the result negligible. Alexander sailed down the river to investigate the condition. In the warm months of the year the water from the depleted river bed did not run into the irrigation canals because the banks, damaged by the floods, did not allow the proper working of the weirs. Alexander decided that it was essential to construct a firm base and for this purpose he dug down to a rock foundation and continued the cutting to join the old canal.

Impressed by the beauty of the country near Pallacopas, Alexander founded a new city in which volunteers soon settled. The position was selected as suitable for commerce and for protection against inroads by Bedouin Arabs.

The funeral rites for Hephaestion becoming due, Alexander arranged to return to Babylon; none of the unhappy predictions having occurred during his first visit, he felt no uneasiness about re-entry into the town. As he piloted his own ship up the river a strong wind blew off the symbol of royalty, the diadem (a linen fillet), which became entangled in the reeds and was rescued by a sailor. The man, fearing to lose it, placed it on his head for safety as he swam back to the ship, and was rewarded with a gift of money. This incident, considered to be of grave import, afforded opportunity for the embroidery of writers who declared that the King ordered the death penalty for the helpful sailor who had dared to wear the royal emblem.

All seemed auspicious when Alexander met Peucestas and Nearchus. Peucestas had brought 20,000 Persian recruits; the phalanx had been modified to include rows of Persians with disciplined Macedonian infantry to maintain control in front and rear. The new battalions passed in review before the King, who sat in splendour, clothed in the royal purple, on a throne of gold, under a canopy of rich tapestry. Representatives of the army, courtiers, ambassadors and important guests had silver seats on a lower platform; the magnificence of this gathering represented the grandeur which the Orientals associate with royalty.

The Macedonian troops were few in number compared with those drawn from many regions. Yet this measure, so necessary for the defence of the empire, has been misrepresented as proof of a desire to gain dominion over the whole world. But the competent Persian recruits collected by Peucestas were only too soon to be in action; after the death of Alexander Perdiccas required the whole Imperial army to subdue Cappadocia and the revolting Greek mercenaries in Iran.

Another curious incident was regarded by the augurs as of evil omen. Feeling fatigued after a military review Alexander bathed in the palace garden, and on his return was startled to find on his throne a stranger wearing the cloak and diadem which had been left on the platform. Forbidden by etiquette to approach the royal tier and dislodge the intruder, the eunuchs left in charge were engaged in noisy argument. To questions put by Alexander, the unknown man, looking dazed, explained that a god had ordered him to ascend the throne. Realising that the invader was insane, Alexander refused to inflict the death penalty advised by the augurs; this was the punishment usual in Persia for any man who dared to occupy the royal seat.

How many days after this event did the banquet in honour of Nearchus take place? If soon after Alexander had complained of fatigue, it is probable that the organism which brought about his fatal malady had already entered his system; the infection may well have originated from the mosquitoes of the marshy plains near Babylon.

THE END, JUNE, 323 B.C.

Then came, without warning, the unexpected tragedy. On three successive evenings the King dined with friends and guests; even after the first gathering it was noticed that he showed symptoms of fatigue. The Diary of Eumenes, his trusted secretary, tells of a steadily mounting temperature and increasing weakness; a pathetic narrative. His suffering was borne with his usual refusal to admit defeat. To a medical reader the diagnosis of Alexander's fatal malady lies between malaria and an amoebic abscess. Both yield to modern drugs; nothing is known of the treatment given to Alexander. During the 1914-1918 war many a strong man afflicted with malaria died within a few days. Strangely enough, even to-day certain writers repeat the story that the death of Alexander was brought about by over-drinking during three late evening banquets.

It was natural that friends of Alexander should wish to see much of him before he sailed to the Arabian coast with Nearchus. For when he set out on a journey who could tell how many years might elapse before they would meet again? He had started off to find Darius, then travelled over Persia, the Punjab and the Gedrosian desert; when all had supposed him lost for ever, he had suddenly reappeared.

At the chief banquet the King recited a scene from Euripides in the presence of Greek actors and other guests. When the company dispersed, an old Thessalian friend, Medius by name, persuaded Alexander to accompany him to his home to meet a few congenial spirits. This happy gathering broke up toward dawn, arranging to resume their talk on the following evening. Alexander bathed and slept soundly, well into the morning. The friends enjoyed their second evening, no doubt interchanging reminiscences of youth and recounting their later adventures. On his return to the palace Alexander felt feverish; this symptom, so disquieting to the medical reader of the Official Diary, is ignored by those who ascribe his illness to late hours and heavy drinking. In his Memoirs, Aristobulus contradicted the rumour that wine had hastened the end; at the last banquet, feeling feverish, the King had tried to allay thirst by drinking more than usual.

Some discrepancy regarding the dates of progress of the malady is due to the fact that certain writers used the Macedonian calendar, but there is no disagreement that the illness lasted about twelve days. Alexander had felt very weary for two days before his friends noticed a lack of his usual energy. He lay quiet all the third day; Medius called to amuse him and they played a game of dice. That night he slept little, and awoke soaked in perspiration, a sure sign that the infection was gaining ground. Yet he sent a message to the infantry to be ready to start in four days, and to the fleet to be prepared to sail in five days. On the following day he was taken in a litter over the river to rest in the royal gardens and revive in that peaceful atmosphere.

But on the next day fever and weakness increased. Lying on his couch he interviewed his generals, then with Nearchus he planned their future voyage. He listened attentively to all that Nearchus told him about the dangers to be encountered along the coast, and said that he would gladly endure these in view of the importance of the exploration of Arabia. After some days in the royal gardens he was carried back to the palace. The fever had not abated; on the contrary, it was steadily rising and his weakness had become so great that it was with difficulty that he could be conveyed to the sacrifices which he had insisted on attending every morning. Now this was no longer possible.

On the seventh day of the illness, shivering and still more exhausted, he gave the order that his generals should assemble in the palace. On the eighth and the ninth days he sent further instructions to postpone the date of the sailing of the fleet. His generals passed by him as he lay on his bed, but though he seemed to recognise them he was too feeble to speak; he could only follow them with his eyes; to some he held out his hand.

For two whole days the town had been alive with rumour and emotion; it was feared that he had died and that the truth was being withheld. At last the army clamoured for admission to the palace; they hammered on the gates and called aloud that they would not leave until they had seen their King. They would not be denied; it was impossible to prevent their entrance; when the doors of the palace were opened many of the people of the town pressed in after the troops. In profound silence they filed through his bed chamber, weeping as they passed his couch. Only by slight movements of his eyes and head could the dying King acknowledge the presence of those faithful and devoted companions of so many years of shared endurance and danger.

On the eleventh day Ptolemy, Seleucus, Peucestas, Peithon and several other generals went to the temple of the God of Healing and spent the night there in prayer and sleep, as was the custom when the verdict of the Oracle was sought in emergency. They prayed that Alexander might be restored to health and inquired whether he should be brought into the temple. In the morning came the response of the Oracle: it would be best for Alexander to remain where he was. This reply was taken to the King; by the evening of that day, June 13th, Alexander died.

He had not reached his thirty-third year; he had reigned twelve years and eight months. In that brief space of time he had changed the whole world and left an indelible mark on its history. Death he had never feared, but he could never have dreamed that the Dark Angel would fetch him except from a field of battle.

Towards the end his generals begged him to name his successor; but none could be certain they had heard aright the whispered reply. "To the most worthy", was one version; "To the strongest", was another; others affirm they heard him murmur that he foresaw much bloodshed would follow his funeral rites. The whole world held its breath in awe that one so mighty should have been carried off so suddenly, at the height of his reputation and his power. Even in Athens there was consternation when the unbelievable news became known; it was as if the world had come to an end. What would the future hold when this godlike personality no longer remained to guide the millions in his empire? Destiny—only the great Greek dramatists could have deciphered the mystery behind the inscrutable darkness.

What thoughts must have passed through the mind of the dying King during that last week of suffering and weakness, surrounded by his friends, grief-stricken, bewildered, and the thousands of lamenting soldiers crying for admission to the palace—"So much to be done—no time—who could carry on his work?—the Habitable Earth—the Ocean which now never would he find." And as the fever and fatigue no longer permitted consecutive thinking?

If indeed the dying pass in swift review the events of a whole lifetime, the King would dwell on memories of his friends—Aristotle, to whom he owed all—Olympias, impetuous, beloved—her letters, one overlooked by Heph-

aestion, perched behind him; to indicate the need for
silence he had pressed his signet ring against the lips of
that dear confidant—Roxane, and their coming child—
Sisygambis, his second mother in Asia—Nearchus, brave
Admiral of the Fleet—who now would sail with him to
Arabia?—their joyous reunion at Carmania—Craterus, his
best general—the loyal team who had followed him for eleven
crowded years—the race to find Darius—Aornos—the Five
Rivers—the ice-crested mountains glistening at dawn and
sunset—Calanuṣ, saying as he mounted the pyre: "We shall
meet in Babylon"—that had come true—Death had been
near at the Malli fortress—and now—the priest at Siwah
had confided what was too sacred to reveal—he had tried
to carry out his mission: to reconcile the world, to teach his
people to be independent and to strive after the Greek ideal,
Excellence. God, the father of all men, who had made the
best peculiarly his own, would understand.

CHAPTER X

DISMEMBERMENT OF THE EMPIRE

Perdiccas and the cavalry generals agree to await the birth of Roxane's child—The infantry prefer an illegitimate son of Philip—Greece repudiates the Corinthian League—Division of the empire—War between the generals—Perdiccas killed, 321 B.C.— Antipater dies, 319 B.C.—His successor, Polyperchon, calls on Olympias as deputy—Death of Eumenes, 316 B.C.—Philip Arrhidaeus and his wife join Cassander and are destroyed by Olympias—Cassander's friends slay Olympias—Cassander removes Roxane and her son—He proclaims that Alexander was not true heir to the throne—Cleopatra is destroyed— Antigonus claims to be Head of the Empire—The generals become kings—Antigonus is killed, 301 B.C. Cassander reigns over Macedonia and Greece

MANY of the books which deal with the life of Alexander the Great dismiss the subject of the break-up of his empire in a short paragraph to the effect that after his death the vast territory was divided between his generals, who fought for predominance for over twenty years, during which time the royal line of Macedonia was exterminated. Many readers have longed for further information about the causes of such tragic happenings. The considerable study entailed is of so much interest that I propose to summarise here the main incidents.

The following chapter shows the other side of the picture: the life-work of Alexander was not wasted; he was the fertilising agent who brought order out of chaos and created a new phase of civilisation which moulded the world, even to this day.

Just before his death Alexander had handed his signet ring to Perdiccas, who soon called a meeting of the generals to discuss the problem of their future relationship. From the first it was evident that no one of these brilliant men could assume the leadership of the great empire. Documents were laid before the meeting which sketched gigantic plans to gain the West as far as Carthage and even Spain. These were unanimously discarded. Tarn and other historians who have studied these hypothetical schemes for world dominion came to the conclusion that they were forgeries dating from a later century; inner evidence, based on the proposed route, supports this verdict.[1] Although Alexander may have from time to time weighed up the pros and the cons of further military advances, he had too much common sense not to have realised that maritime exploration must occupy the next stage in his career, and later, civilian administrative duties would be heavy.

Antipater, left in charge of Macedonia during the long absence of Alexander, had been a staunch upholder of the kingdom, but, severe as a ruler, he had many enemies. On the death of Alexander Greece seized the opportunity to repudiate the League of Corinth which had unified the city-states. They resumed their old quarrels and became separate communities. Athens had always resented the predominance of Macedonia, partly because of the attitude of the Peripatetic school, which had never understood the disappearance of Callisthenes, and also because Demosthenes disapproved of the changes coming about in the world with the advent of monarchic rule. But, so long as Alexander lived, the Athenian authorities had not dared to disregard him; they hated his supremacy; they hoped that the tide might turn and that Athens would be restored to her former high position. No gratitude had ever been shown to Alexander for his gifts from Asia, and his overtures for friendship had been ignored. But his strength had been feared. After

[1] *Journal of Hellenic Studies*, 1939, LIX, 124.

his premature death Demosthenes urged the Greeks to fight against Macedonia; but in the ensuing grievous war Antipater was the victor and Greece came under the power of Macedonia.

At the meeting summoned by Perdiccas all agreed with his suggestion that until the birth of the child of Roxane no irrevocable decision concerning the future could be made. If the infant should be a boy, it was probable that the Macedonian people would choose him as the legal heir to the throne. For the time being, Antipater should remain as Regent. It was the custom in Macedonia that the heir to the throne was elected by the people, and it came to many as a surprise that there was disagreement concerning the choice made by the cavalry and that made by the infantry. The infantry, regarding Roxane as a foreigner, expressed their preference for Arrhidaeus, an illegitimate son of Philip by a Macedonian woman. He was a delicate youth, reported to be epileptic; later he was described as Philip Arrhidaeus. Subsequently, for some time, he was made joint King with Alexander IV, the son of Roxane.

After more or less discussion the empire was apportioned between the chief generals; but the original division did not long endure. Disputes soon arose between the men who had worked so happily together under Alexander. Ptolemy went to Egypt, which he desired to possess; it was easy to defend, as its position protected it against any aggressor. Cappadocia and Paphlagonia were consigned to Eumenes; Thrace to Lysimachus; in Syria the kingdom of Babylon was chosen for Seleucus, who soon made Tigris his capital; to Antigonus was apportioned Lycia, Pamphylia and greater Phrygia; Antipater continued as Regent of Macedonia, and to his son Cassander was given Caria.

This partition of the empire was altered several times after many of the generals had lost their lives while struggling for supremacy. For more than twenty years war became more or less continuous. Alliances were frequently formed and broken off; for a time two or three would stand together, then suspicion, jealousy, economic and trade disputes led to war. Few periods of peace lasted longer than a few months;

the absence of one Governor provided opportunity for another to invade his territory. Ptolemy and Seleucus remained in almost permanent possession of the territory orginally allotted to them, but even they at one time had a quarrel over Syria, which both desired for trade purposes. Ptolemy occupied southern Syria and gained the precious spices from south Arabia.

As the years passed and their countries became impoverished, the people lost all sense of security or permanence. No longer free men, but only mercenaries, the soldiers became demoralised; without interest in the wars between their leaders they fought only from the necessity to earn a meagre livelihood.

Perdiccas, loyal and capable, did not possess the flair for the management of men; he could not maintain the position of authority which his ability and character deserved. Not long after the death of Alexander, Perdiccas required the whole Imperial army to suppress a revolt in Bactria, where some 13,000 Greek mercenaries, who had settled in the new city-foundations, desired to return to their families and homes; they had begun to cause trouble even before Alexander died. Perdiccas also ensured the safety of Cappadocia and adjacent territory which had been neglected during the rush to capture Darius; this had remained a danger to communications with Iran.

Meanwhile Ptolemy, against the will of Perdiccas, had secretly conveyed the body of the King to Egypt. He said that Alexander had expressed a desire to be buried at Ammon; the excuse was plausible, and probably it was wise that the tomb of so great a monarch should be erected in Alexandria, the city which he had founded and for which he had predicted a great future.

During the absence of Antipater in Greece, Perdiccas for some time acted as Regent of Macedonia. He had asked help from Antigonus when sending troops to Cappadocia, but Antigonus, one of Alexander's most trusted generals, paid no attention to his request. On the contrary, he prejudiced Antipater and Craterus against Perdiccas, so that they believed his insinuations that Perdiccas desired to reign over

Macedonia. The story was complicated by the fact that Olympias had suggested to Perdiccas the advisability of marriage with Cleopatra, the sister of Alexander, now a widow. But this was a difficult proposition because Perdiccas had already married a daughter of Antipater. Thus one can realise how the suggestion put forward by Olympias, known to be friendly with Perdiccas, lent colour to the current rumour that Perdiccas was aiming at the throne. Together, therefore, Antigonus, Ptolemy and Antipater formed an alliance and war ensued. Perdiccas invaded Egypt, but after much hard fighting, in which he was unsuccessful, he was killed in 321 B.C. by several of his own men who had given up all hope of final victory.

Antipater continued to act as Regent of Macedonia, the position to which Alexander had appointed him in 334 B.C. He had been a hard ruler, not very popular, but loyal and capable; he had saved the kingdom from Spartan aggression. When he died in 319 B.C., the final partition of the empire remained unsettled.

The ambitious Cassander now comes into the complicated picture of the break-up of the empire. As the son of Antipater, Cassander had expected to follow his father as Regent of Macedonia, but to his chagrin and disappointment, he found that Antipater had selected in his stead Polyperchon, an officer of proven reliability. Knowing the ability of his son and also his ambition, Antipater must have feared that he could not rely upon Cassander to guard the little son of Alexander; future events were to prove that Antipater had been wise when he appointed Polyperchon to follow him as Regent. But the Fates which weave the pattern of human lives could not disperse the clouds gathering densely on the horizon, darkening the future of the family of Alexander.

Determined to become Regent of Macedonia, Cassander approached Antigonus and sought his assistance toward the furthering of his design, the goal of the Regency. No doubt he was a clever persuader; Antigonus responded to his suggestions and thus unwittingly set a torch to a smouldering fire. Polyperchon, obliged to be absent for a time from Macedonia, asked Olympias to act as his deputy. For once

Olympias did not rush in precipitately, but sought the advice of Eumenes, formerly secretary to Philip and then to Alexander. Loyal, wise and unselfish, he had remained a friend on whom Olympias could rely; whilst esteeming her fine qualities he knew her hasty temperament and her son's discouragement of her interference in political matters. He counselled her to be very cautious; indeed it would be best, he advised, if she remained in Epirus and left all details to her generals.

The Macedonian people welcomed the mother of Alexander as a temporary Regent. Olympias began well, with every intention to be discreet, but quiet and reasonable conduct was to her unnatural. Eumenes, in Cappadocia, was too far off to be available for advice and consultation in emergency, and unfortunately had become involved in war with Antigonus, who then was claiming authority over most of the empire. Having learned much from his long association in Asia with Alexander, Eumenes fought with skill, but was taken prisoner after several ingenious escapes from capture. Antigonus hesitated for a time before he could decide how to deal with a captive who not so long before had been his colleague and friend, but, eventually, with apparent reluctance, he ordered the execution of Eumenes. Thus, in 316 B.C., one of the noblest figures among all Alexander's generals passed from the scene of sordid controversy over the partition of the empire. Eumenes had been so consistently loyal that his death was an irreparable loss to Olympias and the remaining members of the royal line.

Cynane, an illegitimate daughter of Philip, arranged a marriage between her daughter Eurydice and Philip Arrhidaeus, hoping thus to secure for her the crown of Macedonia. As Eurydice was a capable young woman, determined to gain the throne, she and her husband joined Cassander against Polyperchon. But when Eurydice tried to force the hand of Olympias her troops deserted her, refusing a struggle which might injure the mother of Alexander. Is it surprising that at last Olympias lost all restraint? By her order Philip Arrhidaeus was murdered, whilst to Eurydice she sent a rope, a weapon and poison, with instructions to choose by which method she would do away with herself. Eurydice was courageous; she said that she hoped Olympias might one day have a similar fate, and hanged herself with her own girdle. She had lost her gamble for the throne.

Guarding carefully the interests of Roxane and her son, during the absence of Cassander Olympias took the opportunity to bring about the death of about a hundred of his friends. Had Eumenes been alive to caution her, this impulsive action, with its disastrous results, would have been avoided. Mob emotion is ever fickle; the slaughter so shocked the populace that they veered round to the side of Cassander, who took prompt revenge by besieging the city in which Olympias was living. The mother of Alexander never lacked courage; the animals died of starvation, but Olympias held out until all the inhabitants of the city were threatened with a similar fate. Summoned to stand a trial, she demanded that she should be permitted to plead her cause before the Macedonian army; but at that time it was far dispersed, fighting in distant countries under former colleagues now at war with one another. Cassander dared not order his troops to execute the mother of Alexander. He had sent some 200 men to slay her, but when she appeared before them, clad in her royal costume, they had stolen away, ashamed. He advised her to take flight in a ship, but she refused, knowing that such action would be construed as an admission of guilt, and that her life would be taken when on the sea. Then some of the followers of Cassander, relatives of the men whom Olympias had slain, relieved him of his task; they destroyed her, it is said, by stoning her to death. Thus one great obstacle to Cassander's ambition had been removed by 316 B.C.

There remained Roxane and her little son. On some pretext, perhaps that they required protection, Cassander placed them in a castle which was in fact the safe custody of a prison. There they lived in obscurity, forgotten, helpless, for several years. When Alexander IV was nearing the age of fourteen the existence of the boy and his mother became a menace to the designs of Cassander. Rumours and questions were heard that it was surely time that the young prince was learning to carry out the duties customary for the heir to a throne. Versions differ as to how Cassander arranged matters; but it is stated that with cold-blooded deliberation the mother and son were poisoned. Nothing is known regarding the personality of this boy, heir to the greatest empire, and son of the greatest king in history.

Cassander was thorough; he issued a proclamation that Alexander had never been the true heir of Philip, because his mother Olympias was not a Macedonian princess; at the time of her marriage with Philip she had been a barbarian. Therefore her son, Alexander, had been only a Pretender, without any legal right to the throne. A new claimant was put forward by Polyperchon, a hypothetical illegitimate son of Alexander by a captive woman after the battle of Issus; his actual age precluded him from being what his sponsors declared. Again the persuasive Cassander succeeded in convincing Polyperchon that he was acting as the pawn of Antigonus. So ably did he put his case that Polyperchon brought about the death of the young lad, and then found that by this action he had placed himself in the power of Cassander, who did not hesitate to take advantage.

But even this did not suffice to satisfy Cassander. He permitted no word to be published which did not disparage the reputation of the great dead; nothing in the Greek language could be read which did not describe him as a drunkard, a megalomaniac and a tyrant. We have seen in modern days how the freedom of the press can be abolished, and how skilful propaganda can influence the young generation which has not known the past; even in ten or twenty years all is forgotten. As all information was inscribed on papyri it is readily understood how the public could be misled. Not till after the death of Cassander in 298 B.C. could the people of Macedonia receive any glimpse of the true nature of the mighty conqueror of Asia. Still more serious consequences to the reputation of Alexander followed: because the Greek tongue was the chief means of communication between men of many nations, the misrepresentations fostered by Cassander were for long believed to be truthful facts.

Cleopatra, Alexander's sister, was now the sole survivor of the family. She had been a widow for some time, and had the choice of several husbands. Leonnatus, whom she preferred on personal grounds, was killed in battle while assisting Antipater in 322 B.C.; Perdiccas fell in 321 B.C.; Eumenes proposed marriage, but Cleopatra wisely convinced him that as such a union might involve civil strife in Macedonia, it must not be considered. Cleopatra had been living in Sardis as a queen, and at one time this aroused the suspicion of Antipater. However, she pled her cause in public before a Macedonian Assembly with such frankness and good sense that she regained his friendship. When she was about fifty years old she realised that she was in the power of Antigonus, and with a desire for safety she proposed marriage with Ptolemy. As it was the custom for a monarch in these times to have more than one wife, Ptolemy agreed that it would be advantageous to marry the sister of Alexander. But this proposal threatened the growing ambition of Antigonus, who in 308 B.C. desired to restore and to be Head of Alexander's empire. Forthwith he arranged for the death of Cleopatra, and to conceal his guilt, her murderers, said to be her waiting women, were executed. Thus, at last, no member of the family of Alexander remained alive to block the path of Cassander to the throne of Macedonia.

It is said that Cassander shuddered when he passed the statue of Alexander at Delphi; did this incident occur before or after the death of his last victim in the royal family?

About 316 B.C. Antigonus had proclaimed himself Lord of Syria; he attacked Babylonia and wrought so much harm to Babylon that Seleucus was forced to flee from the country and hasten to Egypt, where Ptolemy gave him shelter for some time. Antigonus proceeded to take possession of Phoenicia and Palestine on his way to attack Egypt, but as his capable, charming, but evil son Demetrius was defeated by Ptolemy, Seleucus returned to his own country and resumed his popular rule there.

During all the changes in the competition for the various parts of the empire, Lysimachus had remained a close friend of Cassander, whose sister had become his wife. As the possession of power appeared to be a prominent aim of the Diadochi (as the successors of Alexander are called by historians) it was certainly to the material advantage of Lysimachus to attach his fortunes to his brother-in-law, Cassander. The philosophical lessons studied during his time in India were replaced by the disillusioned attitude to life which too often follows the idealism of youth.

In 311 B.C. the Diadochi, exhausted and weary of continual fighting which never brought about any settled agreement, decided to form a truce. Together they framed several conditions for a lasting peace; one of these appointed Cassander as Regent of Macedonia until the young Alexander would be ready to ascend the throne. Antigonus assumed the title of Head of the Empire; the other generals became kings. This agreement did not suit Cassander; nor for that matter did any of the Diadochi look forward to the year when the son of their dead King would become old enough to reign over Macedonia, for that date would spell the end of their position as monarchs. The truce agreement, as all who drafted its clauses must have been uneasily aware, was an indirect suggestion for the removal of the innocent boy before he attained his majority. As already recorded, Cassander lost little time in bringing about the death of Roxane and her young son. One is glad to know that Seleucus was absent in Babylonia at the time of this strangely phrased treaty.

Cassander was also unscrupulous. Although he owed to Antigonus his original advance from obscurity, he had no objection to injuring the old man at this stage of his successful intrigues. He persuaded Ptolemy and Seleucus that a strong coalition could stop the claim of Antigonus to be Head of the Empire. In 301 B.C. a fierce battle ensued and a decisive victory was gained over Antigonus, then verging on eighty years of age. Attacked by Lysimachus, Ptolemy and Seleucus, Antigonus called on his son, delayed on the way to the field of battle; but before the arrival of Demetrius, the old general had fallen, fighting bravely to the end.

In his *Moralia*, Plutarch gives a vivid description of the struggles of the Diadochi; as the book is rare I have quoted from it on page 86. Details of the quarrels, intrigues, coalitions and bewildering changes can be studied in the forty-three pages of the *Cambridge Ancient History*.

I am well aware of the deficiencies of this account of the wars between the Diadochi; no pages have given me more difficulty in extracting the vital from the extraneous events, nor more sorrow to compose. None can read the narrative of the Asiatic and Indian campaigns without admiration. The officers—Craterus, Ptolemy, Nearchus, Coenus, Leonnatus, Peucestas—as one follows them through the years become like living friends. As one reads of the twenty years' internecine warfare one senses the Nemesis described by the Greek dramatists, the undercurrent of terror which lies beneath the apparently smooth surface of everyday existence. The Oracle spoke truly: "it was better for Alexander to remain where he was"; on that bed of death he was spared all knowledge of the destructive future. But were the disasters and the horrors of these Pagan wars more heinous than those of the Middle Ages waged by fanatics under the banner of the Christian religion? Nor can we point a finger of reproach when we consider the atrocities of the post-Victorian "total war" with scientific methods of destruction by land, sea and air.

When one has read much about historical, or even fictitious individuals, one often wonders which of these men and women one would choose to meet if they returned to earth. One forms a definite opinion of their characters; one is attracted by some, repelled by others. Few will agree with my desire to meet Olympias. She was honest and outspoken; she was full of courage; she was probably fascinating in conversation; one can understand why she held the life-long affection of her great son. Impetuous, unable to weigh the pros and cons of her quick decisions and often violent deeds, she was unfitted for government, as her son well knew. But the opinions of Perdiccas and Eumenes, loyal to Alexander, weigh for much, and they remained her friends. She tried to exercise restraint when acting as Regent during the absence of Polyperchon, and she faithfully guarded the interests of Roxane and her son, Alexander IV. Can one blame her because she lost all self-control when Eurydice and Philip, both of questionable birth, ambitious to seize the throne of Alexander, assisted his deadly enemy?

One would like to know more of Cleopatra, the distinguished sister of Alexander. With what pretext did Antigonus bring about the death of such a woman, and how could he hope to conceal his crime by destroying her murderers? With Roxane, surely all must sympathise—far from her native land and relatives, suddenly deprived of the protection of her invincible husband, aware of daily danger, a virtual prisoner surrounded by people who regarded her as a barbarian. Those lonely years in the castle must have depressed the bravest spirit; what memories of past grandeur must have haunted her during the dark months and years as the power of Cassander loomed ahead, a growing menace, death for herself and her son, which might come in any form on any day.

Eumenes and Perdiccas, upright and loyal, attempted all that was possible for the family of their beloved King. Although he could not carry out the dreams of Alexander, Ptolemy was successful as King of Egypt and all historians are grateful to him for his Memoirs, which described not only Alexander's victories, but reclaimed his reputation from the effect of the abusive propaganda which alone could be published during Cassander's life.

Of the popular Craterus, Alexander's second-in-command, we would welcome further records. Apparently at one time Eumenes fought against him, misled by a false report; in the ensuing battle Eumenes was the victor, but on hearing that Craterus had been fatally wounded, he hastened to the side of his old comrade, and though himself seriously injured, held the hand of his dying friend and with tears bewailed the cruel fate which had led them both, by misunderstandings, to unnecessary war.

Cassander interests the analytical psychologist who traces the motives which induce men to commit deeds below their conscious approval. How much did Cassander "know himself"? He had received a good education and is said to have been able to recite most of Homer. In youth his health was so indifferent that Alexander had little use for his services in Asia; his inability to share the sports usual with Macedonian youths placed him apart when athletic games and competitions were held in public. This may have brought about in the boy what is now called an "inferiority complex". A clever sedentary lad tends to brood with jealousy, even hatred, on the feats of gifted relatives who surpass him in physical strength; this reaction is aggravated when they outstrip him also in mental equipment and in personal charm. History records many examples of cruel and unscrupulous methods adopted by those frustrated spirits when in manhood they attain to power. Never could the frank, generous-hearted Alexander have dreamed that one who in early youth had appeared to be a negligible nonentity would become a veritable Iago, able to incite to war the formerly united generals. Still less could he have imagined that this man would bring about the death of all members of the royal family of Macedonia, gain the crown, rule with ability over Macedonia and Greece, and for many years bury under obloquy the memory of the victor of Asia. Not until Cassander died in 298 B.C. could the Memoirs of Ptolemy and of Aristobulus be published. Both men had accompanied Alexander throughout his campaigns; both wrote independently. Only then did the young generation in Macedonia learn the truth about the career and character of their great King.

CHAPTER XI

AFTER-RESULTS

*Extension of Greek culture—Widespread influence of
Greek art—The Foundation cities—Improved conditions throughout Persia—New harbours, towns and
other aids for trade between East and West—Greek
becomes a universal language—Ptolemy in Egypt—
Seleucus in Asia*

APART from the immense increase of international trade
and the fraternisation of many nations, what were the
results, temporary and enduring, of the career of this great
man? Of supreme and lasting importance to the world was
the extension of Greek culture; secondly, a vast territory was
opened up which had been useless as a desert until the
conquered nomad tribes had been trained to follow civilised
ways of life, with the resultant impetus given to the building
of cities, the creation of harbours, ships and other aids for
travel on land and sea; thirdly, financial and economic
reforms; and lastly, the partial realisation of Alexander's
dream of universal toleration for all religions and the
brotherhood of mankind. These results differed in many
regions of the empire; for various reasons the successors of
Alexander had not been able to follow all his visions. Because
their dynasties endured for several generations, the work of
Ptolemy and of Seleucus in their respective kingdoms is
summarised later in this chapter.

Greece and the Greek language were forgotten during the
Dark Ages, but with the Renaissance their natural supremacy
was recognised and became the basis of European culture.
Hellenic culture continues to influence the world to this

day. In Bactria, it left an indelible mark which extended to northern India and parts of the Far East; two large volumes, beautifully illustrated, describe this transformation: *L'Art Gréco-Bouddique du Gandhara*, by A. Foucher. Comparatively recent discoveries by archaeologists show how the technique of Hellenic art was adapted to Indian buildings and statues. Thus, as Foucher says, there was created an intimate union between the genius of antiquity and the soul of the Orient. On the border of India these works of art show an infinite superiority to the native creations in stone. Brief as was the transit of the Macedonian march from the Cophen valley to the delta of the Indus, the refining influence of Greek art can be traced all along Alexander's path from the Hindu-Kush, Peshawar and Taxila to the mouth of the Indus. Even in Turkestan and China, where Alexander never penetrated, the Buddha statues are modified by the gracious style of Greece. In *Aesthetics and History*, Bernard Berenson, the art connoisseur, writes:

> The term Hellenistic covers the art that after the conquests of Alexander captured the entire Mediterranean world and its hinterland. . . . The influence spread much further than even this recognition would imply. Buddhist art, practised in what are now Afghanistan and the Punjab and Java, is fully as Hellenistic as the so-called Christian art prevailing in the West. . . . In Rome the wealthier and more cultivated Romans of the second to the fifth century were so Hellenised that early Christian art was Hellenistic. . . . To this day, twenty-two centuries after his death, we still divide the world between what preceded and what followed Alexander the Great, the individual who more than any other changed the entire aspect of Mediterranean politics, culture and civilisation.

Alexander had started out as a crusader, to avenge the invasion and the destruction of the precious buildings of Greece, but later had as his goal the extension of Hellenic ways of life throughout his empire. In this he succeeded. Greek democratic liberty—freedom to think and to speak, and the duty of the individual to take his share in the government of his city—was instituted wherever he became master.

After the surrender of the robbers and semi-savage tribes of the mountainous regions of Persia, who had for centuries been a persistent menace to life on the plains, Alexander founded new towns and improved communications. The so-called "Foundation cities" were built at the junction of important roads, in positions specially chosen to assist the transit of merchandise and to command the valleys—a precaution necessary for adequate military supervision. The towns were planned on the Greek pattern, with a market square, school, offices, shops, temple, theatre, gymnasium and often a fountain. The young were given instruction in military methods and in Hellenic culture with its ideals of chivalrous courage.

Some records speak of seventy cities having been founded, but only sixteen are certain; those hastily built with mud walls soon crumbled into dust. Six remain to this day: in Egypt, Alexandria; in Aria, Herat; in Arachosia, Ghazni; in Margiane, Merv; on the Oxus, Termez; on the Jaxartes, Chodjend. Seven endured a considerable time: among these—Susiana, Prophthasia, Alexandria-ad-Caucasum and Bucephala. The new cities were placed near enough already existing villages to permit association with the native population, yet so far apart that the Macedonian and Greek settlers could maintain their own custom of life. The new colonists, chiefly Greek mercenaries, old and wounded men, introduced Macedonian methods of farming and agriculture to the mountain tribes. Many married Oriental women; thus began the fusing of the nations according to the plan which had been simmering in Alexander's vision for the future since his winter in Egypt in 332-331 B.C.

The free intercourse opened up from the East relieved some of the economic difficulties which had threatened the West. Disputes between the city-states had led to neglect of the farms; at one time food became so scarce in Greece that its pottery had to be sold to pay for imports of corn. The new cities in Asia provided some solution of the unemployment during the time of financial crisis in Greece.

Alexander had envisaged vast building projects even during his early experience in Egypt. Many great conquerors had visited the coast of that country; how came it about that a youth in his early twenties almost at a first glance grasped the importance of building a town on the site where he founded Alexandria and foresaw that it would develop into a centre for an immense exchange of commerce between Egypt and the western Mediterranean? And later, when he had controlled all the territory as far as Pattala, what far-sighted statesmanship enabled him to search for and to find the sea route which would encourage trade from India to Babylon? And then, just before his death, what filled him with a longing to explore the Arabian shore to seek a safe path which would connect Babylon with Alexandria?

When Destiny cut short his life he had designs for the construction and the completion of buildings for dockyards, harbours, lighthouses; temples to be restored, new cities to be founded; rivers to be opened out for safe navigation; an efficient irrigation system for Babylonia and for other derelict land. Wilcken stated that what had been accomplished were "achievements of colossal dimensions".

Bishop Thirlwall summarised the benefits which resulted from Alexander's expedition in these words:

Let anyone contemplate the contrast between the state of Asia under Alexander and the time when Egypt was either in revolt against Persia, or visited by her irritated conquerors with the punishment of repeated insurrection; when almost every part of the great mountain chain which traverses the length of Asia, from the Mediterranean to the borders of India, was inhabited by fierce, independent, predatory tribes; when the Persian kings themselves were forced to pay tribute before they were allowed to pass from one of their capitals to another. Let anyone endeavour to enter into the feelings with which a Phoenician merchant must have viewed the change that took place on the face of the earth, when the Egyptian Alexandria had begun to receive and pour out an inexhaustible tide of wealth;

when Babylon had become a great port, when a passage was open both by sea and land between the Euphrates and the Indus; when the forests on the shores of the Caspian had begun to resound with the axe and the hammer . . . This part of the benefit which flowed from Alexander's conquest cannot be easily exaggerated.

With the advent of Alexander came new methods of government in civil, military, and financial administration. Just as he was swift to alter and modify his tactics in battle to meet new situations, so also did he adapt new political methods to suit the different regions of his empire. Nor did he ever hesitate to throw aside those which were unsuccessful; failure only stimulated him to consider a more practical solution. The chief positions in government were at first confided to Macedonians, later to Persian satraps; finance and taxation remained in Macedonian hands. In Asia Minor superintendents of finance collected the taxes direct from the peasants and remitted them to the Treasury. In the large towns, such as Susa, Persepolis, Babylon and Memphis, a commandant was appointed, directly responsible to the King. In India the chief princes and rajahs proved to be loyal allies. Persian treasures were converted into useful coinage, and a universal system of currency was introduced, with immediate benefit to trade.

Important and far-reaching consequences followed when Alexander adopted Greek as a universal language throughout the empire. Confusing mistakes had constantly occurred when financial and business transactions were conducted through the medium of interpreters; a uniform currency and tongue simplified commerce and also exchange of ideas. Education in the Greek language extended knowledge of Hellenic culture, so that nations which had followed separate lines of thought, traditions and customs, became members of a common civilisation, citizens of the same world. Just as to-day the French language lends itself to express thought with concise precision, so in antiquity clear thinking was best conveyed in Greek. Greek became the chief agent of the unification of the East and the West.

St. Paul spoke and wrote in Greek; the Gospels were written in Greek so that their message could reach a wide public. It can with truth be said that Alexander paved the way for Christianity; without his spade-work its preachers would have made slower headway in western Europe.

With a common language Oriental knowledge became more accessible to the West. Rapid progress was made possible when Greek and Babylonian scholars collaborated in mathematics, science and astronomy. Babylonia had studied astronomy long before Christ; the distance of the sun and moon from the earth had been calculated with almost exact precision. They knew that the earth turned on its axis, that certain planets revolved round the sun and that the sun was much larger than the earth.

As the city-states in Greece remained at variance, some called on Rome for assistance. The reputation of Athens was so high that Roman visitors regarded it as an honour to be invited to participate in the Olympic Games and to speak at public receptions; some were privileged to witness the Eleusinian Mysteries (p. 271). Rome gradually acquired much of the refinement of Greece; it adopted the alphabet, the art, the literature, even some of the legal methods of Greece.

Alexander's dream of the brotherhood of mankind was not destined to materialise during the short spell of life allotted to him, and without the guidance of his strong personality none of his successors could undertake the task. When one looks back upon a lifetime one can often trace a plan, as of a master designer; behind the scene of the conscious self of the individual a pattern has been woven which during the years of its gradual unfolding could not be seen nor understood. The influence and the example of Alexander lived on, even in the years of warfare between his successors. In their different spheres his generals, who eventually became kings, tried to copy his example, not only in war, but also by encouraging the extension of Hellenic culture and by working for the benefit of their subjects.

PTOLEMY AND EGYPT

Ptolemy had been one of the most capable of the generals throughout the campaign in Asia and India. It is believed that he was connected with the royal family. When Alexander died, Ptolemy knew that no single man could ever replace him and rule over the vast empire which he had created; he had seen that the gigantic task had been wearing out the strength of Alexander, a superman. As he was certain that the empire must be divided, Ptolemy desired that Egypt should fall to his share. It was a fertile country, difficult to attack, having the natural defence of surrounding deserts. During his long reign Ptolemy led Egypt to prosperity before he handed over its management to his son, Ptolemy II. Then only was he free to compose his Memoirs, which could not be published during Cassander's lifetime. In future years these Memoirs, compiled from the Daily Journal to which he had access, provided the main source of accurate information on the campaign in Asia and reinstated the reputation of the King whom he had followed with devotion during eleven strenuous years.

Although Ptolemy conferred many benefits on Egypt, certain aspects not in accord with Alexander's aims should be mentioned. The Treasury became enriched, the soil more fertile, but the people were impoverished and did not possess the freedom and initiative of the democratic Greek cities. All the land was owned by Ptolemy and was farmed for his use, as had been the custom in Egypt for centuries. The fellahin could not leave their villages without special permit; they were obliged to cultivate their territory or farm; they could not cut a tree without official licence and were continually inspected. As a definite amount of their produce had to be given to the King, the loss fell on the peasant when there was a bad harvest. Wheat and oil, the main products of Egypt, were a virtual monopoly of the King. There was no escape from heavy taxation; an immense army of inspectors and officials had thorough registration notes of every individual, his income and possessions.

Ptolemy built only one city, Ptolemais, in Upper Egypt. He encouraged Greek and Macedonian settlers; especially did Greeks flock to Egypt where they could acquire wealth. Housing was speeded up, for not only did the military seek quarters in the land of the Nile, but so also did artisans, lawyers, doctors, merchants and students of art. The Greeks tended to keep to themselves and did not mix much with the Egyptians; they had their own clubs, Hellenic games and competitions, but except in outlying villages these did not influence the native population. Recently discovered papyri describing the daily life of distant small communities prove that Greek gymnasia were widely distributed, not only in towns, but in comparatively limited groups throughout Egypt. Apart from the moral element which characterised Greek games (p. 251), competitions introduce a friendly atmosphere. In France, in 1918, I saw how one British soldier enlivened a French military hospital by inciting rivalry between the wards with the solitary football which he carried about with him. It is now known also that Greek and Macedonian colonists acquainted the native population with the best examples of Hellenic literature: Pindar, Homer and Menander.

Ptolemy developed the Alexandrian museum which made the town a famous educational centre. It resembled a modern university inasmuch as it had Professors who lectured and taught every branch of learning: natural science, physics, astronomy, mathematics and literature. Among its eminent instructors were Euclid and Archimedes, of immortal distinction. For a time the famous scholar Eratosthenes presided as head of the unique Alexandrian library; so high was his reputation that students flocked to Alexandria from all parts of the world. Following the example of Alexander, Ptolemy sent a stream of reports and specimens to Aristotle. He encouraged the study of the arts but failed to induce writers, musicians, artists and philosophers to settle in so busy a town as Alexandria. Theocritus, the poet, born in Sicily, came to Egypt and there he wrote pastoral idylls of such high quality that they are believed to have inspired Virgil, Shelley and Milton. The philosophers, however, found the peace and the calm of Athens more congenial. In that distant century, just as to-day, students preferred the quiet atmosphere of old universities, cloistral in comparison with the activity of the towns in which industry thrives. Sooner or later the philosophers wended their way back to Greece and the satisfying beauty of Athens.

Contrast that peace with the whirling activities of Alexandria when the huge volume of trade opened up between the East and the West. Produce from Ethiopia, Africa and Arabia came through Egypt and was carried by vessels from the Alexandrian harbour to the towns of the Mediterranean coast and the islands of the Aegean Sea. As Alexander had foreseen, the Phoenician ships were displaced by those from Alexandria. Merchandise from the Indus travelled by the sea route discovered by Nearchus and exchanged goods with the towns on the Tigris created by Seleucus and his son. Ships made the circuit of the southern coast of Arabia, whence camels and caravans conveyed their cargo by the Red Sea and the Nile to Alexandria. Egypt imported the spices so much sought after by the rapidly growing population of Asia, Greece and other Mediterranean countries. Egypt also imported wines, wool, marble and horses, and exported woollen textiles, wheat, linen, luxury creams and perfumes. In time came changes: new industries, new towns, and a diminishing output from the silver mines once so productive of wealth for Greece and Macedonia.

Ptolemy introduced Greek banking methods which aided international trade; in this connection Alexander's silver coinage proved invaluable. Even in that century many modern financial transactions were employed, such as interest on money loans, and drafts on banks for payment of bills; those methods for simplifying finance and trade were lost in Europe during the Dark Ages. Volumes have been written concerning the economic developments during the Hellenistic age.

Ptolemy did not interfere with the religious beliefs and customs of the Egyptians; as in India, these had become too deeply intertwined with the lives and traditions of the nation. He introduced the worship of Serapis as a link between the Egyptian and the Greek deities. Many temples were erected, some say forty-two; of these the most important was the Serapium in Alexandria, where the god was represented by a noble statue, coloured blue, with jewelled eyes and an expression of great majesty and also mystery. The worship of Serapis reached as far as Rome and endured until the final extinction of Paganism in 325 A.D. There is an extensive literature on this subject.

Although the poor did not benefit, the Ptolemy Kings were preferred to all previous conquerors because three generations of their line resided in Egypt. Their predecessors had been only passing visitors; tax collectors and other officials had not been slow to take advantage of the people when the supreme ruler lived in far distant countries.

SELEUCUS

In Syria Seleucus tried to follow the example of Alexander and in this he was the most successful of all the generals. Owing to the twenty years of war among the successors, Seleucus could not in the early years of his reign devote time to develop his high purposes. He restored the ancient culture of Babylonia, although at one time Antigonus had almost ruined the town of Babylon and the population had fled to the adjoining country. He fulfilled the promise of Alexander to rebuild the temple of E-Sagila; the work was completed by his son, Antiochus I. When Babylon once more became powerful and prosperous the great temple was again laid in ruins by the Parthian conquerors. To-day neither town nor temple can be traced; excavators seek for their remains beneath mounds of sand and earth.

On the Tigris Seleucus made Seleucia his capital; there it was conveniently situated for the ever-increasing volume of trade between East and West which followed the sea route first navigated by Nearchus. When inland communication was interrupted, the ocean became, as Alexander had foreseen, the chief path from the Indus to the Persian Gulf. The country around Seleucia was fertile, owing to the alluvial deposit from two great rivers, the Euphrates and the Tigris, and the good system of irrigation. Seleucus founded many cities on the Greek pattern, and his example was continued by his son and grandson. When settlers from

Macedonia and Greece came to the new cities, Hellenism in Asia extended to northern Syria, Mesopotamia, eastern Persia and Asia Minor.

By the intermarriage of Europeans and Orientals the age-long distinction of Greek and "barbarian" was broken down. Seleucus was the only general who retained the Oriental wife chosen for him by Alexander at the wedding feast in Susa; as a daughter of Spitamenes, the Sogdian chief, she had been educated with the family of Darius and given a sound knowledge of the Greek language and culture. With such an advantage she would be a true companion to her husband. Her son, Antiochus I, carried on the extension of Hellenism throughout his empire.

Seleucus had none of the monopolies which were the King's privilege in Egypt; as he had a legal right to only one-tenth of the harvest, in a bad year losses did not, as under Ptolemy, fall upon the peasant alone. In Asia Seleucus could not centralise the government as was possible in the compact land of Egypt, which had one people and natural defensive borders. Persia had many races, traditions and religious beliefs; in its mountain regions there was ever-recurring danger; the valleys and gorges invited the unruly spirits of every new generation to return to their primitive habits as roving nomads and bandits. The complications in Asia which Alexander had experienced in administration are thus summarised by Tarn: "In Egypt Alexander was an autocrat and a god. In Asia, he was an autocrat and not a god. In old Greece he was a god, and not an autocrat. In Macedonia he was neither autocrat nor god, but a quasi-constitutional King over whom his people enjoyed certain customary rights. The Phoenician Kings were subject allies; the Cyprian Kings were free allies, who coined gold, the token of independence. To the Iranian landowners he was feudal superior." Although his empire was less extensive than that of Alexander, Seleucus was faced with similar difficulties; the civilian government of the separate cities was so complicated that books have been written on that subject alone.

During the wars of the successors Seleucus could not

attend to the troubles brewing in the Punjab when Chandragupta rose to power and drove out the Macedonian garrisons.
This great Indian King had met Alexander and learned from
him the advantage of a well-trained army. But he had no use
for Hellenic culture; it could not be combined with his aims
for northern India. He overran the whole country from the
Bay of Bengal to the Arabian Sea; his Mauryan empire was
all-powerful from 321-296 B.C. When at length Seleucus
turned his attention to the Punjab it was too late to do other
than come to friendly terms with Chandragupta. He ceded
to the Indian sovereign the land of the Gandhara, from the
Cophen to the Indus; its inhabitants, the "kingless peoples",
had always fiercely resisted Alexander. Some years later
Chandragupta sent 500 elephants to Seleucus to aid him in
the coalition against Antigonus when claiming to be Head
of Alexander's empire.

Chandragupta's efficient but harsh methods of rule had
led to recurring revolts. Taxiles was deposed because of his
sympathy with Hellenism and preference for Persian and
Greek culture. A great change came about when Asoka,
the grandson of Chandragupta, becoming converted to
Buddhism, decided to forego the use of force and to unite
his peoples in bonds of love and friendship; the success of
his missionary zeal is evidenced in the still existing remains
of Buddhist temples, statues and monasteries in Gandhara
and Kashmir.

Some have said that the effect of Alexander's invasion of
the Punjab vanished within seven years of his death. The
two cities on the Indus soon disappeared; but the influence
of Alexander's transit was enduring. With clear insight he
had realised from association with Indian princes, rajahs
and ascetics that Hellenic culture could have no permanent
place in a country of disconnected states, some highly
civilised, some comparatively primitive; they could not have
been run into the mould of his complex empire. The recent
excavations of Sir John Marshall prove that Hellenism left
many traces; in Taxila, objects of Greek art were found which
dated up to the fifth century A.D.

As the centuries passed, the European settlers became

influenced by the Oriental mode of life. For a time Hellenism revived when Demetrius of Bactria, half Macedonian, half Greek, tried in 187 B.C. to reclaim the Indian empire of Alexander. He acquired more territory than Alexander, but he had not to meet the strong opposition overcome by his model. A gradual modification of the characters of the races was in part due to the climate of India, Persia and Egypt. By the second century, said Livy, the Macedonians who dwelt in Alexandria, Seleucia and Babylonia had grown to be Egyptians, Syrians and Parthians.

Seleucus, like Alexander, permitted freedom to practise any form of religion. In that sphere of thought the Greeks had always shown tolerance because they considered that the deities of Nature were the same all the world over, however their names might vary. But the Orientals could not reconcile Greek gods and goddesses with their own religious beliefs. Gradually the Pagan religion became blended with that of the East; in some regions Greek statues shed the refinement, restraint and dignity of Greece and developed into coarse representations of fertility; but in other parts of India the Pagan deities acquired a spirituality foreign to their Greek counterparts. In Bactria and in India some of the coarser Eastern statues took on the delicate charm of the Hellenic deities.

The town of Pergamum rose to prominence and exerted a strong Hellenising influence, preserving the pattern of the Greek city-state, with an Assembly, or Council, and annually elected officers. The chief ruler never interfered with the deliberations of the city, but remained in the background as a friend, ready to give advice when requested. As the Greek language came into general use, Hellenic culture and education brought about a civilising influence. Much of the New Testament bears evidence of contact with Greek thought. As Greek philosophy and science were studied and translated by the Arabs, the teaching of Aristotle had a predominating influence for many centuries throughout the whole of Europe.

In the course of time Rome, unable to prevent recurrence of civil war in Greece and Macedonia, conquered both countries, gathered much from their culture, adopted many of the Greek deities and studied her philosophers. But the expansion of Rome belongs to another story. Within 140 years of the day when Philip had been elected Head of the League of Corinth the Macedonians had forgotten all the lessons of warfare introduced by him and his son, and were forbidden by their Roman conquerors to venture beyond their own borders. Their soldiers had become demoralised, fighting only as mercenaries for any master, Greek or foreign, and practising brutal cruelties such as in former days had been perpetrated only by Oriental warriors.

Yet, by a strange turn of the wheel of Fortune, Hannibal, who was acquainted with the Greek language, studied the methods of war introduced by Alexander, and thus it happened that he taught the military art to the Romans. And long centuries later, Napoleon also devoted much time to analysing the uninterrupted successes of Alexander, and acknowledged the debt which he owed to his great predecessor.

When Cassander died in 298 B.C. the propaganda of disparagement of Alexander, ordered by the man who had exterminated his family and secured his throne, was at last arrested. The new generation, who had heard nothing other than evil concerning the character and achievements of Alexander, were at length able to learn the truth about the greatest of their countrymen. Several great Romans showed a lively interest in the astonishing career of the conqueror of Asia; Julius Caesar, the Emperors Trajan and Augustus longed to emulate his exploits. Caesar was assassinated. Trajan looked at the sea and concluded that he was not young enough to embark on such a journey to the Far East, but he visited Babylon and paid tribute to the genius of Alexander by sacrificing to his memory in the chamber of the palace where he had died. Augustus was the first to bestow upon Alexander the title of "The Great"; he placed the effigy of the Macedonian upon his signet ring and made the decision to try to copy his example in the government of his immense empire. He succeeded in founding a form of policy which ensured a peace which lasted for two centuries.

The latest edition of the *Encyclopaedia Britannica* has a remarkable tribute:

> Alexander's career is one of the turning points in history. He created for the Western world the monarchical ideal. . . . No ruler had succeeded in making the person of the monarch respectable. Alexander made it sacred. . . He founded cities destined to become centres of Greek influence, the great majority in lands in which city life was almost unknown. . . . For many centuries after Alexander's death Greek was the language of literature and religion, of commerce and of administration throughout the Nearer East. His Empire perished at his death, but its central idea survived—that of the municipal freedom of the Greek Polis within the framework of an imperial system. In the East, Hellenism came in the train of the conqueror, and Rome was content to build on the foundation laid by Alexander.

CHAPTER XII

VERDICTS OF HISTORIANS

Cassander forbids all publications which praise Alexander—Quotations from historians, both favourable and unfavourable: Cleitarchus; Polybius; Plutarch—Rooke's translation of Arrian's Anabasis—Quintus Curtius—Aristobulus and Ptolemy—Droysen—Bishop Thirlwall—Ide Wheeler—George Grote—Freeman—Georges Radet—Professor Wright—Lieutenant-Colonel Dodge—Iliff Robson—Ulrich Wilcken—A. Burn—Sir William Tarn—Legend and romance

THIS chapter contains excerpts from both ancient and modern admirers and detractors of Alexander. During the lifetime of Cassander, nothing in favour of Alexander could be published in Greece. As Greek was the universal language of the empire this restriction of literature led to the defamation of his memory; his name became associated with scurrilous tales, magnified by repetition, of drunkenness, tyranny, despotism, cruelty and megalomania. After the death of Cassander in 298 B.C., friends of Alexander took the opportunity to write their reminiscences of his Asiatic campaign. Aristobulus, the Greek architect who had travelled with Alexander throughout Asia and the Punjab, published his Memoirs, probably—Tarn states—between 294 and 288 B.C. About the same time Ptolemy I produced his Memoirs, drawn from the Day Journal, in which had been noted a chronicle of the campaign. As Aristobulus lived in Macedonia, Ptolemy in Egypt, they wrote independently, each unaware of the other's work; distressed by the current false rumours, both men desired to give the public true information concerning the work and character of their King.

The army had two circles, the military and the civil; these had different spheres of interest and were equally over-occupied with their respective duties. Many of the civilian experts who came into personal contact with the King would know him more intimately, being on a different footing from the officers subordinate to his command. It is known that Alexander talked more freely to Aristobulus about his objectives than he did to many of his military suite. After his intricate analysis of the sources from which the numerous histories of Alexander had been compiled, Tarn concluded that the most trustworthy evidence came from Aristobulus and Ptolemy.

In the literature of the second century B.C. the name of Alexander is rarely mentioned; forgotten, he remained unknown to the young generation. Because he was believed to have been a contemporary of Alexander, Cleitarchus' account was long regarded as authoritative. His sensational descriptions were enjoyed by a wide public, but writers of such different quality as Curtius, Strabo and Cicero dismissed him as dishonest. After examining the sources from which Cleitarchus had drawn his information, Tarn decided that he was unreliable, and that he wrote later than Aristobulus and Ptolemy—probably between 280 and 260 B.C. Only fragments of Cleitarchus now exist; unfortunately his writings did much to injure Alexander's reputation.

The Greek communities, no longer united, became a ready prey for Rome; the feats of Alexander remained unknown to a public living in fear of Rome. Soon, however, there arose a desire for knowledge of Alexander's campaigns; the archives were searched to disentangle facts from fiction. Eratosthenes, the Cyrene (born 276 B.C.) recognised as an authority on astronomy, geography and history, had first-hand reports from guests present at the Feast of Opis, who had heard Alexander's prayer for the brotherhood of all men. Although most of the writings of Eratosthenes are lost, later writers quoted many extracts from his work. Arrian, who wrote on Alexander after the time of Christ, compiled a list of books which he consulted; the names which he collected fill twenty closely printed pages, striking proof of the interest the subject had created. He considered Aristobulus and Ptolemy the most reliable of all the authors whom he studied.

Polybius, a Greek historian who lived from about 204 to 122 B.C., had experience of war and of travel; his testimony concerning Alexander is therefore of considerable importance. He criticised the errors in Callisthenes' history of Alexander and stated that "Alexander was a man by universal consent of a superhuman elevation of Spirit". After noting how the work of Philip and his son had raised Macedonia from an insignificant monarchy to the first rank of nations, he added: "Under the rule of Alexander it secured a reputation for valour which posterity universally acknowledged. For although a large share of the credit must be given to Alexander, as the presiding genius of the whole, though so young a man, yet no less is due to his coadjutors and friends who . . . endured numerous labours, dangers and sufferings; and though put into possession of the most ample wealth, and abundant means of gratifying all their desires, never lost their bodily vigour . . . or contracted tastes for violence or debauchery. On the contrary, all those who were acquainted with Philip and afterwards with Alexander, became truly royal in greatness of soul, temperance of life and courage." In another volume Polybius states: "The genius of Alexander surpassed any human measure. His actions and the vigorous logic of his plans are witness to the uncommon power of his will and the superiority of his intellect. To judge his work one must not only look at what he accomplished; he was at the head of the culture and the knowledge of his age."

Plutarch's *Lives* have endeared him to students for many centuries. Yet little is known about him beyond the fact that he was born about 50 B.C. In his popular *Lives* he has a chapter on Alexander; but candidly admits that he was more concerned with his character than the events of his life. J. E. Powell has analysed the sources from which Plutarch obtained his material and expressed his opinion that Plutarch had made an imperfect and carelessly collected epitome from twenty-four writers and from the so-called "Letters" of Alexander. These letters have since been proved to be spurious; they were not even mentioned before the time of Cicero.[1] Plutarch had been delighted to have found what he regarded as trustworthy new material; it is now known that he was mistaken.

Plutarch's life of Alexander begins by praising his attractive and fine qualities, and then, towards the middle of his essay, introduces many superstitions and fables which prejudice the average modern reader. Moreover, it would appear that when he revised his article in later life he had become influenced by those who considered that Alexander deteriorated soon after his entry into Persia; in consequence, some of the incidents recorded are those which were invented by what is known as the "hostile tradition".

But Plutarch wrote other works: in the *Moralia* he has two long essays in which his portrait of Alexander forms a striking contrast to that given in the *Lives*. Even allowing for the fact that these articles are what the Greeks called Rhetoric, presenting all the facts for one side of a case just as a barrister does for the defence of his client, the estimate remains as a veritable paean of praise. I am informed by an eminent Greek scholar that the *Moralia* are genuine. As the *Moralia* are little known, and not now to be procured, no apology is made for quoting liberally from their enthusiastic and beautifully written pages. Much of these essays is believed to come from Eratosthenes who repeated what he had heard from eye-witnesses whom he met after Alexander's death. Strabo also often quoted Eratosthenes as his authority when he referred to Alexander in his volumes of geography.

In the first essay, Plutarch made a strong protest against critics who ascribed to "Fortune" the achievements of Alexander in Asia: "Who was ever better fitted than he for splendid enterprises, with all the choicest and most excelling precepts of magnanimity, consideration, wisdom and virtu-

---

[1] *Journal of Hellenic Studies*, 1939, LIX, 229, Powell. See also Tarn, Vol. II, pp. 196, 301.

ous fortitude, with which a philosophical education largely supplied him for his expedition? . . . We may properly affirm that he invaded Persia with greater assistance from Aristotle than from his father Philip."

Plutarch compares the results achieved by philosophers with those obtained by Alexander. Who, he asks, follows the instruction of the thinkers? But Alexander changed the whole world.

He taught the convenience of wedlock, introduced husbandry amongst the Arachosians, persuaded the Sogdians to preserve and cherish, not to kill, their aged parents; the Persians to reverence and honour, not to marry, their mothers. . . . No sooner had Alexander subdued Asia than Homer became an author in high esteem, and the Persian, Susian, and Gedrosian youth sang the tragedies of Euripides and Sophocles. . . . Plato described an Ideal Commonwealth, but never persuaded any people to make use of it. Alexander, building above seventy cities among the barbarous nations . . . weaned them from their wild and former savage mode of living. Believing himself sent from Heaven as the moderator and arbiter of all nations he laboured thus that he might bring all regions, far and near, under the same dominion.

It was not his design to ransack Asia, like a robber, nor to despoil and ruin it . . . as afterwards Hannibal pillaged Italy . . . but to subdue all . . . under one form of government and to make one nation of all mankind. But if the deity that sent down Alexander's soul into this world of ours had not recalled him quickly, one law would govern all mankind, and they would look toward one rule of justice as though toward a common source of light. But as it is, that part of the world which has not looked upon Alexander has remained without sunshine. . . . Therefore, in the first place, the very plan and design of Alexander's expedition commends the man as a philosopher, in his purpose not to win himself luxury and extravagant living, but to win for all men concord and peace and community of interests.

Again, in the same essay we read:

> Do Alexander's actions reveal the caprice of Fortune,
> the violence of war, the might of conquest, or do they
> rather reveal the great courage and justice, the great
> restraint and mildness together with the decorous be-
> haviour and intelligence, of one who did all things with
> sober and sane judgment? For, by Heaven, it is impossible
> for me to distinguish his several actions and say that this
> betokens his courage, this his humanity, this his self-
> control, but everything he did seems the combined pro-
> duct of all the virtues. . . . Who was ever more hostile to
> wrongdoers or kinder to the unfortunate? Who more stern
> to his opponents or more indulgent to petitioners? . . .
> He believed that he came as a heaven-sent Harmon-
> izer and as a Reconciler for the whole world; those whom
> he could not persuade to unite with him, he conquered
> by force of arms; and he brought together, into one
> body, all men everywhere, uniting and mixing in one
> great loving-cup, as it were, men's lives, their characters,
> their marriages, their very habit of life. He bade them all
> consider as their fatherland, the whole inhabited earth,
> as their stronghold and protection his camp, as akin to
> him all good men, and as foreigners, only the wicked.
> They should not distinguish between Grecian and
> foreigner by Grecian cloak and targe, or scimitar and
> jacket; but the distinguishing mark of the Grecian should
> be seen in virtue, and that of the foreigner in iniquity;
> clothing and food, marriage and manner of life they
> should regard as common to all, being blended into one by
> ties of blood and children.

In another essay of the *Moralia* volumes we find a vivid
description of the twenty years of war between the successors:

> Immediately after Alexander's decease, his forces, as
> they wandered here and there and fell foul of their own
> efforts, were like the Cyclops after his blinding, groping

about everywhere with his hands, which were directed at no certain goal; even thus did that vast throng roam about with no safe footing, blundering through want of a leader. Or rather, in the manner of dead bodies, after the soul departs, when they are no longer held together by natural forces, but undergo dispersion and dissolution, and finally are dissipated and disappear altogether, even so did Alexander's forces, having lost him, maintain a gasping, agitated, fevered existence. . . .

There are several translations of Arrian's *Alexander Anabasis*; one of the most readable is that of J. Rooke (1859). In his preface Rooke begins by confessing that if there had ever been a tolerable history of Alexander in the English tongue, he would not have attempted to translate Arrian; but, he continues, "As most of the Histories of him . . . are full of Errors, Inconsistencies, Incredibilities, and Romance, I thought it might be no unacceptable Piece of Service, to present the Publick with the truest, justest and most accurate Account thereof now extant. . . . Of almost an Hundred and fifty Authors who have handled this Subject, scarce Half a Score have come down to our Times. . . ." Discussing the reliability of the few writers who received wide attention—Cleitarchus, Diodorus, Strabo, Plutarch, Arrian, Curtius, Justin and Crosius—Rooke sums up their qualities: "Diodorus took much upon Trust, without ever examining into the Truth or credibility of the Facts which he related: he swallowed everything . . . and Curtius copies from the same Authors . . . Justin will stand condemned as an injudicious Author . . . Arrian was a Man of a sound Judgment; he took care to chuse only what was most probable, and left the rest as Husks and Chaff." After discussing the other authors Rooke concludes that only Arrian and Curtius need be considered. He points out that even Plutarch, in the *Lives*, admits that he tries rather to "declare the Springs or Causes of Actions, than the Actions themselves. Besides, with regard to Prodigies, Omens, etc. he was extremely credulous, and even his accounts of facts are not always carefully given."

As regards Curtius, Rooke's verdict is: "I think it is a pity that a Brand of Infamy cannot be stamped upon every Author who dares to impose Romance upon us under the specious Title of 'History'." Many commentators, he says, have praised Curtius.

Blinded by the Glare of his Oratory . . . His Periods are generally rounded and well turned, his Cadences sweet and harmonious, his Language pure and elegant. . . . But among so many shining Qualities (fitter for a Declaimer than a Historian) he has many blemishes; for he often runs counter to true History and his Geography is frequently false. One half of his Work is made up of Speeches which were never spoken, Letters which were never sent; and Descriptions of Mountains, Rivers, Towns and Countries, whereof many are false.

Apparently Curtius was a student of Rhetoric, who selected the subject of Alexander

not so much with a design of transmitting just and accurate History as of giving the world a specimen of his Oratory. . . . He took occasion to interlard his History with Speeches . . . not in the style suited to the Macedonian soldiers, who were most of them unlettered. . . . The Narrative parts . . . please us not so much by the Accuracy of Description as by the Beauty and the Brightness of his words and by a certain heat of Style. . . . He greedily snatched at all the Fables which he found in ancient writers which a judicious Historian and a Regarder of Truth would either have omitted or detected as Falsehood, and employed all his Rhetoric to make them pass as Truth. . . . Such is the Fable of Thalestris, Queen of the Amazons, who was desirous of having a child by Alexander . . . and approached his Presence with Three hundred Female Attendants, etc. The rest I shall not take the Trouble of transcribing; those who have a mind, may read it in Curtius. . . . I shall also forbear declaring it a Fable; for whoever cannot smell that out, wants a Nose, and is not worthy to have good Sense thrown away upon him.

Here is an example of Curtius' fables which Rooke calls the "Speeches which were never spoken". Darius is discovered dying of multiple wounds, abandoned in a waggon, and thus addresses a wandering Macedonian who approached him:

"Whoever thou art—by common lot of man, from which this spectacle shows that the greatest Kings are not exempt, I conjure thee to bear my last command to Alexander. None of these calamities which long since overtook me, nor the manner of my death, an unparalleled woe, presses so heavily on me as this one; after that most clement of conquerors has deserved so much from me and mine, I have been forced to live as his enemy, and I die without making him a return. But if the last vows of the unhappy can influence the gods, if the Deity more compassionately listen to prayers poured out with the vital spirit, Alexander will live in inviolate safety . . . in the country of Cyrus, his shall be a more illustrious reign. Constant to his virtue, he will permit my mother and children to live near him, which they shall deserve by their fidelity and obedience. But he will pursue to speedy death the parricides, if not from sympathy with an unfortunate enemy, at least from detestation of a heinous crime, and lest such unpunished enormities should cause the murder of other sovereigns, and even of himself."

To-day, readers demand adherence to facts in preference to the balancing of sentences. It is not generally understood that in olden days a degree of licence was permissible to those who wrote the lives of eminent men. Before the Renaissance, with the revival of learning, it was usual for a historian to put into the mouths of characters the speeches which he considered that they *ought* to have delivered; no attempt was made to report their actual words. For Curtius and similar authors, elegant phraseology was all-important. Thus a modern scholar can tell at a glance that the more eloquent the language the more doubtful is the veracity of an ancient so-called historian.

The reader of Curtius will therefore not be surprised to learn that, after having quenched his thirst, the dying Darius resumed his speech with a further peroration. Similarly long, polished and balanced speeches are reported by Curtius as having been declaimed by Philotas when on trial for conspiracy, and answered by Alexander with equally resounding oratory. Addresses phrased in choice language are presented before the judging tribunal by the accomplices of Philotas, by the royal pages accused of similar plots, and by the illiterate and doubtless inarticulate Macedonian soldiers on the occasions when they disagreed with their King.

Now one must quote from Curtius a sample of the gossip which no doubt thrilled readers who enjoyed scandal: "Alexander, whose genius was more vigorous in war than in peace, as soon as he obtained a respite from military cares, devoted himself to voluptuousness; and he whom the arms of the Persians could not keep in check, was conquered by their vices. Unreasonable banquets, whole nights consumed in drinking and revelling, a retinue of concubines, declared him to have fallen into all the obliquities of the Barbarian manners." It is a curious fact that in some of the translations of Curtius, such as that by Peter Pratt, there is no mention of Alexander having succumbed to the temptations of Babylon; but the folly of many of the army is described.

In a later chapter Curtius sums up the character of Alexander, and here this astonishing writer performs a veritable somersault. *De mortuis nil nisi bonum* does not explain this *volte-face*. From this fact, and also from allusions to eastern regions then under the rule of Rome, Tarn deduced that Curtius wrote after the reign of Claudius. Curtius' final summary reads thus:

> Indisputably, to persons justly estimating Alexander, it is plain that his great qualities were part of his nature; his bad traits, either vitiations of prosperity, or ebullitions

of youth. Half-incredulous, we wonder at the force of his spirit; his perseverance in labour, abstinence, and watching, almost to excess; his bravery transcending that of other kings, and even of men without other endowment. . . . Death, which appals mankind, he habitually despised. . . . How many kingdoms did his moderation and beneficence to the vanquished restore or give? . . . Equally with magnanimity he displayed wisdom and an early policy which mature years sustained. Immoderate appetites he had tempered to a mean . . . he never invaded the conjugal rights of another. These were great qualities. . . . As to his proneness to anger, and love of wine, as fervid youth had increased, so sedate age might have moderated these faults.

It must be admitted that Curtius provides excellent entertainment; escapist literature gives its readers glamour and romance—harmless, so long as one places no faith in its veracity. One can understand how the sick King Alphonse derived so much benefit from the prescription of his physician that he should distract his mind with Quintus Curtius. Tarn finds Curtius: "Clever, careless, cynical, he is about the most maddening writer of antiquity; he could have told us so much, had he been in earnest; instead . . . he exacts the same price—to wade through his rhetoric—for a mere fraction of what he must have known."

Towards the middle of the second century after Christ, a history of Alexander was written by Arrian, a Greek who had held high office in the service of Rome. In a preface, Arrian wrote: "There is no hero on whose life so many pens have been employed or where they disagree so much among themselves. . . . And if any wonder why, after so many writers of Alexander's Acts, I also attempt the task, and endeavour to elucidate the fame, after he has perused the rest, let him proceed to the reading of mine, and he will find less cause of Wonder than before." After having studied all available evidence, Arrian concluded: "Ptolemy and Aristobulus are preferable to all the rest. and more worthy of credit. Their veracity is less to be doubted, because they compiled their histories after Alexander's death, when neither fear nor favour could induce them to relate facts otherwise than really happened."

Although Arrian had had experience of war, he belonged to a later century, when the military names and the army formations had been changed; his accounts of battles and distant territories where there had been much fighting are not always accurate. He had great admiration for the intellect and the character of Alexander, but did not exonerate him from all faults. He gave due credit to the King for his magnanimity, his continence, his care for the safety of captive women, the wounded and the sick, his astonishing hold on the affection and the obedience of his generals and soldiers, and his unique virtue of regret for wrongs committed in anger. Of these Arrian observes: "Other great conquerors have committed crimes in wrath but have always excuses for such acts; only Alexander expressed repentance and remorse when he had done wrong—all antiquity has not produced an example in a King of such sincere repentance as he showed."

Arrian is a little uncertain whether Alexander ought to have adopted Persian dress, but considers that it may have been wise to do so when he presided over his Persian Court, for by such means he proved that he wished to please and to demonstrate his friendship for them. Arrian disposed of the charge of megalomania, which receives acceptance even to-day from certain writers, by pointing out that deification may well have been necessary for political reasons; it conferred authority and was usual with many rulers who had preceded and were to follow him. Arrian did not believe the stories of drunken habits, because Aristobulus, who had known Alexander well and had accompanied him throughout his campaigns, expressly contradicted such gossip, and wrote that "long banquets and deep drinking were not his delights"; instead, he enjoyed conversing at the evening meal.

In his seventh chapter Arrian writes:

In body he was very handsome, a lover of hardship,

quick and untiring; most courageous; most zealous of
honour and glory; most religious; indifferent to sensual
pleasures; insatiable for the noble enjoyments; most
brilliant to seize upon the right course of action, even when
all was obscure; most swift to weigh up the probabilities
for success; most masterly in marshalling an army and
equipping it; without equal in commanding his troops,
inspiring them with confidence and dispelling their fears
by giving them the first example of facing danger with
unshakable courage. In doubtful enterprises his daring
decided the victory; he was most skilled in swift anticipa-
tion and gripping of his enemy before any one had time
to suspect his presence; he was most reliable in keeping
promises or agreements; most guarded in not being
trapped by the fraudulent; very sparing of money for
his own use, most generous in gifts to others. . . . It is
not without the special will of the gods that he appeared
among men, not one of whom can be compared with
him.

Arrian's history concludes with this fine tribute:

If any man consider seriously who he was, what
success he always had, and to what a pitch of glory he
arrived, he will easily conclude, that in comparison with
his great and laudable acts, his failings were few and
trifling . . . and considering his repentance and abhor-
rence of them afterwards, may easily be overlooked. . . .
There seems to me to have been some Divine Hand
presiding over both his birth and actions, insomuch that
no mortal upon earth either excelled or equalled him.
And though I take the freedom in this history to censure
some of his deeds, yet I must own myself an admirer of him
altogether. Let those who reproach Alexander look upon
themselves, examine their own weakness and how they
managed their own narrow sphere, before they venture
to condemn him who raised himself to the highest pinnacle
of glory, the monarch of two continents, whose renown
had extended over the whole world; no nation, no city,

no man had not heard the name of Alexander.

The Memoirs of Aristobulus have been lost, but references and extracts occur in the works of Strabo, Eratosthenes and Arrian. They shed vivid sidelights on Alexander. Many a conversation must have taken place on his special subjects— architecture, engineering and geography. He states that Alexander was always open to reason; one could always tell him the truth even when one disagreed with him. Aristobulus appears to have been a most able man; he restored the tomb of Cyrus the Great and probably was with the King when he consulted other experts concerning dams, wells, canals, irrigation schemes and other technical subjects. Alexander showed keen interest in everything, and always aided his soldiers with the manual labour entailed by the building of mounds, bridges and other means of crossing ravines and rivers. Both Aristobulus and Ptolemy considered that Black Cleitus had deserved his fate and that Callisthenes had been guilty.

J. D. Droysen, a young German historian, was deeply moved when he read that Alexander had visited Ilium to place garlands on the tomb of his hero Achilles. But, said Droysen, Achilles had Homer to commemorate his deeds; he made a vow that he would be the Homer for Alexander. He studied every record, good and bad, and gradually realised that Alexander had changed the whole world during his astonishing career. Subsequent study of Greece convinced Droysen that he had to deal with a subject more wonderful than any in antiquity. No one, he declared, had understood the force of character and the grandeur of Alexander's plans, for not only was he a military genius, but also a far-seeing statesman and philosopher. His book on Hellenism first appeared in 1833, but was laid aside when in later life he was preoccupied with the history of Germany, his own country. In 1934 Benoist-Méchin translated the volume dealing with Alexander; the rhythm of the French language gives to it the heroic beauty of an epic poem. In his preface Benoist-Méchin said that "however one approaches it, the history of Alexander remains a study which enchants men at every stage of life."

In his *History of Greece* (1843), Bishop Thirlwall condemns many of Alexander's deeds, but he concludes: "So passed from the earth one of the greatest of her sons: great above most, for what he was in himself, and not as many who have borne the title, for what was given to him to effect. Great, not merely in the vast compass, and in the persevering ardour, of his ambition: nor in the qualities by which he was enabled to gratify it, and to crowd so many memorable actions within so short a period: but in the course which his ambition took, in the collateral aims which ennobled and purified it, so that it almost grew into one of the highest of which man is capable, the desire of knowledge, and the love of good. In a word, great as one of the benefactors of his kind."

Ide Wheeler wrote in 1900: "No single personality . . . has done so much to make the world of civilisation we live in what it is, as Alexander of Macedon. . . . Whatever lay within the range of his conquests contributed its part to form that Mediterranean civilisation which became the basis of European life. The story of the great Macedonian . . . is instinct with personality . . . when and where the personal Alexander was absent from the scene, history in these days either tarried or moved in eddies; the current was where he was." Of his character, Ide Wheeler writes that from his mother came "passionate warmth of nature which betrayed itself in furious outbursts of temper occasionally, but quite as much in a romantic fervour of attachment and love for friends, a delicate tenderness of sympathy for the weak, and a princely largeness and generosity of soul toward all, that made him so deeply beloved of men and so enthusiastically followed. . . . His respect for women and his moral cleanliness made him an exception in his time."

We now turn to two writers, George Grote and Georges Radet, who admit that they place more reliance on the works

of Cleitarchus, Curtius, Diodorus and Justin, than on the
Memoirs of Ptolemy and Aristobulus. Tarn's analysis of the
unreliable sources from which the first-named drew their
material was not then available. George Grote wrote twelve
volumes on the history of Greece; the last, published in
1856, considers Alexander of Macedon. Grote believed
that even the good deeds recorded by both friends and
enemies were inspired by a desire to gain admiration and to
impress the world; they were calculated from political
motives. Although Grote was obliged to admit that the
treatment of King Porus was generous, he hints that this
was in part due to admiration of Porus' noble stature and
dignified bearing! Of the speech to the mutineers at Opis,
Grote states that it "teemed with that exorbitant self-
exaltation which formed the leading feature in his character". Grote repeats the slander that Alexander, enraged,
crucified the physician who had failed to save the life of his
friend Hephaestion, and became "so irascible that no one
approached him without fear. . . . At length he roused
himself and found consolation in gratifying the primary
passions of his nature—fighting and man-hunting." For the
military aspect of Alexander, Grote cannot find words
adequate to express his admiration. "Together with his own
courage we trace in all his operations the most careful
dispositions taken beforehand, vigilant precautions in
guarding against possible reverse, and abundant resource
in adapting himself to new contingencies. Amidst constant
success these precautionary combinations were never
discontinued. Alexander overawes the imagination more
than any other personage of antiquity . . . as an individual
warrior and as an organiser and leader of armed masses;
not merely the blind impetuosity ascribed by Homer to
Ares, but also the intelligent, methodised and all-subduing
compression which he personifies in Athene." Although,
Grote continues, he knows that some authors have credited
Alexander with "grand and magnificent views on imperial
government and for intentions highly favourable to the
improvement of mankind, I see no ground for adopting
this opinion."

In 1873 Freeman, in his *Historical Essays*, reviewed Grote's *History of Greece* and protested that the character and aims of Alexander were unjustly dealt with. He also pointed out that Niebuhr, the eminent historian who died in 1831, "showed unscrupulous malignity against both Philip and Alexander. . . . Their crimes are exaggerated, their virtues depreciated, their motives distorted; every piece of scandalous gossip raked up against them."

In 1931 Georges Radet gave credit to Alexander's finer qualities: chivalry towards the vanquished, courtesy to women, liberality to both friends and enemies, personal charm and military skill. In contrast, Radet dwells on his wrathful temper and considers that he had an overweening certainty of a divine origin. The mystic sense with which many writers endow Alexander was, in the opinion of Radet, a Dionysiac excitement, as shown by his enjoyment of the orgies of that god. Radet devotes eight pages to the banquet at Persepolis where, so goes the story, an Athenian courtesan suggested that they set on fire the palace of Xerxes (p. 60). But Tarn has proved that this discreditable tale, found in the works of Curtius, Diodorus and the later version of Plutarch's *Lives*, does not stand investigation. Ptolemy and Aristobulus did not mention the presence of Thais. Wilcken (1933) dismisses it as: "One of the fables of Cleitarchus related that after a wild orgy of intoxication, Alexander, incited by the Athenian hetaera, fired the palace. Naturally this was eagerly repeated by later writers and finds credence even to-day." But Radet believes that when not engaged in practical affairs the emotional side of Alexander's nature found satisfaction in such forms of indulgence. Such an interpretation is customary with some psychologists. On the same plane Radet places the competitions and sporting activities which Alexander usually arranged for the relaxation of his troops after periods of hardship. Is it not more reasonable to conclude that Alexander understood the minds of the people? From all time men have loved to assemble in crowds to watch the spectacle of monarchs and soldiers in rich attire, with magnificent chariots. Games, dances, songs and revelry usually follow these processions. Such celebrations after times of endurance, natural in every country and every age, cannot fairly be described as manifestations of Dionysiac frenzy.

Professor Wright, of the London University, wrote in 1934 that Alexander surpassed all other conquerors in that he gave a superior civilisation to those whom he defeated. "In the history of our European civilisation four names stand out from all others: Alexander, Julius Caesar, Charles the Great, Napoleon. All four were so superior to the ordinary level of human capacity that they can hardly be judged by common standards. . . . Alexander, both in his work and in his character, is entitled to the first place. . . . He was the fine flower of Greek civilisation . . . the effects of his conquests in widening the horizon of men's minds can only be compared with the discovery of America."

The verdict of a professional soldier carries authority. In 1890 Lieutenant-Colonel Theodore Dodge, of the United States Army, wrote a lengthy study of Alexander. He agreed with Arrian, whom he considered the most sober-minded and accurate of the ancient historians, that Alexander as a human being was not free from faults, but that his work excelled anything in history. He writes:

> Starting with a handful of men from Macedonia, in four years one grand achievement after another and without a failure, had placed at his feet the Empire of the Great King. Leaving home with an enormous debt, in fifty moons he had possessed himself of all the treasures of the earth. Thence . . . he completed the conquest of the known world, marching twenty-two thousand miles in his eleven years' campaign. And all this before he was thirty-three. . . . No man ever was a great soldier without the most generous virtues of the soul and the most distinguished power of the intellect.

After enumerating other essential qualities of a great captain he adds:

The unconscious habit of ruling men and of commanding their love and admiration, coupled with the ability to
stir their enthusiasm to the yielding of their last ounce of
effort . . . ability to think as quickly and accurately in
the turmoil of battle as in the quiet of the bureau . . .
power to foresee the result of a stratagem or tactical
manoeuvre; the capacity to gauge the efforts of men and
of masses of men . . . the mental strength which weakens
not under the tax of hours and days of unequalled strain.
Alexander was the first man who possessed these qualities
in the highest measure. . . . He was remarkable in being
able to keep the gaps in his army filled by fresh recruits
from home or enlistment of natives, and in transforming
the latter into excellent soldiers. . . . His periods of
inactivity were spent, not in feasts and follies as his critics
say, but in studying the countries he proposed to traverse.
Those who knew him in his own era and called him a
demi-god came far more near the truth.

After his account of the exploration of the Indus and its
delta, Dodge states: "There is abundant evidence in the
stories of the ancient authors that Alexander fully grasped
the extent of what could be accomplished by commerce
and the arts . . . It is the habit of modern writers to reduce
everything he did, excepting his military exploits, to crass
luck. . . . And yet the great among his contemporaries gave
him credit for vast and true conceptions, and there were
giants in these days."

After so many laudatory pages many a reader may, like
Professor William James after his visit to Chatauqua, the
colony of perfect people, long for relief by turning to Iliff
Robson. His biography of Alexander, published in 1929, is
largely based on Curtius, Cleitarchus and Diodorus.
Obliged to admit many extraordinary qualities of heart
and mind, he appears to be somewhat bewildered by the
incompatibility of the excellent with the evil propensities
which he desires to point out to hero-worshippers. Con-
trasting the praise with the criticism of history, Robson asks:

Which is the real Alexander? He was all and none of these pictures, because he never stayed still long enough to be any one of them; and because he passed rapidly from one moment into another. Here we have him in a drunken fury, slaughtering his friend, and there we have him, almost maudlin in his penitence; here we have him storming impossible heights, himself the very soul of incredible valour, there indulging in a grief for Hephaestion which, sincere no doubt in its beginning, lapsed into weak theatricalities—all contradictions from start to finish. He never was the static Alexander whom we see in the neat summaries of historians; he was an idea, a force rushing like a cyclone over Asia; at one time the leader of a crusade; soon he is a triumphant conqueror, now chivalrous, now brutal, but always successful; now he is the uniter of the ever-sundered West and East; then the great scientist, the indomitable explorer, held from reaching the eastern circle of Ocean only by the travel-weariness of his less indomitable men; finally, the deified hero, almost a god amongst gods. . . . Historians will continue to differ; and that means, so long will they continue to re-create their own Alexanders.

This author is certain that Alexander secretly rejoiced over the murder of his father and was apprehensive lest he too might be assassinated. Robson believed that he had solved the problem of Siwah; he knew—what no historian nor friend of Alexander had ever learned—that the Oracle had told the King that he was not the son of Philip, but of a god. Strange that this antagonist of hero-worshippers was obliged to record, in contrast to a long list of faults, an equally lengthy list of virtues rarely met with in the great conquerors of ancient days. He had studied Plutarch's *Lives*, but makes no mention of the *Moralia* (p. 186). Nor was the research of Tarn then available. He wrote during the so-called "debunking" period when it was the fashion to examine the Victorian giants as through a glass which magnified every defect, but left their virtues out of sight.

Ulrich Wilcken (1933), a German historian, studied

Alexander from his early youth and sums up his opinion:

> It is hardly an exaggeration to say that every student has an Alexander of his own. There was in him a super-human quality; genius is never quite capable of explanation, and must remain to us marvellous. His gigantic life-work brings before us a personality of unique genius . . . a mixture of demonic passion and sober clearness of judgment. In this iron-willed man of action, a realist in policy if anyone ever was, beneath the surface lay a non-rational element; his longing for the undiscovered and the mysterious, which with his will to conquer and his delight in scientific discovery, sent him to the ends of the known world. . . . He believed in his Mission. . . . It has been said that a sense of Divine possession is characteristic of the conduct of the great men of antiquity. This is true of no one more than of Alexander. . . . The towering nature of his personality is most clearly shown in the fact that the men nearest him, who after his death showed themselves to be strong rulers, blindly obeyed him during his life. Nearchus said that the Army believed that there was nothing he could not dare nor do.

A. R. Burn (1947) retails Alexander's reputed many faults, but toward the end of his book admits that "he had the untiring persistence of a scientist or an explorer. And with his restraint and moderation . . . in an environment that gave him every temptation to excess and sensuality, it is clear that, born a few centuries later, he could have been a famous and dominating saint."

Sir William Tarn is the most convincing, because the most thorough of the historians of Alexander. His first volume (published in 1947) is a vivid, condensed account of the achievements and the character of Alexander. In his long second volume every statement in history is closely scrutinised, traced to its source, the original text examined, the reliability or the irresponsibility of the author weighed in the balance. Greek and Latin references throughout make this volume a veritable encyclopaedia for students of history.

Several of Tarn's most striking estimates should here be quoted:

> What his force of character was like can best be seen, not in his driving power, great as it was, but in his relations with his generals. Here was an assembly of Kings, with passions, ambitions, abilities beyond those of most men; and while he lived, all we see is that Perdiccas and Ptolemy were good brigade leaders, Antigonus an obedient satrap, Lysimachus and Peithon little noticed members of his staff. . . . To be mystical and intensely practical, to dream greatly and to do greatly, is not given to many men; it is this combination which gives Alexander his place apart in history . . . he was one of the supreme fertilising forces of history. He lifted the civilised world out of one groove and set it in another; he started a new epoch; nothing could again be as it had been. . . . The torch which Alexander lit only smoulders to-day; but it never has been, and never could be, quite put out. . . . His personality was adequate to great tasks. Aristotle had taught him that man's highest good lay in right activity of mind and body both. . . . He gives a strangely vivid impression of one whose body was his servant.

Then followed centuries of legend and romance. Apparently more than eighty versions, in some twenty-four languages, reported his travels and achievements. He was traced to North Africa, Ethiopia, Tibet and China; of course also to Jerusalem, and his advent had been prophesied by Daniel. Russia also he had visited as far as the Land of Darkness and the Well of Life. These fantasies are still repeated in the mountains of Iran and the foothills of the Himalayas. A friend who was in that region in 1949 had seen an excellent Indian film with realistic scenes of the campaign in the high hills, the ravines and the rivers of northern India. Recent travellers in the Punjab tell that many fair-haired members of the tribes proudly claim descent from the Macedonians who dwelt there so long ago.

Those who desire to see the region of the Alexander Romance must mount upon a magic carpet and be transported from the every-day world to the far-off lands of legend. Victorians who recall the glamour of the Arabian Nights' Entertainment which was read to them in childhood can recapture some of that delight from the Ethiopic version of the "Pseudo-Callisthenes". Sir Ernest Wallis Budge has translated the Ethiopic story of the Pseudo-Callisthenes, the chronicle of Almakin, the narrative of Joseph Ben Gorion, and also a Christian Romance of Alexander. This fascinating tale is introduced with a judicial summary of the life of the Great King: "If all history be searched, no character will be found whose life and deeds have appealed so strongly to the admiration and the sympathy of all nations as that of Alexander the Great. His personal bravery, the hardness he endured as a soldier, his indefatigable energy, his military skill, his sound judgment, his magnanimous character, his travels, his conquests and his tragic death, have literally made all the world wonder. After his death professional writers and story-tellers began to exaggerate and to misrepresent the facts of his life and to add fictitious statements of every degree and wildness." This volume is rendered even more attractive with its beautiful illustrations from Persian manuscripts.

In the bulky volume of the Pseudo-Callisthenes those in search of fantasy will be richly rewarded. In its pages Alexander is the TWO-HORNED who flies on the back of an eagle to the heights of Heaven, and his speeches to the magicians, kings, soldiers, prophets and angels are translated from manuscripts in the British Museum and the Bibliothèque Nationale of Paris. The TWO-HORNED also travelled to Jerusalem, Arabia, Ethiopia, the Land of the Darkness and the Well of Life. Even the depths of the sea were explored by the mighty King, who spent many days and nights in a glass diving cage, watching fishes of enormous dimensions swim slowly past.

And now, having stepped off the magic carpet, dismounted from the back of an eagle and ascended from the depths of the ocean, we regain the solid ground of sober truth. We gladly return to the most trustworthy of the scholars who have studied the life of Alexander of Macedon. In the address recorded in the Proceedings of the British Academy in 1933, Sir William Tarn said: "He was the pioneer of one of the supreme revolutions in the world's outlook, the first man known to us who contemplated the brotherhood of man, or the unity of mankind. Alexander, for the things which he *did*, was called Great, but, if what I have said to-day be right, I do not doubt that this idea of his—call it a purpose, call it a dream, call it what you will—was the greatest thing about him."

Not every scholar agrees with Tarn; some consider that he has drawn an idealised portrait of Alexander. Puzzled by the diverse estimates of historians every reader will form his own opinion in accordance with his temperament, his knowledge of character and psychology, and his experience of life.

PART II

CHAPTER XIII

CHARACTER OF ALEXANDER

*His horse, Bucephalus—Alexander's love of exercise—
Persian envoys—Quarrel with his father—Attitude
towards women—Compassion for the suffering—His
generosity—His distrust of Rhetoric—His diet—His
disregard of danger—Causes of his military success—
Refutation of accusations of drunken habits, enjoyment of Persian luxury and of flattery—Impatience and
anger—His speeches—Influence of Aristotle—Indian
ascetics—His love of exploration and interest in
religion—His response to mysticism*

CERTAIN anecdotes reveal the character of Alexander in
his early years; several which are mentioned by every
historian of antiquity cannot be dismissed as hearsay.

The acquisition of his favourite horse, Bucephalus, reads
like a fairy tale. A spirited horse had been offered to Philip
for a price, and was being tried by able riders. Alexander,
then very young, probably under thirteen, watched the
efforts of the trainers with increasing dissatisfaction. Philip
was not pleased by his son's criticism of the methods
employed to break in the horse, which kicked and reared so
that the usual attendants were afraid to approach so savage
an animal. As Alexander continued to protest that he could
succeed, if permitted to try, his father at last gave reluctant
consent. Alexander had observed that the animal had its
back to the sun and was shying to avoid the moving shadow;

he turned the head so that the frightening black shadow fell behind, gently caressed the horse, and with soothing words quieted its fear; then casting off his cloak, he quickly mounted and with superb carriage and complete mastery rode round the course. Astonished and relieved, Philip embraced his son and presented the animal to him. Alexander named him Bucephalus, because his head resembled that of an ox; he treasured him as a constant companion. Bucephalus would never permit any other than Alexander to mount him; in battle his ox-shaped head with the white mark on the brow and his black coat made him a conspicuous object. During the Uxian campaign in the mountains, Bucephalus was stolen one night; Alexander issued a proclamation that unless the horse was restored the tribe would be slain; Bucephalus was brought back to the camp immediately. The horse lived to be very old; in 326 B.C. he fell, worn out, during the battle of the Hydaspes in the Punjab; a town was founded not far off from the field and named in his honour—Bucephala.

All exercises calculated to strengthen the body Alexander delighted to perform, but of professional athletes he did not approve. In youth he refused to take part in the Festival Games because he would not compete except with kings. But during the Asiatic campaign he knew the importance of competitions and other games for the relaxation and the morale of his troops, especially after prolonged periods of heavy endurance and warfare. It must not be forgotten that the Greeks regarded games from a religious attitude which is not considered in that connection in modern times; that aspect is discussed in the next chapter. While in Asia Alexander kept his muscles strong and agile by mounting and dismounting from horse and chariot running at full speed. His favourite sport was hunting; the pursuit of wild boars, foxes and bears provided exercise for the body and also encouraged skill and swiftness of the mind.

While Alexander was still young, some say under ten, Persian ambassadors were received by him during the absence of his father; the visitors were astonished by the mature questions put to them by the boy regarding Persian methods of government. They predicted a great future for so unusually intelligent a young prince. At school he used to sigh on receiving news of the victories of his father, both in diplomacy and war. "What will be left", he asked his companions, "for you to share with me when we grow up?"

The example of Philip, when he decided to divorce Olympias, the dearly-loved mother of Alexander, so that he could marry Cleopatra, the beautiful young niece of Attalus, one of his generals, must have made a deep and painful impression on his son. Philip had been notorious for bouts of intoxication and marital infidelity; the unhappiness this conduct brought to Olympias and the consequent disruption of the home life would create the atmosphere of insecurity now recognised to be so harmful to children. Olympias, coming from Epirus, was regarded as a "barbarian", that is to say, a foreigner; therefore the right of her son to the throne might be disputed. Because Cleopatra, the new wife, was a Macedonian of high rank, any child whom she might bear would, by a section of the people, be considered as the true heir to the throne. At the wedding banquet of his niece Attalus expressed the hope that a legitimate heir to the crown might be born of the union. Alexander, enraged, flung his cup at the speaker, exclaiming that he was no bastard; sword in hand, Philip rushed towards his son, stumbled and fell, overcome with drink. Looking down on him, Alexander scornfully remarked to the guests that there lay the man who essayed to conquer Persia, but lost his way from one couch to another.

This humiliating scene was followed by the banishment of Alexander and several nobly born youths who were his close friends; the Prince at once rode off with his mother to her home country. Soon after, when Philip complained to an envoy about the lack of unity among the Greek states, the officer replied that no good example of concord was shown in the family circle of the King. Impressed by the justice of the remark, Philip recalled his son; in any case he required the aid of the Prince and his friends for military projects.

In Persia, when men remarked upon his self-control, Alexander is reported to have said that it would be shameful if, when he had conquered the men of a country, he were himself to be vanquished by their women. Again: "The beauty of women must yield to the beauty of virtue"; and "The rebellion of the body, sweet at the moment, only leads to trouble". He would have appreciated the lines of George Meredith:

> Or shall we run with Artemis,
> Or yield the breast to Aphrodite?
> Both give bliss;
> Each can torture if derided;
> Each claims worship undivided;
> Youth must offer on bent knees
> Homage unto one or other;
> Earth the Mother,
> Thus decrees.

Alexander forbade his soldiers to violate captured women; once he ordered that two Macedonians who had raped such captives should be killed, saying that they were like wild beasts, destructive to humanity. Aristobulus tells the story of his examination of a Theban woman who had been brought before him on a charge of murdering a soldier who had raped her. She frankly described how she had lured the man into her garden and told him to look down into a deep well, saying that she had thrown into it many valuable treasures. When he bent over to examine the depth she had quickly pushed him in, and thus he had been drowned. Although the prisoner was of his enemies, Alexander so admired her courage that he conferred freedom on her and her family.

Like the detractors of ancient times, some modern writers have tried to explain Alexander's attitude toward women as due to homosexuality. But when Philoxenes told the King that two beautiful boys had been offered for him, Alexander was furious: "What evil has he seen in me that he should purchase for me such shameful creatures?" he exclaimed,

"Tell the dealer to take his wares to hell." The subject is considered in Chapter xv; but here one ought to state that Tarn has proved on what a flimsy basis such an accusation was constructed.

After the capture of Persepolis a command was sent that the women were not to be touched. This was new in war; did any other army leader give similar advice before Kitchener in 1914? Alexander took precautions that young girls should be safeguarded from the troops; women relatives of enemy chiefs fallen in battle were retained under good supervision; it was even ordered that they should not be allowed to hear about evil. The orphaned daughter of his most obdurate opponent, Spitamenes, was one of those young girls who were educated at Susa with the family of Darius.

When Darius learned that his mother, wife and family had been taken as prisoners, he was filled with anxiety about their fate. As it was regarded to be the privilege of a conqueror to take possession of the captive women, at first Darius refused to credit the messenger who told him that they were living in a palace at Susa, and being treated with the honours due to royalty. Moreover, Alexander had accorded to the wife, dying in childbirth, a funeral befitting a queen. After the defeat of Darius at Gaugamela his family had followed the Macedonian advance, but on reaching Susa, Alexander housed them in quarters suitable for royalty. Astonished, Darius exclaimed that if it were indeed his destiny to lose the kingdom of Persia, he knew no man except Alexander to whom he would gladly yield up his throne.

Alexander's consideration for women has puzzled many, not only in ancient but also in modern times. Sisygambis, the mother of Darius, he treated as he would his own mother; on entering her apartments he did not permit her to prostrate herself as was the custom before a king, and he remained standing until she invited him to be seated. The story may be true that after his death Sisygambis was so overwhelmed with grief that she was inconsolable, refused food and died five days later. Some consider that Alexander married from motives of policy, and that his chief reason for this marriage was his desire to fuse the nations; but others believe that he felt for Roxane, the Sogdian princess, the normal attraction of love.

It has long been believed that in the great days of Athens, women, although honoured as wives and mothers, had little freedom; but this has been seriously disputed by recent historians. In Macedonia women associated with men as equals; brave, outspoken, courageous and practical, they shared the faults as well as the virtues of their husbands, sons and brothers. Alexander's attitude to women would be influenced by the fact that Plato had advocated that they should share with men the responsibilities as guardians of the State. Aristotle had taught that a good ruler and his associates must be free from all suspicion of sexual offence and never violate the chastity of any subject,[1] and doubtless Alexander was acquainted with Aeschylus' treatment of the matter in his play, *The Suppliants*.

Another trait distinguished Alexander from the majority of his contemporaries—compassion for the sick and the suffering; such emotion was in those days regarded as unmanly. Again we trace the influence of Euripides, whose dramas show more human understanding of the afflicted than is usual in Hellenistic literature. The unhappy fate of Medea, Cassandra, Electra and the Trojan women is depicted by a dramatist who sympathised with their trials from a human standpoint, distinct from the remote plane of a god.

Frontinus, a historian who wrote during the first century A.D., tells in his *Strategematigon* many anecdotes concerning distinguished men. This story is mentioned by many subsequent writers: As Alexander sat in his tent, watching his troops pass by, he noticed a soldier overcome by fatigue and cold; calling him into the tent he placed the exhausted man on a seat close by the fire. When the soldier recovered warmth he rose, afraid, realising that he was in the presence of his King. But Alexander comforted him, jestingly remarking that if a Persian soldier had occupied the seat of a King

[1] *Politics, V*, xi, 1314b.

he would have been considered guilty of a crime punishable by death, but that privilege belonged to a Macedonian; instead of death as his penalty, he had received life.

Lavish generosity was a characteristic of the King throughout life; he gave freely to his officers and men, reserving little for himself. His custom of bestowing princely gifts on native guides and on chieftains who surrendered to his arms is recounted even by his enemies. Loyalty to friends was another virtue, rare in any age; even after the discovery of treasonable conspiracies and betrayal of confidence which occurred on several occasions in Asia, he would refuse to believe his informants until he received convincing evidence that the reports were based on fact.

His character was so direct that he had no use for quibbles and sophistry; he distrusted men who indulged in "rhetoric", a term employed to describe not merely fluent speech but the ability to maintain in debate or argument entirely opposite points of view. This became a fashionable study in legal and political circles, and constituted a danger to the young and inexperienced who could not judge between truth and falsehood when both were favourably presented in eloquent language. Just as George Meredith condemned sentimentalism as distinguished from genuine emotion, so did Alexander despise insincere discussion which led to confusion between right and wrong.

Clemency toward conquered foes has been so often recorded in the campaigns of Asia and India that one may suitably repeat here his declaration: "I have not come to destroy nations; I have come here that those who are subdued by my arms shall have nought to complain of my victories." In this connection is told a story which may not be true, but is so relevant that it is worthy of repetition. When a relative of King Porus heard of his defeat he hastened to interview Alexander, hoping to obtain some of the territory, but to his astonishment found the conqueror seated in friendly conversation with his recent bitter foe.

Like Napoleon, Alexander was abstemious at meals, and used to reproach young officers who indulged too freely in food and drink; Aristobulus tells us that these spendthrift youths often fed on rich and dainty dishes whilst their King at the same table was taking only fruit and light food. When Queen Ada of Caria tried to coax him to eat more and tempted him with deliciously cooked meals, he said that he had found that the best appetiser was healthy exercise before his morning breakfast.

Critics often stated that Alexander undertook many military operations because he wished to prove that he could accomplish what his predecessors had found impossible; this they regarded as "avid of glory". In one sense it is true that he was "avid of glory", but with this reservation: the brave men of his generation followed the ideals of Homer's *Iliad*. The Greek point of view cannot be understood until one has read the *Iliad* and the poems of Pindar (both treasured by Alexander) which admire as godlike the power of the warrior and the athlete. For those poets arduous deeds were not inspired by vanity nor desire for praise, but by a religious motive, the longing to emulate feats of almost superhuman strength and endurance. The Greeks strove after what they called *arete*, a word not easily translated into English; it implies excellence, the highest quality, great worth, the best which a man is able to attain. The Greek had none of the self-depreciation and undue modesty of the modern Englishman; he was glad to have his exploits recognised; he was proud of success, especially in the field of war. When one regards the heroic actions of Alexander from the Greek attitude, the words "avid of glory" convey no reproach; on the contrary, they describe a quality which is praiseworthy.

There was another side to the glory of warfare, one to which Alexander was not blind; no Greek forgot how the kinsfolk of the slain were bound to suffer. But this grief was not brooded upon with melancholy, for death awaited every man and was accepted with resignation as the inscrutable will of the gods. In the story of the Asiatic campaign we have watched how Alexander gradually developed beyond the limited field which satisfied his ideals of the time when he crossed the Hellespont. But throughout his career death held for him no menace, no terror, and thus with his army he fearlessly undertook tasks of danger which to lesser mortals seemed beyond the power of men. With firm faith in his mission he was confident of the protection of the gods. Thus many of his achievements, which some have said were undertaken with a desire for his own glory, at the cost of unnecessary loss of the lives of his soldiers, are from this angle seen to have been part of a maturely considered policy. Until Sir Aurel Stein proved that it was a strategic necessity to take Aornos, its capture was regarded as an example of a vainglorious feat.

From antiquity to the present day Alexander has been described by military experts as a genius in the art of war. Hannibal, Caesar, Frederick and Napoleon studied his methods and admitted that without his example they could not have accomplished so much. One soldier tells us that the passage over the Hydaspes has ever since been regarded as the model for the crossing of a river. Napoleon advised: "Make offensive war like Alexander, Hannibal, Caesar . . . read and re-read the history of their campaigns. Model yourself on them . . . that is the only way to become a great captain." Alexander modified Philip's military foundations; to meet the varied conditions in Asia, novel tactics and weapons were introduced for the conquest of the fierce warriors and swift horsemen of the mountainous districts in Iran and the Punjab. Several times the army had to be radically reorganised. His success was invariable, whether he fought against disciplined, highly trained troops, or guerilla bands of wild hill tribes, on plains or on mountains, deserts, ravines, marshes or rivers, in winter snow or burning sun; weather and darkness were no obstacles. No time was ever wasted; no marches so rapid; always he arrived before the enemy expected him. His men, knowing his concern for their welfare, followed him over 21,000 miles, certain that he would find for them the essential living conditions, equipment and transport to suit all climates.

Many reasons have been advanced to explain why he never lost a battle. First, he made careful preliminary investigation of the territory over which he proposed to advance; often for this purpose he undertook dangerous exploration in person, sometimes alone, frequently with shepherds or native guides. Before meeting his opponents he studied their psychology, their weapons and methods of warfare. His intellect moved with such rapidity and precision that he could cope with any unexpected emergency. It has been said that no great conqueror more quickly grasped the salient points of a critical situation; no great captain more swiftly translated into action his decisions. At a glance he could size up the weak and the strong elements of an opposing force, weigh the advantages and the disadvantages of every possible manoeuvre. Then, as some historians write, "He rode at the double", or "descended like a whirlwind", and appeared suddenly in the midst of an enemy throng before anyone dreamed that he was in the vicinity.

No matter how long the time absorbed, he never started a project without seeing it through to completion. Thus, at Tyre, when weeks were precious, he devoted months to its possession. In Sogdiana, he postponed the entrance into India until after the death of Spitamenes. In the Punjab, he did not join Hephaestion until he had dealt thoroughly with all the fierce tribes on the northern bank of the Cophen. Nor was the fleet permitted to sail from the Indus until the delta was minutely examined and a suitable harbour built. He never made any advance until certain that both rear and flank were secure; no temptation to haste ever made him swerve from that vital principle.

When in Sogdiana (Chapter IV) Alexander was overwhelmed with anxiety. So many Macedonians had been left to garrison the provinces over which they had travelled that reinforcements were urgently required, and it became necessary to fill the gaps by incorporating Persian troops into the army. Although it was impossible to explain to the grumbling veterans the reasons for this measure, Alexander retained their devotion and their confidence because they saw how he never asked them to make an effort which he was unwilling to undertake himself.

Most distinguished men who live in the public eye have

in all ages been the subject of gossip in connection with wine and women; therefore it is necessary to examine from what basis came the rumours which accused Alexander of having developed a habit of overdrinking. It was said that drunkenness was a hereditary trait in Macedonia to which Alexander became a victim about the time of his adoption of Persian dress and etiquette in Bactria. As the Macedonians were not accustomed to wine so strong as that of Iran, no doubt many, especially on festive occasions, would show some degree of the loss of inhibition which follows the consumption of even small amounts of alcohol. But there is no reliable proof that Alexander indulged in heavy drinking. He had seen so much of the evil results of drunkenness in the person of his own father that he may have determined to avoid that failing. Even if Aristotle had not taught that "drunkards are easily attacked and readily despised", he could not have failed to observe how indulgence in alcohol interfered with the reasoning faculty and led to loss of self-control, especially in the sphere of sex. His practical sense would tell him that the continuous mental and physical work demanded of one in his position could not be satisfactorily carried out by a man with habits of intoxication. During periods of rest from danger and hard mental stress there would, no doubt, be merry parties, but one does not stigmatise as drunkards the young men who enjoy such reunions.

Plutarch states: "He was not so much addicted to wine as he got the credit of being. The notion that he was a hard drinker arose from the length of time he spent at table, but this he protracted not in drinking so much as in conversing. For with each cup he used to start some special topic for prolonged conversation and discussion—this of course only when there was no business at hand." In the seventeenth century Freinshem contributed two chapters to fill the gap left by the lost portions of Curtius' history; it is remarkable that in spite of the fact that Curtius delighted to dwell on stories of drunkenness Freinshem took the trouble to state that Alexander had no distaste for wine, but avoided intoxican.

Lieutenant-Colonel Dodge (p. 200) writes that he would

not deny "occasional indulgence in drink and other failings . . . but too much stress has been laid on these. So
much attention has been paid to his vices that the true
perspective of his portrait is in danger of being lost. . . . his
life, with rare exceptions, was one prolonged period of toil
and danger." In parenthesis, it is obvious that this American
writer uses the term vices where we would speak of faults,
failings and blemishes. After the death of Alexander
Aristobulus contradicted the rumour that the fatal malady
had been caused by hard drinking at the farewell banquets;
only when the King felt fever gaining on him had he
quenched his thirst by taking more wine than usual—a brief
detail which carries conviction.

Another accusation, that of corruption by Persian luxury
and the wealth of great cities, does not stand the scrutiny
of careful examination. Alexander set an example of simple
living except on those occasions when he considered it was
essential to adopt the pomp and show expected by Orientals
from a monarch presiding at Court and receiving foreign
potentates and ambassadors. Often he rebuked young officers
who wore costly garments and delighted in gorgeous equipment, with menials waiting on them; how would they fare
on active service, he would enquire, if in times of relaxation
they left even the care of their horses to their servants?
Many of his officers and men were indeed demoralised by the
luxurious life of the towns in the Persian plains; the warm,
enervating climate of Babylonia conduced to easy-going
habits and undermined the energy of many whose youth
had been passed in the austere mountains of Macedonia.
Alexander was ever on the watch to keep his men occupied
when no danger was at hand to keep them on the alert;
with strenuous games he in such times prevented the laziness
which would have ruined their fighting spirit.

Yet he was no ascetic; as a lover of art, beauty, colour and
craftsmanship appealed to him. After the battle of Issus,
when he entered the tent of Darius and gazed in astonished
appreciation at the beautiful rugs and golden vessels, it is
said that he exclaimed: "So this is Royalty!" He would
have no puritanical prickings of conscience when, during the

last year of his life, he sat upon the gold-canopied throne of the Great Kings of Persia and gave greeting to the messengers who came from all parts of the world to honour him. But the assumption of such regal splendour at public functions is no proof that "success had dazzled him"; Alexander and his generals soon learned that such royal state was necessary in the East. Many of our Viceroys of India admitted that they enjoyed the pomp and magnificence which was customary and expected by Oriental subjects. That enthusiastic crowds waited day and night in rain and cold to watch the coronation procession of Queen Elizabeth II in 1953 proves the strength of the appeal of pageantry to mankind; it stirs the imagination of all classes and ages.

Detractors of Alexander say that he desired the flattery accorded so lavishly by the poets who eulogised his exploits, but with equal authority one hears that he often smiled at their licence. Aristotle warned him that only tyrants liked flattery; free men despised it.[1] To an adulator who saw him bleeding from a wound, the King jested that one must agree[1] that this was mortal blood, not the ichor of the gods. To his Persian wife, who advised him to seek recognition as a son of Zeus, he replied; "I decline divine honours, for I was born a mortal, subject to death, and I must beware of such things, for they endanger the soul." Indeed, it is obvious that he required no flatterers to tell him that he was superior to most men; he could not be unaware that he inspired men to do their best, and that in every emergency they responded to his call. Although he knew that all depended upon him, there was no occasion for undue pride in that fact. Why should any man be "dazzled by his success" when such success was earned only after long preparation and strenuous work? He would know well the teaching of the Hellenes that pride brought down the wrath of the gods. His quiet remark after having watched the death of Calanus on his pyre sheds a truer light upon his character: "That seer has vanquished more powerful enemies than I" (p. 132).

After the passage over the Gedrosian desert and the return to Carmania Alexander must have endured heavy mental

[1] *Politics*, V, xi, 1314a.

stress which he could share with no confidant. No human being could long continue the pace which he set as his duty toward his subjects; he was occupied from morn to night with military, scientific, civilian and other expert advisers. Like the great British pioneers who 2,000 years later dedicated their lives to govern India, Alexander used to sit outside his tent all day listening to the suppliants who awaited his judgment concerning the misdeeds of the satraps who had oppressed them. Nor could he delegate much of this work to any subordinate when even Harpalus, a friend of his youth, had so grievously betrayed his trust. It is recorded that when completely exhausted he recuperated with long spells of sleep, sometimes for thirty-six hours on end.

Critics have made the reproach that at this time of his reign Alexander became "more prone to wrath", as if this were a criminal characteristic. But every man who has been obliged to carry on, pressed by overwork and constant interruptions, will understand and sympathise. With ever-increasing responsibilities, years of fighting, serious wounds and consequent impairment of strength, the King was bound to become more peremptory, more impatient, more subject to outbursts of rage. In these moods it is said that his eyes flashed, his lips were contorted, his aspect became so menacing and so terrifying that it was never forgotten by the wrongdoer whose conduct had evoked his anger. Every great commander has experienced how hard it is to maintain composure when decisions on vital matters involving the lives of thousands must be swiftly made, orders issued instantaneously, and their performance ensured. He could consult on equal terms with no one; for in that century who could have understood his projects for the future of his empire? Living always with a moving army, constantly revolving in his mind the enormous problems of both military and civilian administration, he must have learned the impossibility of attempting to share his anxieties with any of his officers; probably not even Hephaestion could have given more help than that of a sympathetic listener. He rarely spoke about his plans until they had been considered and matured; once he had formed his resolutions, his persuasive faculty gained the obedience of his officers and men.

In Persia Alexander had suffered many injuries and periods of illness which affected his physical reserve. His skull had been so heavily hit by a stone that his sight had been impaired for a time; a bone in the leg had been splintered; his neck, shoulders, arms, ankle and body had received many wounds. At the Malli fortress an arrow had pierced the chest so deeply that he fainted and lost much blood. In the 1914-1918 war in Europe many wounds became so septic that amputation was necessary; soil contamination was the chief cause. In the pure air and the uncultivated mountains of Asia, wounds would not be thus infected and therefore could heal without widespread poisoning of the whole system. On several occasions, though poisoned by drinking the impure water of marshy regions, Alexander had been obliged to ride on, even to fight, while tortured with dysentery. It is now known that one of its organisms can lie latent in the body for many years, and then give rise to internal abscesses which invade the blood stream and are fatal without prompt treatment with modern drugs. Some say that in the last year of his life the King looked unwell and moved with stiffness; with such a history it would be surprising if so many wounds and illness had not left their mark upon the strong constitution of the Alexander who crossed the Hellespont.

Alexander wrote frequently to his mother, to Antipater, to Aristotle and other friends, but after his death in Babylon his correspondence fell into the hands of his enemies in Macedonia and bears certain evidence of having been altered to suit the purpose of his calumniators, especially of Cassander, the usurper of his throne. It is now established that practically all the supposed letters were forgeries (p. 186). With clever omissions, additions and modifications, letters can convey meanings entirely different from those intended by the writer.

Only fragments of the addresses which inspired his army have reached posterity. From time to time he called a council of war to whom he explained his plans and invited discussion; as a rule his exposition was so concise and practical that he carried all with him. Napoleon, too, had that gift of eloquence combined with clear and rapid thought which appears to be a feature possessed by the great captains in history. Seven of the speeches reported by Arrian have been analysed by Tarn, who decided that two can be regarded as true accounts—the practical, to-the-point explanation given before the siege of Tyre (p. 36) and the conclusion of the lengthy address to the mutineers at Opis (p. 134).

Strabo (born about 64 B.C.) was a widely travelled and prolific author. Although most of his work has been lost, his seventeen treatises of geography have come down to posterity almost intact. His references to the life and character of Alexander occur most often as quotations from the writings of Aristobulus and Eratosthenes; as only fragments of these writers now exist, Strabo's allusions have considerable interest. Incidentally, his information concerning Alexander's sojourn in Eastern Persia, the Khyber Pass and the Punjab affords further proof, if such is needed, of the civilising effect of the Macedonians on the tribes who became adherents of Alexander, as did the majority after experience of his clemency.

Alexander was profoundly influenced by the wise education received in early youth from Aristotle. This great thinker, as a student of Plato, taught his royal pupil to discuss with his tutor subjects which to-day are learned only in universities: natural science, philosophy, religion, politics and government. Throughout Asia the King, interested in every branch of knowledge, never failed to despatch to Aristotle samples and reports of the plants, the animals, the soil, and information concerning the conditions of the people of every country through which he passed. Aristotle wrote for the guidance of Alexander a special treatise on the duties of a monarch toward his people; a king was bound to work for the benefit of those whom he ruled. There is ample evidence that Alexander endeavoured to fulfil that duty when he became the Great King of Asia.

Aristotle believed—as, indeed, did most thinkers of that

time—that a slave population was necessary, and that some men and races were "natural slaves". Greek civilisation being regarded as the highest, defeated enemies should be treated as subjects or slaves; but with experience of a wider world, Alexander no longer upheld that division of mankind. After Alexander's death Eratosthenes wrote that he agreed with the victor of Asia that it was more true to divide mankind according to their good and their bad qualities, for many Greeks were bad and many barbarians were good. As Alexander had declared that "God is the Father of all men, but the best he made peculiarly his own", this explained, said Eratosthenes, why he "disregarded his advisers and welcomed as many as he could of fair repute".

Of supreme importance was the moral training received during adolescence from Aristotle; a man's whole life can be made or marred by the instruction he receives during those impressionable years. Alexander was taught that the body should be the servant, never the master of the spirit; self-control, greatness of soul and intellect should be the constant aim of every man. We have seen that during his campaign he had endeavoured to live in accordance with those ideals, and how bitter had been his repentance and remorse when, overcome by wrath, he had slain Cleitus. Although his friends attempted to persuade him that he had been tried beyond endurance, he never made any excuse for his evil deed.

Another principle maintained by Aristotle was that the "pursuit of the Good" demands the energising of the soul in excellence (*arete*) during a full life of action. Moments of insight should never be permitted to go to waste, but be utilised by being harnessed to practical deeds. Ideals firmly planted in youth provide, as it were, a coat of armour which cannot be penetrated by the temptations to self-indulgence which assail most of those who rise to power. The often quoted "Power corrupts" does not hold true when it has been gained by the conscientious work of one whose aims are noble, based upon a foundation of solid rock. Such men have proved to be incorruptible, and of these Alexander provides a historic example. Both Plato and Aristotle stated that as power in the hands of the best men ensured the best type of government, the people should entrust supreme authority to such outstanding individuals. Jung has pointed out that the collective unconscious of a community appears to demand the leadership of a great man, a superman, a hero to whom they desire to look for guidance.

Aristotle, renowned for his researches in natural science, was equally interested in politics, art, ethics and religion. His attitude towards religion appears to have deeply influenced his royal pupil; testimony comes from the historian Polybius, a Greek officer taken prisoner when Rome overran Macedonia. He wrote (Book V, 10)[1]: "Alexander the Great was so enraged with Thebes that he sold its inhabitants into slavery and levelled the city with the ground; yet . . . he was careful not to outrage religion, and took the utmost precautions against involuntary damage being done to the temples or any part of their sacred enclosures. When he crossed into Asia to avenge on the Persians the impious outrages they had inflicted on the Greeks he did his best to exact full penalty from men, but refrained from injuring places dedicated to the gods; though it was precisely with such that the injuries of the Persians in Greece had been most conspicuous." Those who dismiss Alexander's scrupulous care to carry out all religious observances as a proof that he was "very young", and "had a simple piety", do not realise that he was bound to follow the ritual customs of his time. Being the giant that he was, there can be little doubt that he held the higher vision which underlies the external or public ceremonies of religion. This is confirmed by the fact that he once remonstrated with Aristotle for having written lines which revealed to the average man the esoteric meaning which should be entrusted only to initiates (p. 265). Aristotle replied that what he had written could be understood only by those who had attended his lectures.

When in India the Macedonians met a strange religious sect; naked, penniless, yet content, several of them approached Alexander and stood before him, striking the

[1] E. S. Shuckburgh, Vol. I.

ground with their feet. Asked to explain this unusual form of activity they replied: "No man possesses more land than that on which he can stand. With all your conquests you will at length have no more ground than that on which your body will rest." Strabo tells how Alexander showed interest in another community of men who went about naked, practised fortitude, and were highly respected for their wisdom. Those who desired to speak with them were obliged to go to see them as they lay, stood or walked, ever unclothed, even on the warmest days when the ground was so hot that it caused pain to the bare feet. Alexander despatched Onesicritus as his messenger to converse with them. The wisest man in the group declared that he admired this King who, although head of so great an empire, yet desired to acquire wisdom; he declared that never before had he seen a philosopher in arms. The example of these ascetics may have provided one of the many subjects introduced by the King for discussion during the evening meal. The life-denying principles of the Indian ascetics would appear strange indeed to the alert, inquiring minds, life-affirming, of the Greeks and the Macedonians. When one recalls the debates of university students one would give much to have some record of the talk of those eager young men when they contrasted the results of the active and the contemplative existence. As the *Maha-Bharata*, the Indian epic poem which corresponds with the Greek *Iliad*, had been known about 1,500 years before Christ, it is probable that Calanus, the Indian hermit who had accompanied the Western army all the way to Susa, would have held conversations with Alexander on the subject of its teaching in the *Bhagavadgita*, the Lord's Song. In that noble poem Arjuna, the warrior hero, reluctant to slay his kindred in battle, is at last convinced by Krishna, the supreme god, that war is not inconsistent with the duty of the individual to cultivate the highest spiritual ideal. Certainly in Alexander the activity of the conqueror and the dream of the mystic existed side by side.

The achievements of modern science have blinded many to the reality of the spirit moving along inexorably below the conscious mind; but when we consider life's pattern in silence, as in a wilderness, we find that history records many examples of outstanding individuals who say that they felt driven by a power within which urged them on to undertake tasks demanding superhuman strength. Some great military leaders believed that they felt as if drawn by a guiding or a beckoning hand—Caesar, Napoleon, Gordon, Joan of Arc, were certain of that fact. Sir Francis Younghusband— politician, soldier, explorer, mystic—and even some of our living soldiers expressed a similar conviction. And many great statesmen, as our Empire developed, shared that sense of a divine guidance.

On his return to Babylon in 323 B.C. Alexander threw himself with zeal into preparations for the exploration of the Arabian coast. He had lost his confidant, Hephaestion, and apparently felt less certain about the immediate future; the warnings which had preceded his entry into Babylon must have contributed to depression. In those days the oracles were often accurate: presentiment, precognition, sub-conscious awareness of destiny, "Coming events casting their shadows before"—call it what you will; in antiquity it was recognised that "there's a divinity that shapes our ends, rough-hew them how we will". Before the nineteenth century, prophecy, dreams and other manifestations were regarded with respect; but it is only in recent years, owing to the work of the Society for Psychical Research and Jung's Institute of Analytical Psychology, that we have begun to understand how important a part these have played and still play in the history of mankind.

The subject of geography absorbed the attention of the civilisation of ancient Greece; even the poets and the philosophers desired to know the position of the sun and its relationship to the earth. From many sources we learn that Alexander, sharing that interest, sought to discover the limits of the Habitable World and the Ocean then supposed to surround it. Explore he must! "The Habitable World!" The very words possess a lure, a magical quality of appeal. During the last days of his life, sleepless, racked with fever, still the King talked of exploration with Nearchus, postponing the date of departure from day to day as his malady made new inroads on his physical strength. And after Arabia there remained his promise to Pharasmanes that together they would sail over the Caspian Sea and find whether it had any communication with the great encircling Ocean.

The excitement of war and danger appeals to youth; with the passage of the years this is often replaced by a love of adventure, such as is experienced by the mountain climber who on the summits is filled with an exaltation rarely known to the dweller in the crowded cities of the plains. To-day we admire and wonder at the courage of those who strive to reach the Polar regions and the peaks of Everest. Such men are of the mystic temperament, and respond to an emotion beyond the grasp of the intellect; only dimly do they understand the attraction of these goals; humanity lives and vanishes, but these remain for ever, symbols of the Eternal. Alexander was one of that company. Often he walked in mountain solitudes, sometimes seeking hidden paths to victory on the hills but also, it is said, hoping to reach the majestic heights of the Olympian gods. That abode of the deities he would know to be but a poetical fantasy, but the call to wander ever higher endures throughout life in men of his emotional nature. The *Iliad* was Alexander's military guide, but as a lover of the Muses he would also understand the magic of its descriptions of Nature. Often from the high passes on the Punjab he must have watched the daily miracle of the rising sun as dawn irradiated the snowclad pinnacles, and the clouds moved above or shrouded the peaks of the vast outline of the Himalayan panorama; the sublimity of those towering mountains strikes every traveller with awe.

Historians mention that Alexander often exclaimed that he was "seized with a longing", an expression denoting that he felt impelled to attain some apparently impossible goal and must translate his emotion into practical achievement. There is no evidence that any of his generals, strong and brilliant men, were ever "seized with a longing". Few have understood this proof of Alexander's mystic temperament. Socrates, believing in his mission, told how he was guided by his Daimon at critical junctures of his life. And Joan of Arc, following the direction of her Voices, also succeeded in her mission.

The response to the mystic was so prominent a feature in the character of Alexander that it demands some examination. Bergson stated that many look on mysticism as a form of insanity or an irrational illusion. Admirably has he summarised the attitude of the sceptical: "Some are impervious to mystic experience, incapable of feeling or even of imagining it. But we also meet with people to whom music is nothing but noise, and some will express their opinion of musicians with the same anger, the same tone of personal spite. No one would think of this as an argument against music." In his illuminating volume, *Two Sources of Religion and Morality*, he writes: "The great moral figures who have made their mark on history join hands across the centuries, above our human cities; they unite in a divine city which they ask us to enter. We may not hear their voices distinctly, but the call has nevertheless gone forth, and something responds from the depth of our soul." And William James has proved that the famous Christian mystics were individuals of high mental calibre who translated their visions into useful activity. He admitted that he had no personal experience of mysticism, but that when he heard of it, he "felt an echo in his soul". Most of us, in this age dominated by science, in that respect probably belong to his company.

The word "mystic" has many meanings. The famous explorers belong to one group of mystics; we have seen that Alexander was one of these. The artists, the poets and the musicians form yet another type; their visions of Beauty lie beyond the avenue of the senses and arouse emotions of awe and reverence which convince mankind that there exists a reality beyond the confines of the intellect. We know how the Muses appealed throughout life to Alexander. Certainly no one would imagine that he resembled in any respect the Christian mystics who strove for communion with the God whom they worshipped; such rapture and ecstasy has been attained by few in any age. His mysticism lay in his firm conviction that he had a mission to extend the high ethical standard of Greek culture throughout his immense empire, and so reconcile all nations in one brotherhood.

One would have a deeper understanding of Alexander if one knew the response of the Oracle to his questions at Siwah. It is recorded that he emerged from the temple with a radiant countenance; the answer which he there received was throughout his life so sacred to him that any profane allusion to the subject aroused his intense anger. It is difficult to believe that so strong and so enduring an emotion would have been caused by a promise of personal or material benefit; the priest may have spoken of a spiritual duty, a sacred command. To no one did Alexander ever reveal the message; though aware of the rumours, guesses and conjectures concerning the Oracle, he neither denied nor confirmed them. Perhaps at that interview the seed was sown which blossomed into flower when at the Feast of Opis he spoke of his desire to be the "Reconciler of the World".

Ujfalvy's volume contains illustrations of every known bust, statue and coin considered by ancient and by modern students to represent Alexander. The bust in the British Museum is probably an idealised portrait, showing the joyous confidence of his youth, before the battle of Chaeronea (Plate II). In later years this happy expression is replaced by the lines of thoughtful maturity and authority which characterise the Hermes statue in the Louvre found in 1779 (Plate III). The Pergamum bust, discovered in 1901, now in the Acropolis at Athens, was considered by Ujfalvy to be of high value. Though long immersed in soil and water it has his special features—the furrow across the brow, deep-set eyes, leonine set of the hair and slight inclination of the head to the left (Plate IV). These points are emphasised in the well-known Lysimachus coin which ancient writers acclaimed as a faithful representation of the profile of Alexander (see Plate I).

In 1937 a book was published in which many contributors gave their memories of T. E. Lawrence, whose work in World War I gained for him the title of "The Uncrowned

King of Arabia". The aspects thus presented clearly indicate less of Lawrence than of the character of the writers who had known him. So too with so mighty a personality as that of Alexander the Great. Who among his followers was competent to form an estimate of the many facets of his character? He so far eclipsed his generals that they existed chiefly as reflections of their leader.

What is the explanation of the perennial attraction of the great men of history? Berenson introduced the word "life-enhancing", which he defined as "the ideated identification of ourselves with a person, state of being or of mind that makes us feel more alive, with zest for life, living with a more intense and radiant a life, physically, morally and spiritually, to the highest limit of our capacity". This definition describes a reaction which has been evoked in many who have studied the career of Alexander the Great.

There will always be many who look at genius through dark-coloured glasses. They do not believe in heroes; they distrust outstanding individuals and search for feet of clay when the radiance of virtue shines too brightly. None can deny that we all have feet of clay, but in the great men of history these are so insignificant that they should not be dwelt upon as if they formed the most prominent part of their stature. From the seekers for clay is born, and will ever endure, the so-called "hostile tradition" concerning Alexander of Macedon. Others prefer to believe in his "surpassing excellence"; among those was Arrian, a historian of sound judgment, who, after compiling a list of all the faults of Alexander, summed up his virtues, and pronounced as his conclusion: "He excelled all men and had no equal".

Many explanations have been advanced by thinkers who have tried to fathom the psychology of genius, but it will ever remain a mystery. Myers' definition is in keeping with modern thought: "Genius should be regarded as the power of utilising a wider range than other men can utilise of faculties innate in all." He believed that an inspiration of genius is an emergence into consciousness of ideas which have shaped themselves beyond the will, in profounder regions of the being.

Alexander provides an example of this theory. The complexity of his personality calls out a response which differs with the temperament of those who endeavour to assess the qualities of his heart and brain. From the *Iliad* one can follow the aims of the early years of his reign, but for even a dim understanding of the growth and rapid development of his character one must know something of his background and of the influences which moulded his spirit. Without some acquaintance with the history, the thought and religion of ancient Greece, it is not possible to form a just estimate of a man who in so short a span of life changed the whole world. It is for that reason that Chapters XIV and XV have been written.

CHAPTER XIV

THE CITY-STATE (THE POLIS)

Europe's debt to ancient Greece—Tributes to the city-state—The growth of communities—Beauty of Greece and Athens—Position of slaves—Types of tyrants—The work of Solon—Persian invasions of Greece—Democracy—Duties of the citizen—Religion in the city-state—Position of women—Work of Pericles—Sparta — The Peloponnesian war — The Thirty Tyrants—Rise of Macedonia—Special features of Greek culture: games; education; the theatre

THIS chapter is addressed to those who have not enjoyed the education in the classics which until recently provided a common foundation of knowledge in schools and universities. Many men and women of to-day, eminent in their own spheres of work, are unaware of the immense debt which European civilisation owes to ancient Greece. In modern days the classics tend to be more and more neglected; science has usurped the honoured position so long held by the literature of Greece and Rome. Industrialism, with its monotonous yet hurried existence, has replaced the grace, dignity and beauty which characterised the civilisation of Greece many centuries before Christ; Hellenism set an example of the Art of Living which has never been excelled.

Rome gave us Law; Greece gave us Art and Thought. Most of our culture and much of our science have been borrowed or derived from ancient Greece. The Greeks honoured pastoral and agricultural pursuits, and that attitude to life, Ruskin tells us, raised them to the highest rank of wise manhood ever reached. "Take away from us", writes Ruskin, "what they have given, and we hardly know how low the modern European would stand." At the same time the warrior was held in high esteem; the best qualities of men—their swiftness of eye and hand, coolness of nerve, self-denial, fearlessness—are called out when the struggle may end in death; a man's character is tried to the utmost when he has to confront that issue. Those who have followed Alexander's eleven years' campaign know how valiant was his response to that demand. For he was Greek in spirit; he had their alert, inquiring intellect and capacity for strong emotion. Greek civilisation was unique inasmuch as it was the first to realise the importance of educating every man to understand that he not only had a duty to the State, but should also follow a high standard of personal integrity—self-control, moderation, avoidance of excess.

For an adequate study of the Greek city-state a large book is required, but a brief summary of its history sheds light on the plans of Alexander and also on the political problems which afflict our distracted modern world, dividing nations into hostile and suspicious camps, each claiming that it alone possesses the key which will bring about the happiness of humanity.

The rise and the decline of the Polis (city-state) has attracted distinguished philosophers, politicians and historians. In Egypt, Persia and India civilisation had reached a high level long before Greece had emerged as a nation, but none has aroused so much admiration as that of the Polis. Professor Alfred Zimmern, in his exhaustive volume on the Greek Commonwealth, writes: "The city-state was the centre and inspiration of all the most characteristic achievements, culminating in the great outpouring of literature, art and practical energy, of great men and deeds, in fifth-century Athens. The world has seen nothing comparable to it either before or since."

Writing in the *Cambridge Ancient History*, Sir Ernest Barker thus concludes his survey of the city-state: "The Greek cities might never have achieved their unification by their own efforts; a larger instrument was perhaps needed for the diffusion of Greek culture. But those who have been touched by the philosophy of the Greek city-state may be permitted to stand by its grave and remember its life; and to wonder what, under happier auspices, it might have achieved, and to lament that it was not given to Greece, inspired by Athens, to lead the Mediterranean world to a unity more deep and pervading . . . larger and more permanent . . . than Rome was ever destined to achieve." Certainly there never existed so brilliant a galaxy of eminent men of intellectual distinction as those who worked in one small city before and after the fifth century B.C. Dramatists, poets, philosophers, architects, sculptors, painters, engineers, mathematicians, astronomers, historians—all were represented. It is not generally known that Europe also owes much to Greek science. Before the time of Socrates the speculation and pioneer experiments carried out by Anaximander, Thales and Democritus foreshadowed many of the discoveries of modern physics.

Aristotle described the development of the city-state. In the early days of social life small village communities consisted at first of families and their kindred; as these became more numerous, friends joined to aid each other in their daily tasks. Later, when laws were arranged for the village and surrounding country, one or more members were elected as representatives to express the will of the community. The land was divided, one part being reserved for a family, its animals and pasturage; the other, cultivated for the use of the whole village, was known as the common land. In time, the most able men came to own the portion near their homes, and as the population increased, houses and comforts were gained by the most industrious; such individuals usually save for old age and future emergencies. In different regions the laws regulating property varied according to the character of the people.

The village community framed its local legislation concerning arable land and building, also special religious rites and ceremonies. Every community united in the worship of its own guardian deity. Because the gods were believed to dwell in the hills, woods and rivers, they could mingle with mankind, and therefore outstanding men were thought to be descended from heroes, who were regarded as the children of the gods.

From the union of adjacent villages a city developed. Modern authorities have traced that similar gradual stages occurred not only in Greece and India, but also in France, Italy, Britain and many other countries. In small cities men had to struggle to gain a minimum of food and shelter; they had no time to develop art, culture and abstract thought. After the union of many cities possessing common traditions, laws and deities, a State developed. In the small community there could be only what Aristotle called "bare life"; in the State, what he called "the good life" became possible. Only then could labour be divided, so that some members performed the manual work and thus left the time necessary for the work of philosophers, artists and professional classes.

Greece is a beautiful country, with mountains and hills, often flat-topped, with precipitous cliffs, well-wooded, but with few forests. Its soil is not fertile; its cultivation entailed heavy labour. Almost surrounded by the sea, Greece had fine harbours and became a great sea power. The climate is good, for though the winters are cold there is little snow; the summers, warm by day, have refreshing breezes at night. Athens became the chief city of Attica, a region extending some twenty-five miles round the town; owing to the barren nature of its land, Attica had not attracted the attention of predatory neighbours. Athens has a situation of unusual beauty, sloping to the south with a panoramic view to the sea; on the north the Acropolis dominates the city just as Arthur's Seat rises in rocky majesty behind Edinburgh. The atmosphere has a peculiar radiance, exhilarating and inspiring. Thus Nature bestowed on Athens the stage on which the architects and artists created a material loveliness which has never been surpassed in any age or land.

In the great time of Athens the people lived very simply, chiefly on bread, cheese, eggs, fish and light wines. Even when buildings of imperishable beauty were being erected on the Acropolis there was no ostentatious display, no luxurious housing or rich furnishings in the homes of the citizens, and strict economy was practised in the construction of the temples and other architectural masterpieces which adorned the town.

The history of Greece has many lessons for the modern politician. It is believed that the Homeric era, with its great kings, ended about 1000 B.C. and was followed by a time when the people were ruled by Aristocrats, men of high integrity, culture and traditions. Later, the wealthy few took over the reins of power, established an oligarchic form of government which in many cities led to revolt, and so began the age of a model form of democracy.

SLAVERY

It is a common, but mistaken, belief that the high standard of Greek civilisation was based on slavery. Most countries of the ancient world had, in fact, more slaves, but not the fine culture of the Greeks. The Greek nation was the first to question the justice of slavery and to take legal measures to protect the interests of slaves; it was illegal to treat a slave with violence. In Greece the word slave did not convey the modern meaning; the relationship resembled rather that of master and servant.

The number of slaves varied with the influx of prisoners of war, piracy and their birth rate; at one time they accounted for a fourth of the population; at another they were more numerous than the free men. Many citizens farmed their own limited property, as they could not afford to employ more than one or two slaves; even in the great days of Athens, home life was so simple that little domestic help was needed.

Although slaves had no right to vote, those who were skilled artisans, bakers or tailors, were treated as were free men in similar occupations. Slaves could buy their freedom, or gain it as a reward for special service. They were often employed for police, military and other public duties. Vase paintings prove that in the streets they could not be distinguished from citizens; some became more wealthy than their masters. Demosthenes said that in Athens slaves received better treatment than did the citizens of many countries. Plato urged that there should be a distinction between Greek prisoners and those of other nations; Aristotle pointed out that where Hellenes and foreigners worked together, the foreigners obeyed the Greeks and acted as if "natural slaves". Slaves were treated with brutality in Egypt and Syracuse, but in Greece only in the silver mines did slaves—men, women and children—suffer so severely that many succumbed and died.

TYRANTS

The title of Tyrant is so often mentioned in histories of Greece that it is advisable to have a clear understanding of its significance in those distant centuries. To-day the name denotes a strong ruler who governs with harshness and uses his power for his own benefit. But in antiquity a tyrant was not necessarily a ruthless ruler. In his book, *Politics*, Aristotle describes at length the various types of tyranny recognised in his time. In the early days of a State people were content to serve a hereditary monarch; when the King had fine qualities of mind and character this form of government made for stability and gained the willing obedience of all his subjects. For permanently successful rule the King must possess a degree of almost superhuman unselfishness, always placing the benefit of the community above his personal interests, but too often it happened that his son, or other successor, less able and worthy, lost the respect of the community. Such rulers belonged to the self-seeking type of tyrant who took advantage of his power. As even the higher grade of tyrant tended to forget that it was his duty to aid all citizens to gain sufficient leisure for the "good life", the name tyrant came to have so evil a reputation with the Greeks, lovers of the liberty of the individual within the State, that it was considered a meritorious deed to rid the world of self-seeking tyrants. Yet another type of tyrant was recognised—one who encouraged trade with other cities and even with foreign countries, thus introducing into Greece fresh vistas of thought as well as the material benefit accruing from intercourse with distant lands. Hence such rulers as

Pericles and Alexander could be called tyrants without any reproach implied.

About 594 B.C. Greece entrusted all power to a great statesman, Solon, noted for his tact and fine character. During an economic crisis all classes clamoured for his election as Archon, the chief office in the State. He revived industry so that there were no unemployed, and instituted novel reforms so important and far-reaching that Athens became the greatest city in Greece. Fathers were obliged to educate theirs sons for useful work; women were forbidden to wear extravagant clothing. None could possess more land than they could cultivate, and when a man proved that he could enrich the soil he was given the right to own it. So successful was this measure that toward the end of the Peloponnesian war it was estimated that only 5,000 of the voters were not freeholders.

Solon divided the citizens into four groups, rated according to their incomes. Even the poorest had the right to be admitted to the meetings of the Assembly, and to vote for the election and the annual review of the conduct of the magistrates. Thus, as Aristotle said, the foundation was laid for democracy. Perhaps Solon's most important innovation was the institution of courts of justice, the jury and the magistrates being chosen by all the citizens. It was considered a duty incumbent upon the citizen to know the character of the magistrates whom he could elect for executive posts; this stipulation disqualified from voting those who were illiterate and impoverished. Solon advocated a strong middle class, with moderate means; wealth was not permitted to accumulate in the hands of the few nor to be acquired by those in authority; that always led to a class who lived in luxury, and that spelt oligarchy. Another feature of Solon's rule was his discouragement of party strife and invective in public life; passion and anger were banished from political discussion; problems had to be considered in an atmosphere of calm reasonableness. This attitude, typical of the Greek spirit, provides a marked contrast to the abusive language and the insinuations contained in many modern political speeches and propaganda.

Under Solon's reforms the average citizen was content, for he had a full share in the government of his own city; if worthy, he could be one of those selected to serve on the Council which legislated for his city. On the other hand, under an oligarchic system a citizen lost interest, having no responsibility; he could not choose those in authority, nor vote on subjects which concerned his life and work. When Solon departed on a long journey to the East, hoping that all would be carried on as he had arranged, so many disputes soon arose among men ambitious of power that after twelve years his classification was reversed. His position was taken by Peisistratus, an example of the good tyrant who placed the community first. He advanced education, religion, art and commerce, and ended the conflict between the rich and the poor; but after his death in 527 B.C. his sons developed the characteristics of the evil type of tyrant, and oligarchy threatened to undo much of Solon's work. But once against the reasonable spirit of Greece came to the rescue, and under Cleisthenes wealthy members of the community could not gain undue representation or influence in the governing council of the city-state.

Athens underwent many crises after the time of Solon and his successors. In the Peloponnesian region the Lacedae-monians had grown so strong that Athens acknowledged that Sparta had earned the right to lead Greece when the Persians attacked the country (p. 21). But, when the great struggle came in 490 B.C., it was the Athenians who sacrificed themselves—throwing their army against the invaders with unexampled bravery they won the famous victory of Marathon. While Xerxes, the son of the defeated Persian King, Darius I, was preparing for a third invasion, Themistocles, an Athenian statesman, advocated the building of a fleet, and fortunately succeeded in persuading Athens to adopt his at first unpopular advice. In 480 B.C. Xerxes bridged the Dardanelles and, with an immense army, ravaged Attica and destroyed much of Athens. Acting on the advice of the Oracle of Delphi, the Athenians fled to the island of Salamis and placed their army on their newly built ships. From his throne on a hill overlooking the sea, Xerxes watched the destruction of his fleet by the Greek navy. His army wintered in Greece and in the spring again sacked Athens; this outrage was never forgotten by Greece or Macedonia. When at last Sparta and Greece combined their forces, the Persians were driven out. But the courage of the Athenians had made them supreme; Athens became the glory of Greece. This led to so much jealousy that the competition for leadership between Athens and Sparta flared up in 431 B.C. with the Peloponnesian war.

Athens in the fifth century B.C. is said to have presented the perfect example of the city-state; not only on account of its method of government but also because art, literature and every form of intellectual achievement reached a level higher than that of any previous civilisation. But this ideal condition could not endure for ever. After the war with Sparta and the disastrous failure in 415 B.C. of the Sicilian invasion instigated by Alcibiades—extravagant, ambitious, and traitorous—Athens faced difficulties resembling those which confront the modern politican. What system can alleviate, except temporarily, unequal distribution of wealth and opportunity for culture when men are not born equal in intellect or character? Even in one family some rise to high positions by assiduous devotion to work; others, idle or careless, fall into poverty. Aristotle maintained that the solution lay in wise education in ethics and the duties of the citizen. Admission to citizenship, especially in Athens, was a jealously guarded privilege. A citizen was not at liberty to travel without permission nor was he welcome in distant towns. Hence the despair of men who had been banished from their native cities; especially after a long life in Athens they were never reconciled to dwell elsewhere.

Both Plato and Aristotle desired a strong middle class, because it maintained the institutions and preserved the traditions on which depend the customs and manners of social life. Greek thinkers emphasised the importance of agriculture and the need to aid those who work on the land; politicians who rarely leave our large modern towns too often forget that the basis of human existence lies in the correct management of Mother Earth. Knowing this, Alexander always ordered that the nomads and semi-savage tribes whom he subdued should be instructed how to render their territories fertile.

No serious Greek thinker would have advocated universal suffrage, which places power in the hands of those least qualified to judge the ability of those whom they elect. Every citizen was free to speak and to vote in the meetings of the Assembly; he did not elect paid representatives whose decisions, however unwelcome, the modern democrat must obey. This encouragement of political discussion led to precision of language and the brilliant oratory characteristic of Greece. Aristotle considered that the voter ought to be acquainted with the character of the men whom he chose for high office, for history provided the lesson that when a community became too numerous, it could not be governed with wisdom; he suggested 100,000 as the ideal number of citizens.

The citizen of the Polis, obliged to give active co-operation in civil and military duties, could not be absent from the Assembly during debates on local government and on military defence. This system worked admirably until the communities became numerous, when jealousies and irreconcilable points of view were bound to arise. As the local councils could not always agree about the interchange of goods and the importation of food-stuffs, free communication was hampered with distant countries and even throughout Greece. Still greater divergence of opinion occurred when practical details for defensive measures against foreign enemies were considered. The age-old puzzle then arose: how could a deliberating committee of citizens formulate the instantaneous decisions required when war is threatened? Time was lost in discussions when every minute was precious. Graver consequences followed when the Assembly of one city decided to resist the foe, whilst another community, not far distant, preferred to aid that enemy.

Although free to think, to speak and to vote, every Greek citizen was bound to conform to the religious rites and ceremonies of the State of which he was a member. Greece had no State Church, but no man was permitted to omit his duties to the gods, nor could he forget their prevailing influence on his life. The predominant role played by religion in every sphere of daily work is described in the following chapter.

In the great days of Greece, Athenian women had no say in political affairs. The Hetaerae class, often the mistresses of distinguished men, were sought as hostesses and companions. Some were highly educated; Aspasia was renowned for her political wisdom and her teaching of rhetoric. She became the wife of Pericles (illegally, as she was not Athenian by birth). It has been assumed that the majority of women had little freedom outside the home, but recent scholars have found ample evidence from vase-paintings, sculpture and monuments that women, loved and honoured as wives and mothers, also enjoyed outdoor activities, and led a varied social life. Long before the fifth century Homer had delineated women of outstanding character and attainments; later, the great dramatists portrayed them as so noble and courageous in times of endurance that they commanded the respect of men and gods. Plato was not the first nor the only thinker who urged that women should be educated to share the administrative duties of the citizen.

Democracy in Athens reached its zenith before and during the first period of the rule of Pericles; he always explained to the citizens who elected him the reasons for his decisions, and convinced them of the wisdom of his policy. Many writers have analysed the perfection of that Golden Age when the interests of the State and the individual were identical. Under Pericles, Athens became a strong naval power, which gave her many advantages during the early part of his reign. It is difficult to avoid exaggeration when one considers the amazing outburst of energy brought about during the fifth century. Scholars say that the general level of intelligence in that age was never surpassed during later centuries in Europe. Greek methods of reasoning had not made further progress, and after Pericles their knowledge of science and mathematics was greater than that of the Middle Ages, when Greece and the Greek language had been forgotten.

In 431 B.C. came the long-drawn-out tragedy of the Peloponnesian war. The full story of that struggle, with its terrible consequences, is narrated in the vivid pages of the historian Thucydides. An epidemic of plague added to the horrors of the devastation wrought by the war with Sparta and with Sicily; it carried off a quarter of the population of Attica, and in 429 B.C. Pericles himself fell victim to its ravages. Under his noble leadership democracy succeeded; without his guidance the Golden Age of Greece soon passed.

PERICLES

Pericles (490-429 B.C.) used his power for the best purposes of the State. He was a man of noble birth and of such outstanding ability that he was many times elected ruler of Attica. Thucydides states that he derived his authority from his transparent integrity; he controlled the multitude, leading rather than being led by them; and thus, though "still in name a democracy, Athens was in fact ruled by her greatest citizen". Under him Athens became the greatest of all the Greek cities, and gained immortal fame.

Pericles hoped to bring about the unification of the Greek communities, so that they would combine to withstand foreign invaders, but the jealousy of Sparta prevented the realisation of this policy. The city-states numbered about 250; some had the 100,000 citizens considered by Aristotle as the ideal maximum for the perfect functioning of the Polis; others had few citizens, and only four or five miles of surrounding land. But each clung firmly to its complete independence and decided its own measures for trade and war. Just as we see today in modern Europe, communities with separate traditions, customs and beliefs could not agree to unite and present a solid front to a foreign enemy who in times of peace is regarded only as a distant hypothesis. In the fourth century the question arose again when Isocrates urged Philip of Macedon to bring about the unification of the city-states (p. 5).

Thucydides has recorded the famous funeral oration of Pericles which has evoked the admiration of the world for over 2,000 years. In books dealing with the fifth century many authors cite only a few lines from that great speech, and then remark that it is too well known to require repetition. But in modern days, the literature of the classics is so little known that it is advisable to give a longer excerpt here. Pericles spoke thus:

> Our form of government does not enter into rivalry with the institutions of others. We do not copy our neighbours, but are an example to them. It is true that we are called a democracy, for the administration is in the hands of the many and not of the few. But while the law secures equal justice to all alike in their private disputes, the claim of excellence is also recognized; and when a citizen is in any way distinguished, he is preferred to the public service, not as a matter of privilege, but as the reward of merit. Neither is poverty a bar; a man may benefit his country whatever be the obscurity of his condition. There is no exclusiveness in our public life, and in our private intercourse we are not suspicious of one another, nor angry with our neighbour if he does what he likes; we do not put on sour looks at him, which, though harmless, are not pleasant. While we are thus unconstrained in our private intercourse, a spirit of reverence pervades our public acts; we are prevented from doing wrong by respect for authority and for the laws, having an especial regard for those which are ordained for the protection of the injured, as well as for those unwritten laws which bring upon the transgressor the reprobation of the general sentiment. And we have not forgotten to provide for our weary spirits many relaxations from toil; we have regular games and sacrifices throughout the year; at home the style of our life is refined; and the delight which we daily feel in all these things helps to banish melancholy. Because of the greatness of our city

the fruits of the whole earth flow in upon us, so that we enjoy the goods of other countries as freely as of our own. Then, again, our military training is in many respects superior to that of our adversaries. Our city is thrown open to the world, and we never expel a foreigner or prevent him from seeing or learning anything of which the secret if revealed to an enemy might profit him. We rely not upon management and trickery, but upon our own hearts and hands. And in the matter of education, whereas they from early youth are always undergoing laborious exercises which are to make them brave, we live at ease, and yet are ready to face the perils which they face. . . . And here is the proof. The Lacedaemonians come into Attica not by themselves, but with their whole confederacy following; we go alone into a neighbour's country; and although our opponents are fighting for their homes and we on a foreign soil, we have seldom any difficulty in overcoming them.

If then we prefer to meet danger with a light heart but without laborious training, and with a courage which is gained by habit and not enforced by law, are we not greatly the gainers? Since we do not anticipate the pain, although, when the hour comes, we can be as brave as those who never allow themselves to rest; and thus, too, our city is equally admirable in peace and in war. For we are lovers of the beautiful, yet simple in our tastes, and we cultivate the mind without loss of manliness. Wealth we employ, not for talk and ostentation, but there is a real use for it. To avow poverty with us is no disgrace; the true disgrace is in doing nothing to avoid it. An Athenian citizen does not neglect the State because he takes care of his own household; and even those of us who are engaged in business have a very fair idea of politics. We alone regard a man who takes no interest in public affairs, not as a harmless, but as a useless character; and if few of us are originators, we are all sound judges of a policy. The great impediment to action is, in our opinion, not discussion but the want of that knowledge which is gained by discussion preparatory to action. For we have a peculiar power of thinking before we act, and of acting too, whereas other men are courageous from ignorance but hesitate upon reflection. And they are surely to be esteemed the bravest spirits who, having the clearest sense both of the pains and pleasures of life, do not on that account shrink from danger. In doing good, again, we are unlike others; we make our friends by conferring, not by receiving favours. . . .

To sum up, I say that Athens is the school of Hellas, and that the individual Athenian in his own person seems to have the power of adapting himself to the most varied forms of action with the utmost versatility and grace. This is no passing and idle word, but truth and fact; and the assertion is verified by the position to which these qualities have raised the State. For in the hour of trial Athens alone among her contemporaries is superior to the report of her. No enemy who comes against her is indignant at the reverses which he sustains at the hands of such a city; no subject complains that his masters are unworthy of him. And we shall assuredly not be without witnesses; there are mighty monuments of our power which will make us the wonder of this and of succeeding ages. For we have compelled every land, every sea, to open a path for our valour, and have everywhere planted eternal memorials of our friendship and of our enmity.

Pericles made Athens the most beautiful of all the Greek cities. The edifices constructed on the Acropolis, the hill overlooking the clustered houses of the town, although now in ruins, remain to astonish and delight the architects and the artists of to-day. Especially is the exquisite beauty and the architectural design of the Parthenon Temple recognised as an unequalled masterpiece. The statues on its frieze were executed by Pheidias, whose sculpture represents the Greek spirit at its zenith: calm, dignified, restrained, beautiful. Other buildings on the Acropolis—the Erechtheum, gymnasium, concert hall and baths—designed by the architect, Ictinus, were adorned by Pheidias, who controlled and supervised every detail of the work.

Even the mutilated sculpture of ancient Greece is valued by connoisseurs and given a prominent position in the museums of modern Europe. In 1801 Lord Elgin rescued part of the Parthenon frieze from enemy gunfire; artists travel far to-day to study it in our British Museum. Not all the Greek statuary is executed in cold white marble; the Greeks enjoyed colour and sometimes added paint, or encased it in ivory and gold. Especially were the representations of the great gods richly adorned. The Olympian Zeus, forty feet high, was clothed in gold, the throne and pedestal studded with precious stones, with free use of ivory, ebony, and exquisitely chased figures.

Many artists have learned the anatomy of the muscular system from the Greek statues of athletes. The relationship of strength with nudity is little realised in a climate where exposure to the open air and sunshine is too often an invitation to catarrhal maladies. When sunlight cures were investigated early in this century by Rollier in Switzerland, he was astonished to find how the muscles developed, even in children who lay motionless in bed for many months. But in ancient Greece it was taught that health of the body contributed to the growth of the spirit, and five centuries before Christ Herodotus extolled exposure to sunlight as one of Nature's most potent remedies.

As the Peloponnesian war dragged on the people became less virile; a new generation criticised its great predecessors. "Call no man happy until he is dead" was an oft-repeated saying in Greece; examples of its truth were provided by the fate of many of the famous men of Attica. Themistocles had saved Athens by persuading the authorities to build a fleet, then cunningly induced Xerxes to meet it at Salamis and witness the defeat of his own navy. Yet not so long after this service Themistocles was condemned to banishment and fled for shelter to Persia. Anaxagoras, the Ionian philosopher (500-428 B.C.) taught natural science in Athens for thirty years. Then his doctrine that objects were created, not by chance, but by an unknown power which shaped them, gave rise to suspicion; he was accused of impiety and sentenced to death—only the pleading of Pericles altered the decree to one of lifelong banishment from his beloved Athens. Pheidias was indicted and tried for theft, accused of appropriating for his own use materials supplied from public funds. When the gold and ivory covering of his statues was removed, weighed, and found to be correct, he was acquitted. But his detractors, searching for further defects, found that on the back of the shield of the statue of Athena, visible to ships entering the harbour, were portraits of himself and Pericles; this was construed as "an insult to the goddess". Pheidias was imprisoned in 432 B.C., banished, and died from poison or other unknown cause. Even Pericles was attacked; accused of extravagant expenditure on the adornment of Athens, he was able to refute the reproach by proving that every item had been planned and executed with thrift. Then the evil-minded spread scurrilous calumnies about Aspasia, his beloved and brilliant companion; as being of foreign birth, she could not plead her own cause, but was defended with such sincerity and deep emotion by Pericles that the judges unanimously pronounced in her favour. That such baseless charges could be made against the great men of Athens showed how the spirit of the people had degenerated during the years of warfare. Thucydides' description of the decline of democracy under the rule of lesser men, swayed by ambition, is summarised in Chapter XV (page 275).

SPARTA

In order to understand the long supremacy and rivalry of Sparta, it is necessary to know something about the austere manner of life of the Lacedaemonians in the fifth century. Men, women and children belonged to the State; the discipline was so severe that home and family life were practically non-existent. Sparta was the only city in Greece which had no walled defences; it lay in a fertile plain on the bank of a river and had the natural protection of a chain of mountains, some 8,000 feet high. Nominally, two Kings ruled Sparta, but its oligarchic government was in the hands of five elected Ephors. A circle of Aristocrats had unlimited power over a large slave population, the Helots, whom they exploited and treated with extreme severity. In the communal life of Sparta the men took their meals in a Mess; although marriage was encouraged, the husband only visited the wife, and returned to his camp life. Women and girls were taught to wrestle, throw quoits and javelins, and run races; during pregnancy women underwent a eugenic training so that they should produce a stalwart nation. A committee examined newly-born infants and decided whether they should live or, if weakly, be exposed to die; the babes who passed the test were reared with regular hours for food and sleep, and trained not to fear solitude nor darkness. At the age of seven the children lived with other young companions, taking their meals in tents on the streets, fighting and playing together, often unclothed.

In the seventh century, Sparta had had a high artistic standard, but this declined when war drill became compulsory; men had no time to cultivate the Muses when from twenty to sixty they spent most of their lives preparing for war. After victory the Lacedaemonians did not pursue their enemies to destroy their towns and ruin their land. Friendship between men was encouraged, as it was considered valuable for boys to have the guidance of older men. Spartan soldiers were well-groomed as they marched to battle chanting martial songs; at the Pass of Thermopylae the Persians watched 300 of these youths combing their long hair before the contest, but with their King Leonidas they died to a man rather than submit.

With this manner of upbringing Sparta grew so strong that she was regarded as the leading Greek community. Jealous of Athens she engaged in rivalry, but found that although artistic and highly educated, the Athenians were also brave warriors. In 479 B.C. the forces of Pericles and Sparta combined to defeat the Persians at Plataea, but soon after that date the old animosity returned and Sparta accepted Persian money. Many Spartan nobles and generals had become corrupted when they saw the riches of the Persians whom they had defeated; some introduced luxuries into their homes, but concealed their treasures from the austere majority of the nation. An important general, Pausanias, made treacherous overtures to Persia, but when his intrigues were discovered he had to flee for his life to a temple; the outraged populace blocked the exit with stones till he died in the sanctuary which they dared not enter.

Only Persian bribes had enabled the Lacedaemonians to continue the Peloponnesian war until Athens, exhausted, in 404 B.C. came under the dominion of Sparta, who promised to dispel tyranny; instead, she placed a Governor in every city and selected thirty Athenians to rule Athens under a constitution based on oligarchy. The actions of these men aroused so much hatred that they were known as the Thirty Tyrants. They destroyed the laws, banished those who ventured to disagree, even executed one of their number who suggested moderation. In 402 B.C. Thrasybulus, whom they had exiled, restored democracy, but although the new government lasted long it lacked the noble ideals which had characterised that of Pericles. The overtaxed rich emigrated, and unemployment became so common that many sold their services as mercenaries to foreign masters. The people were given material assistance; Aristotle calculated that at one time 20,000 were receiving State payment. Voluntary duty on the Assembly became so unpopular that members were paid for attendance. Yet commerce increased and many fine new buildings arose in Athens during the fourth century.

Fresh disputes continually recurred between the cities. Thebes and Athens combined against Sparta and defeated her in 371 B.C.; this victory was due to the great Theban leader, Epaminondas. He had formed a special company of enthusiastic young men united by romantic attachment, known as the Sacred Band, much feared because sworn to fight to victory or to death. When Thebes became powerful under Epaminondas, Athens and Thebes gradually drew apart, and with Sparta as her ally Athens fought against Thebes. In 362 B.C. Epaminondas was slain just as he had achieved victory at Mantinea.

Athens, worn out by war and plague, still retained her unique reputation, and was the centre of attraction for students of philosophy, science and literature. But an unexpected menace loomed ahead when, as described in Chapter 1, Philip of Macedon, trying to unite the city-states, took over regions of Sparta and other parts of Greece. Demosthenes warned Athens of this encroaching power. Orators had great influence over audiences listening spellbound to arguments persuading them that only by friendly relations with Persia could they keep inviolate their exemplary civilisation. One recalls the policy of appeasement preceding the European World War II. When war followed, Philip was the victor at Chaeronea; in that battle, which decided the fate of Greece, Demosthenes fought as a hoplite, and Alexander made his début as a cavalry leader.

The progress of the world would have moved along a different course if Demosthenes had come to an understanding with Alexander, who had saved Greece from Persian rule and fused the East with the West. Isocrates and others had foreseen that the independent city-states were doomed to become the prey of any foreign invader, but could have flourished under the protection of a wise monarch. Yet, as we see to-day, nationalism prevailed; Demosthenes and his colleagues clung to an outworn system of government. Many scholars maintain that Greece, united in a federation of States or included in Alexander's empire, would have developed a higher type of civilisation than that which later was provided by its Roman conquerors. Arnold Toynbee indeed suggests that if Alexander had lived longer he would have allied himself with Zeno and Epicurus (p. 288); his vision of the brotherhood of man might then have become a reality.

Several features special to the city-state should receive brief mention here.

GAMES

Moderation, balance and dignity characterised the games and athletic competitions in ancient Greece; the rough and tumble movements of modern sport would not have been tolerated. The Festival of the Olympic Games was instituted about 776 B.C. and continued at four-yearly intervals for twelve centuries. The athletes who competed in these games were highly esteemed; their only prize was a wreath of wild olive, the symbol of courage and of virtue. The name of the victor and of his community were acclaimed with honour and he was led through the city with a triumphal procession; exemption from taxation and other privileges were accorded to those of special distinction.

The association of games with religious observances strikes the modern citizen as a strange combination; to the Greek it was natural, because the gods entered into every realm of human activity. Sacrifices and holy ceremonies, speeches and epic verses, delivered by illustrious orators and poets, formed the introduction to the Olympic, Pythian and other famous festivals.

This attitude of reverence for games is understood when we know that in ancient Greece the body was regarded as an expression of the soul within, and should therefore be trained to become an object of strength and beauty, revealing in every movement dignity, poise and restraint. For his strength the athlete praised the gods and dedicated the power of his body to the service of heaven. Competitors were examined as to their qualifications for entry and took an oath that they would honestly abide by all the rules; the judges of the games were specially prepared for their office and were obliged to swear that they would carry out their duties to the best of their ability. Before the decline of the Polis on only few occasions were such sacred promises broken. At the time of the Festival a truce was made; all disputes between communities were laid aside. The competitions consisted of many types of races—between individual hoplites (men in heavy armour) and chariots with four horses. Contests took place with boxers, wrestlers (often naked), trumpeters, quoit and javelin throwers. Professional athletes were unwelcome because they did not conform to the sacred traditions of the Festival.

EDUCATION

Philosophers in ancient Greece devoted profound thought to the question—what was the right life for man? Plato and

Aristotle agreed that wise education alone could solve political difficulties. Striving after *arete*, excellence of character and work was the aim to place before the young, for the citizen should have a nobler goal than learning how to gain a living. A parade of wealth was not respected. Shelley wrote that "no other epoch in history is stamped so visibly with the image of divinity in man . . . the world owed to Greece not merely great literature and art, but a pattern of life." Music played an important role in education; it included poetry as well as melody and sound. When people had little to read they enjoyed poetry, sung or chanted, and demanded correct rhythm and accent in verses recited from generation to generation. Greek notation has been lost, but it is known that the trumpet, harp, flute, cithera and lyre were in common use. Both Plato and Aristotle carefully analysed the effect of music on health and character—a subject usually ignored in modern life.

In the *Republic* Plato wrote:

As there are two principles of human nature, one the spiritual and the other the philosophical, some god has given to man two arts, music and gymnastic. . . . And therefore musical training is a more potent instrument than any other, because rhythm and harmony find their way into the inward places of the soul, on which they mightily fasten, imparting grace and making the soul of him who is rightly educated graceful. . . . Neither are the two arts of music and gymnastic designed, as is usually supposed, the one for the training of the soul, the other for the training of the body. The teachers of both have in view chiefly the improvement of the soul. . . . The mere athlete becomes too much of a savage, and the mere musician is melted and softened beyond what is good for him. . . . And who mingles music with gymnastic in the fairest proportions . . . may be rightly called the true musician and harmonist in a far higher sense than the tuner of strings.

The Greek musical scale had at least four distinct modes;

both Plato and Aristotle recognised that these aroused different reactions in the listener. The Phrygian mode was animated and stirring; the Lydian, soft and slow; the Aeolian, soft and soothing; the Doric, simple and powerful. Plato describes their action upon the spirit:

> And when a man allows music to play upon him and to pour into the soul through the funnels of his ears those sweet and soft and melancholy airs . . . in the first stage of the process the passion of spirit which is in him is tempered like iron and made useful. . . . But if he carries on the softening and the soothing process, in the next stage he begins to melt and waste, and he becomes a feeble warrior. If the element of spirit is naturally weak in him the change is speedily accomplished, but if he has a good deal, then the power of music weakening the spirit renders him excitable.

Aristotle also devoted much consideration to the influence of music; recognising the debasing quality of certain types, he concluded: "What we have said makes it clear that music possesses the power of producing an effect upon the souls of the listeners."

Although the *Iliad* was studied by the young because it taught courage and chivalry in warfare, Plato and Aristotle condemned all poetry which dwelt on cruel and immoral deeds of gods and heroes. Stories orally transmitted from 1500 B.C. had been collected by Homer and woven into his poem of immortal beauty about 700 or 800 B.C. With the passage of the centuries its evil episodes had become modified, or expurgated, to accord with the ideals of advancing stages of culture. Although regarded as a military model, Achilles had never been a favourite; Homer had not condoned his brutal mutilation of the corpse of Hector. Alexander called Achilles his military guide, but the version of the *Iliad* which he treasured had been edited by Aristotle.

THE THEATRE

Unversed in the classics, a student once asked me why a theatre was always included in the cities which Alexander founded in the East. The market square, the temple, offices and school were necessary; but why a gymnasium and a theatre? The gymnasium of the Greek city was not only a building in which youth could take exercise; it had also bathing facilities and rooms set apart for discussions, for races and other athletic pursuits. The theatre was of great importance; it was a national institution wherein serious dramas were presented. In Athens, on two occasions in the spring of each year, the immense theatre below the Acropolis was filled with visitors who came from far and near to honour the god Dionysus.

Greek theatres were usually constructed along the side of a hill or rock. The seating accommodation in a large town such as Athens was sufficient for about 30,000 spectators; in small towns for 7,000 to 10,000.

The seats, usually built of stone, rose in tiers along a semi-circle facing the stage, which stood on the ground, or slightly raised above that level, and was backed by great doors from which issued the actors and chorus in the course of the play. There was no roof. Knowledge of acoustics was apparently more advanced than in modern days, for every word spoken on the stage was heard by the spectators in the most distant tier. Gangways with easy steps enabled the audience to gather early in the morning to take their places, carrying their baskets with provisions for the day. During the intervals between the two or three dramas which it was customary to present on the one day, the audience moved about and ate their simple meal of eggs, olives, dried fish, fruit and cheese.

To a visitor from our cold, damp, northern land, the first sight of the Greek theatre is an astonishing experience. I shall ever treasure the memory of the theatre at Epidaurus, nor shall I forget the unique beauty of that resort, which was indeed a place of healing. The invalids sent there, as to our modern spas, received more than drugs and physical methods of cure; their minds were soothed by the beauty, the peace and the radiant atmosphere of the surrounding country. The psychological effect of so much loveliness—the thickly wooded outline of the distant hills, the shepherd boys piping to their flocks of sheep and goats in fields glowing with the white trunks of slender birch trees and the pale, pastel-hued blossoms of the asphodels on their tall, fairy-like stems—all combined to aid the labour of the physicians, the priests and the attendants who in ancient times guarded the snakes which crawled by night over the bodies of the sufferers in the temple and healed their maladies while they slept.

The theatre in Greece was not primarily a place for entertainment, but for education, especially in all that concerned the relationship of the gods to mankind. In the theatre the audience learned the history, the myths and the religion of their country. Although they loved life, the Greeks never forgot the unpredictable character of the rule of the gods, which might bring to the most prosperous and powerful unexpected tragedy or death. Although plays were usually subsidised by a group of wealthy citizens, the prizes to be awarded were decided by the humble classes who formed the majority of the audience and were well able to criticise the performances; even mistakes of accent and pronunciation did not escape their attention. No radio, cinema or evanescent journalism existed to distract the mind, a circumstance which probably explains the high level of intelligence which prevailed throughout the population.

In the dramas which have descended to posterity there were few characters, often not more than two or three, the main part being taken by the Chorus. In the early dramas there were songs and dances by the Chorus, the leader of which was a poet who presented a story in honour of a god; later, dialogues took place between the leader and the Chorus. Scenery was added at a still later date. The Chorus consisted of a group of three, twelve or any number up to fifty old men, soldiers or maidens marching abreast in rows of three to the strains of vocal hymn or chant accompanied by solemn music. The dance made no sensual appeal, but evoked an emotion of awe and reverence; its stately dignity represented the thought of the deities as well as the characters of the actors. Every movement of the body, of the head, eyes, limbs, hands and fingers, was designed to convey to the initiated spectator a special meaning.

As music can arouse a depth of feeling beyond the power of language, it was employed to explain what the words and poetry were inadequate to tell. Greek drama did not so much describe the despair of victims doomed to misfortune, as show the courage or resignation with which they met the destiny they could neither alter nor avert; the tragedies displayed not only a contest between good and evil, but also the qualities called out in human beings when there is a conflict between two right courses of action and the result of a choice cannot be foreseen. The moral lesson was summarised towards the end of the play by the Chorus. The training of the Chorus must have involved much rehearsal in order to ensure that the recitation of their lines corresponded with the dance and the chant. Posture and dance; song and chant; music and poetry were so co-ordinated that all contributed to the formation of the perfect and harmonious whole characteristic of the Greek drama. The arts were honoured because they manifested not only beauty, but also an ethical or spiritual ideal unequalled by any other civilisation.

Serious plays occupied the morning; in the afternoon comedies relaxed the audience with boisterous laughter. The chief exponent of comedy was Aristophanes, who is regarded by many as the greatest of all comedians. Born in 448 B.C., he lived through the great days of Athens, the war with Sparta, and watched the decline and the lower standards of the new democracy. Of his fifty-four plays, eleven still exist. His outspokenness and ribald humour could not be presented on a modern stage; but the Greek audience relished his jests, with their references to fertility rites (often obscene) which translators now omit or modify to suit modern tastes. Yet, as a critic of public morals, Aristophanes held up to ridicule many of the leading thinkers and dramatists of his age; in his choruses he expounded his opinions of current speeches and writings. He preferred the older form of government, cultured and aristocratic, and contrasted its dignity with the blatant self-seeking tendencies of the new authorities. In *The Clouds* (423 B.C.) he protested against the fashionable teaching of the professional Sophists whose Rhetoric confused the minds of their pupils so that they could not distinguish right from wrong.

Of the tragedians, the immortal trio are Aeschylus, Sophocles and Euripides. Aeschylus (525-455 B.C.) fought in the battles of Marathon and Salamis and retired late in life to Sicily. He wrote at least seventy plays, of which there remain extant: *The Suppliants, The Persae, Seven Against Thebes, Prometheus Bound*, and the group of three which form *The Oresteia*. His dramas have the impressive utterance which we associate with the Hebrew prophets. In depicting the dealings of the gods with mankind he endeavoured to prove that the sufferings borne by successive generations were not, as generally believed, due to the wrath or jealousy of the deities, but to the presumption and pride of the victims. All Greeks were familiar in daily life with examples of prosperous and powerful men hurled from their high positions into an abyss of suffering. For his plots Aeschylus used the traditional myths and sought to explain their significance. He believed there had to be an eternal struggle between the limited capacity of the human intellect and the Divine Purpose which surveyed the whole world with all-embracing understanding. Man, he sought to prove, could avert evil consequences by curbing his ambitious passions. The characters of Aeschylus therefore move on a heroic plane, high above ordinary humanity; he was popular because he drew an audience up to the religious level desired in the theatre.

Sophocles, born in 496 B.C., lived to be over ninety and had active experience in war against the Persians. He, too approached his work from a religious aspect, and it is interesting to compare his treatment of the myths with that of Aeschylus. It is said that during his long life he produced 113 plays, but only seven of them survive entire, and fragments of others. Sophocles taught that men had infinite possibilities of greatness, and that the fall of the mighty was occasioned chiefly by their own errors. His plays were very popular and the judges awarded him many prizes.

As Euripides was Alexander's favourite dramatist, special reference must be made to his life and work. Plutarch tells us that the King could declaim whole scenes from some of his plays; at the banquet in Babylon a few days before his death he recited a scene from *Andromache*. By his order many of the uncivilised tribes in Iran learned to enjoy and repeat these verses. Euripides was born in 480 B.C., the year of the great victory of Salamis. He was the friend of Pericles, Socrates and Anaxagoras; he lived to witness the fall of Athens, the rule of the oligarchic Thirty Tyrants and the restoration of democracy. But with what a difference! Gone was the striving after *arete* (excellence) and *sophia* (wisdom); no longer was authority in the hands of men of culture, loyal to the traditions of a high standard in public life. Such men had been replaced by demagogues eager for power and wealth. So, at the age of sixty, disillusioned and free at length from the duties of a citizen of Athens, Euripides sought the fresh atmosphere of Macedonia, and there composed some of his best work before he died in 406. He had not been very popular either with the public or with the judges who selected which plays were to be performed and which to be awarded prizes. The average audience preferred dramas which depicted humanity on a noble level, meeting with courage the immutable destiny decreed for them by the gods. Euripides was considered to be too sympathetic with human suffering and too critical of the Olympians, whose infallibility he questioned when they inflicted sorrow on men unaware of having committed any wrong deserving of punishment. Aristophanes made him one of the objects of his satire. However, with the intellectual spirits of his own and subsequent ages Euripides was a first favourite: Socrates would travel far to hear his plays; Horace, Virgil and Ovid praised his work; Milton, Shelley and Browning were his enthusiastic admirers. His plays are a success in the modern theatre; doubtless the beautiful translations of Dr. Gilbert Murray have contributed to the popularity of a dramatist whose work, 2,000 years after his death, expresses in noble language many of the thoughts of the modern world.

It is fitting to conclude this brief summary of the theatre of ancient Greece with a few verses from Dr. Murray's translation of that pathetic masterpiece, *The Trojan Women*, which describes the agony of Hecuba, widow of Priam, King of Troy, and of her daughter-in-law, Andromache, widow of Hector, slain by Achilles. The Heralds tell these unhappy women that they have been assigned as slaves to the conquerors of Troy; their despairing lament is thus drawn by Dr. Murray:

HECUBA   To slavery . . . God! Oh, God of Mercy! Nay,
                Why call I on the Gods? They know, they
                    know
                My prayers, and would not hear them long
                    ago!
                Even so . . . I in my sorrows bear me low,
                Nor curse, nor strive that other things may be.
                The great wave rolled from God hath con-
                    quered me.
                An old, old slave woman, I pass below
                Mine enemies' gates; and whatso task they
                    know
                For this age basest, shall be mine; the door,
                Bowing, to shut and open . . . I that bore
                Hector! . . . and meal to grind, and this
                    racked head
                Bend to the stones after a royal bed.

                . . . What hope have I
                To hold me? Take this slave that once trod
                    high
                In Ilium; cast her on her bed of clay
                Rock-pillowed, to lie down and pass away
                Wasted with tears. And whatso man they call
                Happy, believe not ere the last day fall.

ANDROMACHE   . . . Achilles' son
                So soon as I was taken, for his thrall,
                Chose me . . . I shall do service in the hall
                Of them that slew . . . How? Shall I thrust
                    aside
                Hector's beloved face, and open wide

My heart to this new lord? Oh, I should stand
A traitor to the dead! And if my hand
And flesh shrink from him . . . lo, wrath and
   despite
O'er all the house, and I a slave!

CHAPTER XV

RELIGION AND THOUGHT OF
ANCIENT GREECE

*The Greek religion—Origin of myths—Jung's study
of the Unconscious—The Oracles—Dr. Gilbert
Murray on Greek religion—Dionysus—Eleusinian
Mysteries—The philosophers: Socrates; Plato—Love
—The Phaedrus—The Symposium—Aristotle—Later
philosophers: the Cynics; the Stoics; Epicurus—
Astrology—The spirit of the age—Modern philoso-
phers: Jung; Bergson; William James—Conclusion*

SOME may regard this chapter as a digression from the
main subject, Alexander of Macedon. But one cannot understand him unless one knows something about the spirit of his
time and for that it is necessary to have some acquaintance,
however superficial, with the literature and the thought
which moulded his character and influenced his lifework.

Many modern readers are prejudiced by their schoolday
recollections of the Pagan gods and goddesses supposed to
have been worshipped by the Greeks even when their
universally acknowledged noble civilisation was at the height
of its glory. The modern mind, trained on scientific lines
of thought, questions how a people of such high culture could
have a religion with deities credited with crimes so repulsive
as murder, parricide, incest, and other violations of the
moral law. How could the Greeks reconcile such a religion
with their precepts of self-control, courage and the other
virtues which characterised their civilisation? But thinking
men in the fifth century before Christ regarded the numerous
deities as the relics of an old and crude society, round whom

legends had gradually been woven; they had come to believe that the world was created for some high destiny by a supreme god who, as Aeschylus declared, was called by many names. It is not generally realised that at its zenith the high standard of Greek life is understood from its philosophy, not from its so-called gods.

THE MYTHS

To understand the Pagan religion it is essential to have some knowledge of the origin of myths—an intricate subject to condense in a few pages. Mythology dates from prehistoric times when stories and allegories about heroes and gods were widespread throughout the world. From a study of the myths scholars can tell the stage of civilisation of the races who believed in or paid lip-service to them. As man in the early days of history could have no knowledge of the physical series of causes of storms, violent winds, thunder and lightning, it was natural that he should regard them as manifestations of the wrath of an angry god or of an evil spirit, superhuman beings whom he might propitiate with songs of praise or with sacrifices of valuable objects or animals. Even to-day many children believe that fairies dwell in woodland glades, and malignant creatures haunt forests and dark caves; primitive man had similar ideas, which he did not outgrow during his lifetime. Sunrise, sunset, clouds, caverns, rivers, waterfalls, rocky gorges and high mountains were looked upon as the abodes of spirits, some good, some evil, all having a special inflence on mankind, friendly or antagonistic.

In an early stage of civilisation man would not regard as cruel or discreditable the behaviour of gods whose conduct resembled the low standard which he was accustomed to see with his neighbours; his gods would be as primitive as himself. In the Old Testament we find many examples of unjust and vindictive conduct on the part of the god of the early Hebrews. Myths began in small communities, all of which had their own special deity; as the civilisation evolved, the myths altered with the changing customs of the people. New symbols were adopted: thus the sun might indicate the father, the moon the mother, and stars their children; they were assumed to represent heroes or gods. At a more advanced level of social life men began to enquire into the causes of the phenomena of Nature and the literature of the period reflected the gradual change of attitude towards the traditional mythology. Thus we find Socrates, Aristotle, Plato and Euripides questioning the authority and the existence of the Pagan deities, even though they carried out the ritual ordained to be practised by every citizen. Bergson stated that as religion supplies discipline it requires repeated exercises such as are given by rites and ceremonies. Jung also stresses the need of dogma and ritual as supports which focus the faith of the average man.

The following brief summary on mythology and the work of C. G. Jung may assist the general reader to understand the force of the subconscious drive in outstanding men, and the part it played in the drama of Alexander's life.

A study of language sheds some light on the origin of myths. Speech came from Central Asia, and mankind, it is believed, emigrated from Asia to Europe via Persia, Asia Minor, the Hellespont and also by the Caspian and the Black Seas; others went east to the Punjab. In Sanscrit the Hindus were Aryans (the name indicates noble); in Persia the word became Iran. The Aryan myths included homage paid to natural phenomena, especially the dawn, the sun and other shining objects. Yet such worship could not be called polytheism because men prayed to one god only; the others being considered inferior, resembling human beings. In India at one time prayer was offered to powers of Nature, such as darkness, storm and drought. Some deities were thought to be placated by songs of praise, whilst evil powers, sources of dread, became friendly when their anger was averted by suitable chants and processes of magic.

Recently, independent testimony concerning the origin of myths has come from the Swiss Professor of Analytical Psychology, C. G. Jung, and from anthropologists. It is easy to understand how man's reactions to frightening or pleasing aspects of Nature led to the formation of myths. But there is another source of mythology, less simple to explain. The mind of man, as Myers pointed out in his book, *Human Personality*, is like an iceberg floating on the sea; its greater part lies below the surface of the water. So also does the greater part of the mind lie below consciousness; beneath its awareness is the submerged region, usually now described as the subconscious self. Freud taught that therein dwell the animal instincts and feelings which, though often repressed and forgotten, sway the conscious intellect. Jung, on the other hand, traced to that region not only the evil, but also the religious and artistic aspirations of humanity. Myths within the personality come from what Jung has termed the Collective Unconscious. His research into the Collective Unconscious of both primitive and civilised men proved that certain myths, common to all mankind, are expressed by symbols which have similar features throughout the centuries; these he has named Archetypes. From this deeper level of the unconscious spring evil forces, such as are shown by an angry mob, when even the mildest men behave like savage brutes. Alexander experienced that during the mutiny at Opis, and Napoleon dreaded that type of violence more than any field of battle. From analysis of his German patients, long before 1930 Jung foresaw the coming war of 1939.

Myths born of the struggle within the self are the material from which religion and creative art emerge; in some individuals these have a dynamic power. The founders of the great religions can explain these spiritual truths to the average man only by parables, symbols or allegories. That Alexander understood the distinction is shown by his letter to Aristotle (p. 224).

Jung's investigations were very thorough. From patients drawn from every class, educated and illiterate, and from a sojourn with primitive peoples in Africa, New Mexico and Arizona, he gained a fund of information concerning the unconscious. He soon found that the thinking processes of simple men did not follow the scientific civilised approach which attributes events to antecedent causes; the native started off with the hypothesis that invisible spirits or sorcerers are at work. We all have days when everything goes wrong, and we blame ourselves for fatigue or clumsiness. Is our deduction always right? Primitive men explained that they knew in advance that troubles would accumulate all that day; a stumble at the beginning of a march or the fall of a beast of burden showed them that a wrathful spirit had been offended. Similar happenings occurred during Alexander's campaign and even in the logical century of Napoleon and the two recent wars in Europe.

In both primitive and civilised societies Jung found a religious faith and a moral code which could not have originated from an intellectual formula. From some Pueblo Indians he tried to discover the religion of their tribe, but found them reluctant to answer questions on that subject. At last one very old man confided that when the sun rose, they left their huts, spat on their hands and raised them to the sky with the wordless prayer that they offered their spirits to God, the supreme spirit. They believed that the spittle contained the force or the breath which sustains life. Jung compares this custom with our own: "Lord, into Thy hands I commend my spirit", and concludes with these words: "Was the thought already incubated and purposed before men existed? I must leave the question unanswered."

Anthropologists have confirmed Jung's findings. Primitive men possess a complicated system of social life, with strict codes of etiquette, manners, laws of justice and instruction of the young; their religions have creeds and dogmas. Some recognise witchcraft, prophecy, oracles, myths, and the leading men of some races believe in the significance of dreams and the power of suggestion. Other tribes even examine the entrails of animals for omens.

In ancient Greece and Rome the oracles were held in high respect; their prophecies and advice so often proved correct. Plato stated that the prophetess at Delphi and the priestesses at Dodona "when in the throes of a divine madness" conferred benefit on Greece; but when they returned to their ordinary senses they did little or no good. Of recent years the phenomena of the uprush of the subconscious have received searching investigation by the Society for Psychical Research which was founded by Myers,

Gurney and distinguished scientific men. Modern mediums, clairvoyants and foretellers of the future have certain features in common with the oracles and the seers of antiquity and cannot be dismissed with the incredulity customary in scientific circles. Throughout the ages there is evidence of facts obtained by other channels than the intellect; reliable officials from India, Egypt and distant islands tell strange instances of insight into past and future and of both evil and good events brought about by native witchcraft or sorcery.

With knowledge of the origin and gradual modification of the Pagan religion, one understands why it was so long treasured in antiquity. In the seventh century it was believed that men were subject to the ruling of the gods who inflicted suffering on mortals for errors committed in ignorance. Such men might be haunted throughout their lives by an undeserved doom; this undercurrent of Nemesis is the theme on which were based many of the tragic dramas of Greece. It reminds one of the throbbing repetitive accompaniment in the bass, so often heard in modern orchestras, resembling the shuttle of Fate weaving a pattern beneath the apparent calm of our daily life. The poets and philosophers of the fifth and fourth centuries denounced the repulsive myths; Euripides indeed declared that if the gods did what was shameful they were not gods, and Plato stated that many sacrifices and offerings were merely attempts to curry favour with heaven. Educated men in that time admitted that the good were not always rewarded nor evil-doers punished, and that children often suffered for the sins of their parents; but they believed that the world was created for a good purpose and that evil was not pleasing to the divine source.

The development of the mythology of Greece is described by Dr. Gilbert Murray in his volume, *The Five Stages of Greek Religion*. While the cities were awakening to a higher standard of life and thought, the communities in outlying country districts still adhered to their primitive deities, local gods who represented Nature cults associated with increase of food and population. To placate such gods cruel and obscene rites were usual, and implied worship of the emblems of generation. But in the greater cities in the fifth and fourth centuries the Olympian gods were gradually replaced by worship of the Polis. In the fifth century many Athenians could not find words adequate to express their reverence for the Polis: Pericles and Thucydides found no language vivid enough to describe the emotion with which they regarded the city-state; it had become irradiated with almost a religious halo. Educated thinkers were moving toward monotheism. Dr. Murray remarks: "Certainly Greek monotheism, had it really carried the day, would have been a far more philosophic thing than the tribal and personal monotheism of the Hebrews. . . . If there had been some Hebrew prophets about, and a tyrant or two, progressive and bloody-minded, to support them, polytheism might have been stamped out. . . . But Greek thought, always sincere and daring, was seldom ruthless or cruel . . . great care was taken not to hurt other people's feelings."

So it happened that the old and the barbaric gods of outlying communities were gradually modified to become romantic legends within the Olympic circle. Although no longer supposed to represent real deities, the myths supplied a foundation for poems and dramas. Regarded only as symbols of divinity, the old gods grew luminous; transformed by their passage to the mountains of Olympus they remained serene examples of morality and strength and in time were adopted in part by Rome.

Dr. Murray analysed the stages by which the authorities gradually raised the primitive deities to the heights of Olympus. First, there was a purge of the amoral rites, evil orgies and obscene fertility ceremonies which still lingered in a few isolated villages. A systematic attempt was made to bring order into the chaos of polytheism. Many goddesses were modified or eliminated, the coarser entities combined with their finer counterparts; thus Athene, an outstanding creation with her wisdom, calm and purity, replaced many lesser goddesses. As every city had its own guardian deity, some with distinctive characteristics, such as Diana of Ephesus and Aphrodite, were retained. The gods were similarly reduced in number, their attributes and names modified; Zeus, Apollo and Hermes survived. Thirdly, as people tended to migrate to the cities, where the Olympian deities took precedence, the country as a whole accepted the more evolved gods. Although in some small outlying districts Zeus deteriorated, and scandals collected about him, the endeavour to bring order out of chaos did eventually have a refining effect on the religious concept.

The most tender of the deities were cherished; who does not feel the comfort of the lesson conveyed by the harvest myth as personified in Demeter, Mother Earth, and her daughter Persephone, bound to return once a year to visit Pluto, who carried her off to dwell with him in his dark abode below the ground? The sowing of the seed, the sprouting of the wheat, the growth to the full grain—all are represented in this gracious, illuminating allegory, characteristic of the Greek spirit. Critics of the Pagan religion must admit its charm and that it avoided the sad manifestations of intolerance of other creeds which occurred in subsequent centuries. In its later stage the Greek religion had no Inquisition, no dogmas leading to merciless war between sects, few punishments for heresy, no compulsory Church, no fanatic priests.

It is difficult for us to-day to realise the relationship of a Greek citizen with his religion in daily life. Social life was permeated by the deities in a manner hard to be understood by a generation less accustomed to wandering in woody glades than to hasty speeding over land, sea and air; the material benefits gained by the monotonous processes of industrial civilisation do not inspire the recipients with a sense of religion in routine occupations. But in Greece the gods were very human; they so much resembled mankind that men felt no impassable gulf between them. Almost every family, clan and tribe could trace its origin from some hero, and as heroes were regarded as children of the gods many claimed to be descended from a god, and outstanding men received the title of deification when considered to have accomplished work worthy of the god who was their ancestor.

The Greek religion was characterised by delight in Nature and in all the activities of the body and the mind; its essence lay in its artlessness and in the friendly attitude of intimacy with the deities who shared with humanity their joy in the beauty of the earth, the soft breezes, the sunlight playing over the leaves of the trees, the streams and waterfalls, the clouds and the valleys where nymphs, fauns and deities had their dwelling places. George Meredith, a worshipper of Mother Earth, has been called a Pagan; in his poems, *The Spirit of Earth in Autumn,* and *A Reading of Life,* we recognise the Greek attitude to life. And always, as did the Greeks, he insisted on the importance of self-knowledge, self-control, harmony of body, mind and soul. In ancient Greece, not only was Nature peopled with deities; religion was not confined to a watertight compartment. A special god presided over every private and public function, and was the patron of all political and financial transactions; so too in the spheres of medicine, law and education, all citizens were united in a common cult. Every community had its own particular deity; over Athens, for example, Athene reigned supreme.

Dionysus is a god who has been gravely misunderstood and misrepresented for centuries. His name is associated with ivy, grapes and wine; his other name, Bacchus, has been used to describe him as the god who encouraged excess. In Athens two annual festivals were held in his honour: one in January and one in April, when strangers came from all parts of Greece and from foreign lands to join the celebrations. The image of Dionysus was carried at the head of a procession to the temple; after the ceremonies came a banquet, during which wine was more or less freely taken, expressly for the purpose of loosening the inhibiting intellect, with resulting gaiety, lively talk and laughter, singing and dancing. Those who had drunk heavily became excited and boisterous; hence the reputation of Dionysus as the god of frenzied revels.

But Dionysus was also the god who could call out in his worshippers a divine rapture. William James, the American psychologist, pointed out that the ecstasy of the mystic could be imitated when the reasoning faculty of the brain was inhibited by drugs, anaesthetics or wine. Visitors to the theatres of ancient Greece are often puzzled on seeing the statue of Dionysus near the stage. But, as the god who encouraged deep and elevating emotion, his bust rightly presided over the theatres where the great dramas brought the spectators into contact with characters who had lived nobly, enduring suffering and death with unflinching courage. Always the audience judged the dramas from an ethical standard, and thus for long after the political power of Athens had passed away her literature continued to influence the world and to evoke a religious response.

The religion of ancient Greece had another form of expression in the Mysteries. The Eleusinian Mysteries remained as secret as the rites of the Freemasons; no one who witnessed the ceremonies ever revealed what had been seen and heard. After the time of harvest, the festival was continued over several days; on the final evening a procession travelled from Athens, some twelve miles away, and arrived at Eleusis about midnight. Only those whose "hands were pure and who spoke with intelligible tongue" were permitted to enter the great hall, with its many pillars. The significance of seed-time and harvest was celebrated by chosen actors, who presented the myth of Demeter and Persephone, accompanied by sacred song, chant and dance. Many have told of the ennobling effect of the spectacle upon all who were privileged to watch it; the greatest men of Greece—Socrates and Aristotle among them—attended the ceremony. Pindar the poet said that the man was happy who had seen these Mysteries before he left this world. Cicero wrote: "Much that is excellent and divine does Athens seem to have produced and added to our life, nothing better than the Mysteries, by which we are formed and moulded from a rude and savage state into humanity; and indeed, in the Mysteries we perceive the real principles of life, and learn not only to live happily, but to die with a fairer hope." There can be little doubt that Aristotle would pass on to Alexander all that it was permissible to repeat.

THE PHILOSOPHERS

Philosophy to-day is studied chiefly in the universities, but before Alexander it had reached the market-place. The famous philosophers of Athens collected their students in the streets, the gymnasia and other public places where men gathered for conversation. Socrates, Plato and Aristotle taught during the decline of the Polis, when they were disillusioned by the defective government which had succeeded Pericles. The Athenians had lost their high standards during the Peloponnesian war and the naval disaster when Sicily was attacked on the instigation of Alcibiades. But even before the end of the war Socrates had reproached the democracy which had discarded the ideal that education in nobility of spirit brought more happiness than did the provision of the free gifts which tended to lower the morale of the people.

SOCRATES

Socrates (469-399 B.C.) wrote no books, but fortunately he had as pupil Plato, who, in his Dialogues, has preserved for all time the attractive personality of his Master, the wisest of men, also witty and genial. Convinced that human life must be based on spiritual values, he was himself an example of the noble principles which he preached. In youth Socrates had fought as a heavy-armed infantry soldier in three campaigns, and had been a brave warrior, unmoved by cold, hunger and fatigue. Even in those early years he had been a contemplative; Alcibiades told how Socrates had been standing still, wrapped in thought, during a whole day, and when dawn arrived he was found in the same position, motionless, deep in meditation. Some of the troops had slept on mats all night, filled with curiosity, wondering how long Socrates would remain; they vouched for the truth of his long spell of thinking.

Socrates' method of teaching was unique. He refused to call himself a man who educated pupils. He invited discussions with his "companions", young or old, who sought him in the streets or the gymnasia. He liked to propound a subject for debate, humbly ask the opinions of those near him, and after listening patiently to their replies he would suggest further inquiry. Then question followed question in rapid succession; with rapier lightning logic he pushed home the truth that their arguments betrayed confused thinking on matters which should have been simple to explain, such as "What is courage? What is virtue?" Then, finding that they were becoming entangled in a mass of contradictions, with laughter the majority of his victims usually confessed that they had learned from the dialogue that they knew nothing at all. Socrates joined in their merriment, and with expressions of mutual esteem they would part, promising to resume their talk on the following day. Sometimes these dialogues occurred at an evening banquet, when Socrates was accustomed to drink even more than the young revellers, but wine never impaired his power of reasoning. Even when some of the company fell asleep Socrates continued to talk all night with those who were so desirous to learn his system of logical pursuit of a selected topic that they stayed on till dawn. When young men fell under his spell so deeply that they became over-affectionate, Socrates took control of the situation and used his power for their good.

Although Socrates invited discussion about the Pagan deities, he never neglected the religious duties of a citizen. Deeply religious in the esoteric sense, he studied the doctrines of Orpheus and Pythagoras, who regarded the cultivation of the soul as all-important. He believed that he had a mission to educate the youths of Athens in the Greek standard of *arete*, excellence. To few only did he speak of his religious experience, but he never concealed his certainty that he had a Daimon, a guiding spirit which told him the right course to follow in difficult circumstances. He followed the ideal which he counselled to others; twice, although aware that it might cost him his life, he refused to obey an order of the government which conflicted with his sense of justice. At last, knowing the immense ascendancy which Socrates wielded over his disciples, the authorities indicted him, in 399 B.C., on the charge of "corrupting the youth of the city, neglect of the gods and the practice of religious novelties". This verdict was influenced by the fact that Alcibiades and Critias, who deserved distrust, had once been his pupils and studied his methods of debate from the unworthy motive of gaining power.

Few have time to study all the Dialogues of Plato, but his account of the trial and defence of Socrates and his last words concerning the soul after it "left the Tomb of the Body" should be treasured by everyone. In the *Phaedo* Plato described the last day of life of the philosopher and the manner of his death, and concluded with these beautiful words: "Such was the end of our friend, a man, I think, who was the wisest and justest, and the best man that I have ever known."

Many of the sayings of Socrates are quoted to-day. One describes many politicians: "A statesman is an advocate who is clever enough to carry the day; people will regard him as superior to the expert; rhetoric is just a knack of pleasing an audience." "To suffer evil is evil, but to inflict it is worse." "Life is but a preparation for death." Virtue, he assured his listeners, is knowledge, for no man, knowing what is good and the result of failure to follow it, would willingly choose to do wrong. The supreme business of life was to strive after the good, the perfecting of the soul. In comparison with that object it was foolish to worry about possessions, about money or bodily satisfactions; body and soul were one; the physical must become spiritualised.[1] The good, to Socrates, implied *arete*, excelling in all noble qualities; true happiness was acquired only when the highest capacities of the soul were developed.

Some readers of the Dialogues of Plato ask how can one be certain which speeches represent the ideas of Socrates and which those of his pupil. Scholars consider it improbable that Plato would put into the mouth of his Master any opinions contrary to those which he held; such would be written as if spoken by one of his questioners. Sometimes the date of publication provides the clue. Professor Jowett, who translated Plato, suggested that those written before the death of Socrates must have been known to him and would have been contradicted if inaccurate. The accounts of the trial and the long discussion on his last day of life would have been studied by the disciples who had been present on that occasion and would not have been recorded if

[1] "And flesh unto Spirit must grow" (George Meredith).

untrue. Many of the thoughts expressed by Plato long after
the death of his great Master are identical with those which
scholars regard as typical of Socrates; the two men were in
agreement on most subjects concerning ethics and politics.
Socrates had less faith in immortality; his speech at his trial
proves that he felt no more certain as to the after-destiny
of the soul than do we so many centuries later.

PLATO

Plato (427-347 B.C.) was about twenty-three years of age
when the Peloponnesian war came to an end, and during
his long life he witnessed many changes in Athens. He
had been a devoted follower of Socrates for ten or twelve
years and had been present at the trial, but prevented by
illness from being one of the visitors who had watched the
Master on the fatal day when he drank the lethal dose of
hemlock. Fortunately, Plato had the gift of imaginative
writing, and his understanding of the temperament and the
philosophy of Socrates enabled him to convey to posterity
a faithful portrait which explains the esteem and the
affection with which the Master was regarded by his disciples. The injustice of the trial caused so much grief to
Plato that he left Athens and travelled for some time; on
his return in 387 B.C. he founded the Academy, where he
lectured for many years. Twice he was persuaded to go to
Sicily, and attempted first to aid Dionysius I, the tyrant of
Syracuse, and later, the young Dionysius; but both experiments failed.

The unsettled and demoralised condition of the government of Athens during the lifetime of Plato is thus described
by Thucydides:

And Revolution [change of constitution] brought on
the cities of Greece many calamities, such as exist and will
always exist until human nature changes, varying in
intensity and character with changing circumstances.
Later, the whole Greek world was affected; there was a
struggle between the leaders of the oligarchic and the
democratic parties, the former wishing the support of

Athens, the latter that of Lacedaemon. . . . In peace and prosperity States and individuals are governed by higher ideals because they are not involved in circumstances beyond their control, but war is a rough teacher that brings most men's dispositions down to the level of their circumstances. . . . The cause of all these evils was the love of power, due to ambition and greed, which led to rivalries from which party spirit sprang. The leaders of both sides used specious phrases, championing a moderate aristocracy or political equality for the masses. They professed to study public interests, but made them their prize, and in the struggle to get the better of each other by any means, committed terrible excesses. . . . Religion meant nothing to either party, but the use of fair phrases to achieve a criminal end was highly respected. . . . So civil war gave birth to every kind of iniquity in the Greek world.[1]

Indeed human nature is still unaltered. Thucydides' description fits many of the party political speeches of the present day.

In youth, Plato wrote *The Republic*, a book full of wisdom and suggestions for politicians of every age when the world is as unsettled as was Athens during the unhappy years after the Spartan victory. The popular legend that Plato advised that philosophers should be rulers is not strictly in accordance with his counsel; here is the Jowett translation of the passage so often misunderstood:

Now, I go to meet that which I liken to the greatest of the waves; yet shall the word be spoken, even though the wave break and drown me in laughter and dishonour; and do you mark my words. . . . Until philosophers are kings, or the kings and princes of this world have the spirit and power of philosophy, and political greatness and wisdom meet in one, and those commoner natures who pursue either to the exclusion of the other are compelled to stand aside, cities will never have rest from their evils—

[1] Sir Richard Livingstone's translation.

no, nor the human race, as I believe—and then only will this our State have a possibility of life and behold the light of day.

Among the subjects considered in *The Republic* were property, education, sex relationships, the family and the respective roles of men and women. The guardians of the State were to be drawn from a restricted circle of men and women who were highly trained thinkers or philosophers, but the producers and the military could, with suitable education, rise to the highest level. The guardians must lead model lives of austerity, caring only for the good of the city-state; sharing everything, they have been described as a communistic society. Even the wives and children were to be in common, the unhealthy infants exposed to die, the healthy to be placed under the care of nurses so that their mothers would be free to undertake public and military service. Economic difficulties were foreseen when there was growth of population, with increased demand for goods; this, as we, alas, know to-day, both Socrates and Plato recognised would lead to war. Plato's views on education were considered in the preceding chapter. Having witnessed the problem presented by democratic government, Plato gave a clear picture of its usual progressive stages—the plundering of the rich, the ensuing reaction, then the demand for a single capable ruler to take the reins, and often a resulting tyranny.

In later life Plato wrote *The Laws*, in which he advocated that women should be trained in physical exercises, including horse-riding, and that they should take their part, equally with men, in the duties of citizenship. He upheld family life and monogamy; for the good of the race he advised that men should marry between thirty and thirty-five, and women between sixteen and twenty. Discarding the ascetic communism of *The Republic*, he concluded that humanity required a solid foundation of religion; only a firm ethical ideal could save Athens. In this connection it is difficult to make a choice from his writings; many passages contain phrases which veritably glow with enthusiasm; his prose becomes poetry. Thus, for example: "And whenever the soul receives more of good and evil from her own energy and the strong influence of others—when she has communion with divine virtue and becomes divine, she is carried into another and better place, which is also divine and perfect in holiness; and when she has a communion with evil then she also changes the place of her life." He warns the young who turn to evil that there will be no escape from the just punishment decreed by the gods. To quote again: "If you say I am small and will creep into the depths of the earth, or I am high and will fly up to heaven, you are not so small or so high but that you will pay the fitting penalty."

In the literature of Greece, except in poetry and the drama, there is comparatively little about the love of man for woman, but much concerning strong attachments between men. Women, busy with their household tasks, could not accompany their husbands to the gymnasia, the favourite meeting places for discussion and recreation. And, like the Victorian women, they could not converse on the subjects which interested men—the affairs of the Polis, philosophy and war. Friendship played a great part in Greek social life; community of interests often led to a lifelong sympathetic companionship which urged both men to high endeavour. Too many writers have believed that these friendships always comprised a physical basis.

In the early days of Greece homosexuality was tolerated in certain regions, but condemned and punished in others. From time to time allegations appear, even in modern days, stating that such a practice was so common that it contributed to the downfall of ancient Greece. But this is by no means an adequate interpretation of the many enduring friendships which are recorded in the history of Greece. The Greeks loved beauty; as is evidenced by their statuary, it was often combined with nobility of soul, strength and health. The restraint, dignity and loveliness of their statues induce in the beholder an emotion of reverence; it is not surprising that men were attracted by the charm and beauty of boys and sought their companionship. The association might be temporary or lasting, degrading or elevating, according to the temperament of the individuals. In Sparta attachments between a boy and an older man were encouraged because it was considered that the young gained instruction from their experienced companions. In Sparta, Boeotia and Elis, communities with primitive culture, crude homosexuality was recognised as respectable; but when Sparta declined from her high position, homosexuality was regarded as dishonourable, as indeed had already been decided by many Greek cities. As a custom it died out, except in a few vicious haunts, just after the *Symposium* had been written. In *The Laws* Plato denounced pederasty as unnatural; Aristotle also spoke strongly about its corrupting influence in a community.

Lasting friendships were esteemed because they prompted both men to nobility of life. It was recognised that friendship incited them to reach the highest excellence (*arete*); with the years this affection led them beyond the limits of their personal lives, uniting them in unselfish toil for the common good. The famous Theban Band was renowned for its heroism; the lovers swore to live or die together and were invincible in war. To gain the admiration of his friend, a young man attempted deeds of valour; the praise of his companion was to him more precious than that of any relative or superior officer. When Philip saw the bodies of the fallen lovers after the battle of Chaeronea, he exclaimed with tears: "Perish the man who suspects that these men ever did or suffered anything base." Their devotion resembled the romantic love of later centuries which inspired a lover to noble deeds for the sake of the one woman whom he worshipped as almost divine.

Plato considered many types of love in two of his most beautiful Dialogues. He anticipated many of the findings of modern psycho-analysts when he represented love as "one of the great powers of Nature . . . the principal forms having a predominant influence over the lives of men; those two, though opposed, are not entirely separated, one being easily translated into the other; but the noble yet fleeting aspirations may return into the nature of the animal, the lower instinct, which is latent, always remaining." Even the crude contents of the unconscious, so recently discovered by psycho-analysts, were known to Plato, who said that unless the thoughts which occupied the mind before sleep were noble, impulses from the animal region were apt to invade the conscious, higher part of the soul in the form of evil dreams.

Socrates discussed male love with Phaedrus, a young man who asked his opinion of an article composed by his teacher of rhetoric, Lysias, whom he greatly admired. One lovely morning Phaedrus had enticed the Master into the country; on arriving at a shady nook under a large plane tree beside a rippling stream, they reclined on the grass and engaged in conversation. After tactfully expressed admiration of the essay to which he had quietly listened, Socrates cast doubt on Lysias' definition of love. "Love, a word in many mouths, not often explained", wrote George Meredith over two thousand years later. When Phaedrus pressed for honest criticism of Lysias' advocacy of surrender to a lover who did not truly love, Socrates replied that he would hurry through a speech, but with his face veiled, because the subject was shameful. Lysias' degraded conception of love would cause deterioration of the character. The lover who sought selfish satisfaction became jealous and exacting, the beloved became effeminate, useless in war, and deprived of normal life with home, wife and children. When an old man pursued a young man for his beauty, their association led to results too painful and unpleasant to mention.

Phaedrus, impressed, begged Socrates to continue. The philosopher rose to go home, but felt impelled to deliver a second speech concerning the attitude of the unselfish and spiritual lover, who longed to aid the growth of the beloved. Then followed the famous allegory of the soul as a charioteer driving two horses, one good, one depraved. When the evil horse dragged the other toward wrong desires and deeds, the charioteer, Reason, pulled him back. When the charioteers maintained control over both horses, the finer elements of the souls were able to master all wanton desires incompatible with an orderly and noble life.

Careful study of the many and difficult pages of the

Phaedrus dialogue does not confirm the too prevalent opinion that physical surrender was honoured in that age. On the contrary, in his second speech Socrates said that when such intimacy occurred with friends overcome by their evil steeds, they suffered from the knowledge that their action had not the approval of their whole soul. But those who had gained complete mastery over the wanton desires incompatible with a well-regulated life set out on a heavenward path; their love was a divine emotion, which inspired the friends and influenced the entire community for good.

One excerpt must be quoted from this famous dialogue:

> For every soul of man has in the way of nature beheld true being; this was the condition of her passing into the form of man. But all souls do not easily recall the things of the other world . . . or they may have been unfortunate in their earthly lot . . . and have lost the memory of the holy things which once they saw. Only a few retain an adequate remembrance of them; and they, when they behold here any image of that other world, are rapt in amazement; but they are ignorant of what that rapture means, because they do not clearly perceive . . . for there is no clear light of justice or temperance, or any of the higher ideas which are precious to souls, in the earthly copies of them; they are seen through a glass dimly.

Words so similar to those of St. Paul: "We see through a glass darkly"[1]; his writing bears evidence that he was much influenced by Greek philosophy. And Wordsworth's *Intimations of Immortality* convey the same thought of previous existence.

The heat of the day having passed, Phaedrus and his teacher decide to return home after a prayer by Socrates to the gods that he "should be granted to become beautiful in the inner man. May I deem the wise man rich, and may I have such a portion of gold as none but a prudent man can either bear or employ."

Jowett stated that only those to whom mysticism appealed could appreciate Plato. Under the marble exterior of Greek

[1] *Corinthians*, iii, 12.

literature there lay concealed a soul thrilling with emotion. In both the Symposium and the Phaedrus dialogues Socrates teaches ideals comparable with those of Christianity.

In the wonderful dialogue, *The Symposium*, six speakers discuss Eros from many aspects. The second speech contrasts sensual and heavenly love. Many believe that crude homosexuality was honoured in Athens at that time, but in truth it existed only in a limited circle and was soon discouraged. Werner Jaeger drew attention to the consummate art with which Plato arranged the speeches to follow in an ascending scale to the climax, when Socrates soared to the starry heights. He told the company that he gained his knowledge from Diotima, a woman famous for wisdom and observation of humanity. All men desire to find a beloved with both beauty and goodness; when these qualities are combined love becomes an incentive to strive after the noblest aims. Diotima taught that rightly educated young men started with a love of beauty and virtue, and thence proceeded to search for a more comprehensive type of love, that of the whole world, its laws, its institutions, its greatest deeds and its noblest thoughts; from these, man ascended from the love of earthly things to the contemplation of Absolute Beauty. Thence Socrates rose to the vision of the mystic, the love of God. "Such were the words of Diotima; and I am persuaded of their truth. And being persuaded of them, I try to persuade others, that in the attainment of this end, human nature will not easily find a better helper than Love. And therefore I say that every man ought to honour him as I myself honour him, and walk in his ways, and exhort others to do the same, and praise the power and spirit of Love according to the measure of my ability, now and ever."

After Socrates' inspiring conclusion Alcibiades broke in on the *Symposium* and on finding, to his dismay as well as his joy, that Socrates was present, he told the company what he thought about the philosopher. Alcibiades, a nephew of Pericles, able, ambitious, eloquent, possessed also much charm and beauty which to most men proved irresistible. And of all these attributes he was well aware. He had shared several campaigns with Socrates; at Patidea, the philosopher had saved his life. He both adored and hated Socrates, who was his conscience, always drawing him off protestingly when he preferred to do evil rather than good. Thus runs Jowett's translation:

And now, my boys, I shall praise Socrates in a figure which will appear to him to be a caricature, and yet I speak, not to make fun of him, but only for truth's sake. . . . He is exactly like the busts of Silenus which are set up in the statuaries' shops, holding pipes and flutes in their mouths; and they are made to open in the middle. and have images of gods inside them. I say also that he is like Marsyas the satyr. . . . And are you not a flute-player? That you are, and a performer far more wonderful than Marsyas. He indeed with instruments used to charm the soul of men by the power of his breath, and the players of his music do so still; for the melodies of Olympias are derived from Marsyas . . . and whether they are played by a great master or by a miserable flute-girl, have a power which no others have; they alone possess the soul and reveal the wants of these who have need of gods and mysteries, because they are divine. But you produce the same effect with your words only, and do not require the flute; that is the difference between you and him. When we hear any other speaker, even a very good one, he produces absolutely no effect upon us, or not much; whereas the mere fragments of you and your words . . . amaze and possess the souls of every man, woman and child who comes within hearing of them. . . . This Marsyas has brought me to such a pass that I have felt as if I could not endure the life which I am leading . . . if I did not shut my ears against him and fly as if from the voice of the siren, my fate would be like that of others—he would transfix me, and I should grow old, sitting at his feet. For he makes me confess that I ought not to live as I do, neglecting the wants of my own soul, and busying myself with the concerns of the Athenians. . . . And he is the only person who has ever made me feel ashamed, which you might think not to be in my nature, and there

is no one else who does the same. . . . For I know that
I ought to do as he bids, but when I leave him the love of
popularity gets the better of me. . . . Many a time I have
wished he were dead, and yet I should be much more sorry
than glad if he were to die; so that I am at my
wits' end.

Half drunk, Alcibiades continued to enlarge on the virtues
of Socrates, a man who considered position and wealth as
nothing, but valued only goodness. When one listened to his
discourses they at first seemed ludicrous, concerning asses,
tanners, leather-cutters and copper-smiths. "But", he went
on, "he who beholds his discourses when they are opened,
and gets within, in the first place finds that they alone possess
an inner meaning, and in the next place, that they are most
divine, and hold the most numerous images of virtue, and
extend . . . to everything which is fitting for him to consider who intends to become a man at once beautiful and
good." Alcibiades warned the young men that they might
flatter themselves that they were beloved by Socrates, but
they would find that they would suffer as he had suffered
when they found that they became his victims as they lost
their hearts to the wonderful man. When they had shared
danger in war together he had found Socrates was a brave
soldier who endured cold, hunger and other hardships better
than most men and now, when old, in spite of his intellectual
superiority to all men, enjoyed feasts and was the life and
soul of any party; for although he could take more wine
than most guests, he was never in the least intoxicated.
Alcibiades then proceeded to confess his failure to entice
Socrates as a lover. Knowing how Socrates was attracted
by his beauty, he described how he had on several occasions
made sensual advances, but had gained nothing by his
methods. Feeling ashamed and dishonoured by his ignoble
conduct, he had become more than ever a slavish admirer of
the great man.

For over 2,000 years this record of Plato has continued to
delight the civilised world. And what was the end of that
memorable *Symposium*? During the night most of the guests

fell asleep, others went home. At dawn, some awoke to find Socrates still discussing the resemblance of Tragedy and Comedy with Agathon and Aristophanes. Then they too dropped to sleep, and when he had laid them comfortably on their couches, Socrates went away, bathed, and spent the rest of the day as usual in Athens.

Turning over the pages of Lowes Dickinson's *Greek View of Life* I found a paragraph which might have been written to-day; it was a summary of the conclusions of Plato!

He traced the evil in social life to the decay of religious belief. Though no one was more trenchant than he in his criticism of the popular faith, no one, on the other hand, was more convinced of the necessity of some form of religion as a basis for any stable policy. The doctrine of the Physicists that the world is the result of matter and of chance has immediate and disastrous effects in the whole structure of social life. To reconstruct religion he was driven back on metaphysics and elaborated the system which from his day to our own has never ceased to perplex and fascinate the world, and whose rare and radiant combination of gifts, speculative, artistic and religious, marks the highest reach of the genius of the Greeks and perhaps of mankind.

ARISTOTLE

Aristotle, born in 384 B.C., was the son of a physician who had been the friend of the King of Macedonia, the grand-father of Alexander. In 367 B.C. he went to Athens and became the pupil of Plato, who soon considered him the chief intellect in the school. When Aristotle left Athens after the death of Plato in 347 B.C., Philip invited him at the age of forty-two to undertake the education of his son, Alexander, then only thirteen years old. When the royal pupil went to Asia, Aristotle returned to Athens and started his Peripatetic school, thus named because of his habit of walking about during his lectures. After Alexander died, there was trouble between Macedonia and Greece; Aristotle was charged with impiety, and with the fate of Socrates before him, he escaped to a place of safety where he soon afterwards died at the age of sixty-two.

In this age of specialisation it is difficult to realise over how vast a range of subjects Aristotle was the acknowledged authority for many centuries and in many lands. All knowledge was his province, but his chief reputation rests on his research in natural science. From his Peripatetic school there flowed a steady stream of publications on every branch of science: astronomy, botany, zoology, biology, archaeology and mathematics. From his study of animals Aristotle foreshadowed an evolutionary purpose in Nature; he believed that the vital principle, instinctive in plants and animals, became in man the soul. Nor did his students imagine that their reports were final; they had the true scientific attitude which assumes that further investigation may confirm or modify their work. Aristotle provided an example of sanity and calm in the Hellenistic age, when all was changing, unsettled, disturbing. Although Aristotle and Alexander did not meet after the young King set out for Asia they maintained a regular correspondence. There may have been a temporary coolness after the death of Callisthenes, but there is certain evidence that Alexander continued, to the end of his life, to despatch specimens of plants, animals, insects and other objects which interested his tutor, and that he contributed princely financial aid to the school of science.

On politics Aristotle wrote at considerable length. He taught that the State existed to provide the citizen with opportunity for the leisure and culture necessary for "the good life"; he did not approve of the subjugation of the individual to the State, for the comfort thus obtained was at the cost of the freedom of the spirit. But neither had democracy, except when under the guidance of great leaders, promoted the good of the Polis; it placed too much power in the hands of the more numerous but less intelligent. Plato, and Socrates also, formed the conclusion that government proved more beneficial when led by aristocrats. In those days, it must be remembered, aristocracy implied not noble birth, but excellence of spirit; such men were above temptation to gain wealth from their position of power in the

Assembly. When a King had marked superiority of intellect and character, monarchy was beneficial for the State. Both systems had disadvantages; aristocracy might degenerate to oligarchy, monarchy to tyranny (p. 237).

Aristotle has several references which have intrigued historians; although he does not name Alexander, it is possible that he had him in mind when he wrote: "If there is one man superior in goodness and political capacity to all others such a person may be like a god among men. . . . Men pre-eminently superior cannot be treated as if part of the State . . . but should be gladly obeyed, for they are permanent Kings."[1]

Dr. Gilbert Murray writes: "To people accustomed to the conception of a god-man it was difficult not to feel that this conception was realised in Alexander. His tremendous power, his achievements beggaring the fables of the poets, put people in the right mind for worship. The Kings whom he had conquered had been regarded by their subjects as divine beings. . . . Naturally therefore the man who had conquered the Kings must have been a still greater god. If you judge a man by his fruits, what god could produce better credentials? Men had often seen Zeus defied with impunity . . . but those who defied Alexander, however great they might be, always rued their defiance; and those who were faithful to him always received their reward."

Until the Middle Ages Aristotle was regarded as the supreme authority on both religion and science, even during the centuries when the Greeks and their language had been forgotten and Aristotle's work could be studied only from indifferent Arabian translations. Had he not written so much on science, he would have been considered a great religious teacher. He taught that there was a Divine First Cause who, unmoved himself, moved the universe. Even in Homer allusions are found to a supreme god who showed tenderness and sympathy with the afflicted and at times modified the wrathful moods of Zeus.

[1] *Politics*, III, 1283b.

LATER PHILOSOPHERS

When the decline of belief in the circle of the Olympian gods reached the average citizen, men's minds suffered from the void. After the death of Alexander continuous warfare racked the world for over twenty years, and unsettled conditions prevailed not only in Greece and Asia Minor, but extended over Persia and the Mediterranean countries. Mankind, despairing, seeking certainty and comfort, turned to ascetic and mystic creeds which came from the Orient. Humbled, baffled, hopeless, humanity sought help from many a spiritual source.

Owing to the decision of Alexander to make Greek a universal language, the philosophers of Athens exerted a profound effect upon the thinkers of that century and have continued to influence philosophers and educationalists even to this day. In spite of her exhaustion after the Peloponnesian war, Athens attracted distinguished men who offered a substitute for the outworn mythology. The disciples of Antisthenes lived in poverty, clad in poor raiment, maintaining that they were free men because they had no possessions and no desires. His foremost pupil, Diogenes, the Cynic, dwelt in a large earthen vessel, called in legend a tub, and preached that his way of life was the sole means of freedom. He begged for his bread; nothing, he said, was of value in this world except virtue and goodness. All Greece discussed his oratory and his mordant wit, but as his eloquent advocacy of a return to Nature taught that one should live like an animal, the drawbacks were so great that few of his followers practised his precepts for long.

One of the most important teachers in this Hellenistic age was Zeno (342-270 B.C.) the founder of the Stoic philosophy; its noble tenets are still admired in the modern world. He taught that man's highest aim was the acquisition of wisdom, fortitude, temperance and beneficence; the last named, a new conception, embraced sympathy for all humanity. Epictetus, a notable member of this school, taught that we should forgive injuries. Many of the finest Stoic doctrines were known to St. Paul and were preserved in his Christian teaching. Zeno, it is believed, was the first philosopher to make popular the principle that the world should be a universal brotherhood, that men were the children of one good and wise god; as a direct consequence no distinction should be made between Greeks and other nations, nor between men and women, free men and slaves. But the great Alexander had anticipated that ideal; he had spoken of the brotherhood of all mankind and declared that God was the father of all men. The Stoics advised mankind to make a habit of daily self-examination, thus measuring the improvement or deterioration in their moral state. As perfection, not happiness, was the Divine Purpose of the universe, no blow of Fortune should disturb the equanimity of the mind; pain and sorrow could be borne when a man had learned self-discipline. Such doctrines made a wide appeal; many Romans adopted Stoicism, among them the Emperor Marcus Aurelius and Seneca.

Epicurus, gentle and kindly, founded a school which later bore his name. In his community men and women, rich and poor, lived happy and ascetic lives. His assertion that happiness could be attained by all was gravely distorted by those who adopted it as an excuse for physical indulgence; whereas in truth he advocated only the happiness of the spirit. So long as men did not fear the wrath of the gods, he did not object to belief in the old mythology. His disciples were not allowed to anticipate disasters which might never happen; such anxiety clouded the peace of the mind. Epicurus brought comfort to many who had never realised that, as happiness lay within, men could rise above the sad circumstances of their lives. Epicureans and Stoics had much in common, for both pursued virtue and had faith in a Divine Purpose. But whilst the Stoics taught that men should fulfil the responsibilities of a citizen, the Epicureans took no interest in politics.

Both schools had been influenced by Alexander, who had been the first of all kings to advocate that a monarch ought to bring into harmony all his subjects. Moreover, as he had made Greek a universal language, the philosophy of the Stoics and the Epicureans reached a wide public.

In Babylonia Alexander must have come in contact with

the astrological cult. In the East, for many centuries, students of Nature had observed the connection of the sun, moon and stars with the fertility of the soil and changes of weather. In the lore of the Chaldeans the influence of the planets took definite shape; by the correspondence of their positions in the heavens with the date of a man's birth it was believed that the main trend of his destiny could be foreseen. Astrology existed in Babylonia from 3000 B.C.: by the fourth century it reached Greece, and later passed to Rome. Although some Stoics advocated its adoption as a proof of the forethought of the Divine, Rome eventually took steps to arrest the extension of the cult. Yet it continued to attract followers, and has existed in India, China and parts of Persia and Arabia since its origin in Babylonia. Jung tells us that it has disciples even in modern Europe, and that it is "knocking at the doors of the universities from which it was banished some 300 years ago". It is beyond the scope of this book to discuss the recurring faith in astrology.

THE SPIRIT OF THE AGE

The attitude of science prevailing in the Western world demands proofs and regards intuitional knowledge as only an emotional reaction. Many consider that the soul—or the mind, if that term is preferred—is a product of matter, the brain cells providing the material field for its activity. Science has advocates who maintain that the personality is fully explained by the condition of the endocrine glands, the organs and the circulation. Just as in a school a child dreads to appear different from his companions, so an adult fears to disagree with the dominant opinions of his era. Men used to believe that the soul dwelt in, but was not the product of the physical body, being part of a system which, pushed to its ultimate source, proceeded from God. In the Graeco-Roman world men believed that the communications received from augurs, oracles and some dreams emanated from a spiritual origin. In the scientific nineteenth century men distrusted the intuitional knowledge which is found in both primitive and civilised nations; it contradicted their usual lines of thought. Yet is it indeed less probable than the hypothesis that mind is the product of matter? If matter can evolve so far, it cannot be crass matter, but must possess a buried potential which can expand into an entirely different manifestation of the vital force.

MODERN PHILOSOPHERS

Within comparatively recent years there is evidence of a reaction against the enthronement of matter. Henri Bergson, William James and C. G. Jung testify that intuition can convey valuable wisdom. Bergson first explained clearly the respective spheres of operation of intuition and intellect. Intuition, like sympathy, reaches to the heart of a subject; the reasoning intellect can deal only with the relationship between objects. For the conquest of matter the intellect was so necessary that the intuitional knowledge was sacrificed; thus we find that in the modern world its insight is apt to be fleeting and vague. Bergson believed that the mystic sense lay dormant in all men, but could be stirred into action under the influence of deep emotion, such as is aroused by suffering, heroic deeds, transcendent joy, and contact with human beings who bear the stamp of the Divine.

Socrates told his judges that he always obeyed his Daimon; in every critical situation of his life this intuitional advice had guided his intellect to form a correct decision. That fact would be known to Alexander, but did he realise that he also had similar direction when, as he often said, he was "seized with a longing"?

Perhaps William James has best expressed in simple language this awareness of another world than that which is detected by the senses and the intellect.

The further limits of our being plunge into an altogether different dimension of existence from the sensible and merely 'understandable' world. Name it the mystical or the supernatural region, whichever you choose. Yet the unseen region . . . produces effects in the world. When we commune with it, work is actually done upon our finite personality. . . . But that which produces effects within another reality must be termed a reality itself, so I feel as if we had no philosophic excuse for calling the unseen or mystical world unreal. . . . Our normal waking consciousness . . . is but one special type of consciousness, whilst all about it, parted from it by the filmiest of screens, there lie potential forms of consciousness entirely different. We may go through life without suspecting their existence; but apply the requisite stimulus, and at a touch, they are there. . . . No account of the universe . . . can be final which leaves these other forms of consciousness disregarded. . . . If then there be a wider world of being than that of our everyday consciousness, if in it there be forces whose effects on us are intermittent, if one condition be the openness of the subliminal door . . . at these places at least . . . it would seem as though transmundane energies of God, if you will, produced immediate effects within the natural world to which the rest of our experience belongs.

When Alexander of Macedon was "seized with a longing" he was driven to action, the outcome of which he could not foresee. His expressed desire to extend Hellenic culture did not imply worship of Pagan deities, but the Greek ideal of excellence, *arete*. With this aim he strove to extend knowledge of Greek art, science, philosophy and the many high qualities which characterised that gracious civilisation. When the "urge" from the unconscious is accepted by the intellect, it has a clear path; in that personality there is in truth a vocation, a call to follow, a mission. This intuitional drive in such individuals as Alexander is an imperative demand; it cannot be pushed aside for lesser claims; it is the man's destiny, and for aught we can tell, it may fulfil the purpose for which he was created. As Arrian, the careful historian, concluded: "There seems to have been some Divine Hand presiding over both his birth and actions."

INDEX